BASIC
WOODWORKING

By the Editors of Sunset Books

Sunset Books
Director of Sales & Marketing: Richard A. Smeby
Editorial Director: Bob Doyle
Production Director: Lory Day

Sunset Publishing Corporation
Chairman: Jim Nelson
President/CEO: Robin Wolaner
Chief Financial Officer: James E. Mitchell
Publisher, Sunset Magazine: Stephen J. Seabolt
Circulation Director: Robert L. Gursha
Editor, Sunset Magazine: William R. Marken

Basic Woodworking was produced by
St. Remy Press
President: Pierre Léveillé
Managing Editor: Carolyn Jackson
Senior Editor: Heather Mills
Senior Art Director: Francine Lemieux
Art Director: Solange Laberge
Assistant Editor: Neale McDevitt
Designers: François Daxhelet, Hélène Dion,
    Jean-Guy Doiron, Maryse Doray, Michel Giguère
Picture Editor: Christopher Jackson
Contributing Illustrators: Michel Blais, Jacques Perrault
Production Manager: Michelle Turbide
System Coordinator: Jean-Luc Roy
Photographer: Robert Chartier
Proofreader: Judy Yelon
Indexer: Christine M. Jacobs
Administrator: Natalie Watanabe
Other Staff: Lorraine Doré, Dominique Gagné,
    François Longpré, David Simon, Rebecca Smollett

Book Consultants
Giles Miller-Mead
Don Vandervort

Acknowledgments
Thanks to the following:
A&M Wood Specialty Inc., Cambridge, Ont.
American Plywood Association, Tacoma, WA
Jon Arno, Troy, MI
Black & Decker Canada Inc., Mississauga, Ont.
Black & Decker Inc., Towson, MD
Borden Packaging and Industrial Products, Columbus, OH
Delta International Machinery/Porter-Cable, Guelph, Ont.
Dewalt Industrial Tool Co., Hampstead, MD
Emerson Electric Co., Hazelwood, MO
Franklin International, Columbus, OH
Hardwood Plywood & Veneer Association, Reston, VA
Hitachi Power Tools Ltd., Norcross/Atlanta, GA
Jet Equipment and Tools, Auburn, WA
Makita Canada Inc., Whitby, Ont.
McFeely's, Lynchburg, VA
Milwaukee Electric Tool Corp., Brookfield, WI
National Particleboard Association, Gaithersburg, MD
National Retail Hardware Association/*Do-It-Yourself
    Retailing Magazine*, Indianapolis, IN
Northwestern Steel and Wire, Sterling, IL
Pratt & Lambert/United Solvents of America, Sumter, SC
Ryobi North America Inc., Anderson, SC
Sears/Craftsman, Hoffman Estates, IL
Sherwin Williams Co., Cleveland, OH
Skil Canada, Markham, Ont.
Taller Manufacturing, Madison, IN
3M Canada Inc., Dorval, Que.
Western Wood Products Association, Portland, OR
Woodcraft Supply Corp., Parkersburg, WV

For more information on *Basic Woodworking* or any other
Sunset Book, call 1-800-634-3095. For special sales, bulk
orders, and premium sales information, call Sunset Custom
Publishing Services at (415) 324-5577.

Picture Credits
Photos courtesy of the following:
p.   5 Woodcraft Supply Corp.
p.   9 *(upper)* Skil Canada
        (middle) Milwaukee Electric Tool Corp.
        (lower) Dewalt Industrial Tool Co.
p. 10 Delta International Machinery/Porter-Cable
p. 11 *(upper)* Ryobi North America Inc.
        (lower) Delta International Machinery/Porter-Cable
p. 15 *(upper)* Ryobi North America Inc.
        (middle) Sears/Craftsman
        (lower) Jet Equipment and Tools
p. 17 *(upper left)* Dewalt Industrial Tool Co.
        (upper right) Black & Decker Inc.
        (lower) Sears/Craftsman
p. 21 *(upper)* Dewalt Industrial Tool Co.
        (middle) Black & Decker Inc.
        (lower) Milwaukee Electric Tool Corp.

CONTENTS

TOOLS OF THE TRADE

K nowing the right tools for the job is the starting point for any woodworking project. This chapter will introduce you to the best tools for such basic procedures as measuring, cutting, drilling, and fastening. You will find the techniques for using all of these tools on pages 40 to 69.

Woodworking principles haven't changed much over the years, but technology has. Faster, more expensive, and often more precise ways have been found to do the most basic tasks. However, expensive power tools are not necessary for first-rate work; hand tools still produce exceptional results when they're used skillfully. In general, however, power tools perform faster and more accurately for the average woodworker who's had some practice with them. The choice is yours.

One principle is still true: Buying good tools will save you money in the end. And generally, you get what you pay for. When sorting out brands and models, weigh the advice of experienced friends, professionals, and knowledgeable dealers. Whenever possible, get hands-on experience with tools before you buy. To find quality tools, look in woodworking specialty shops, hardware stores, and home improvement centers. Some top-quality or specialized tools may be accessible only by mail-order; for these, check with other woodworkers or thumb through woodworking magazines and craft publications.

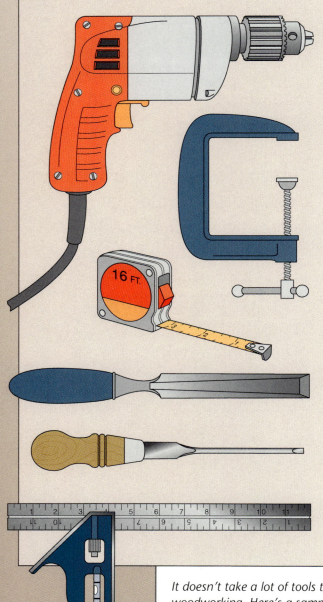

It doesn't take a lot of tools to set yourself up for basic woodworking. Here's a sampling; browse through this chapter before deciding how to stock your workshop.

THE WORKBENCH

No tool is more important in helping you work safely and efficiently than a good workbench. It provides a flat, sturdy surface and, with the right accessories, an extra pair of hands.

Probably the most important feature of a workbench is that it be rock steady, with careful joinery, durable hardware, and heavy proportions. The top should be at least 1½ inches thick; ideally, it should be built from solid hardwood. A typical bench is between 5 and 8 feet long and up to 3 feet in depth. If you work primarily with hand tools, the top of the bench should be at wrist height; otherwise, it should be about 6 inches higher than wrist level.

Built-in clamping devices—vises, bench dogs, and bench stops—distinguish the woodworker's bench from an ordinary worktable. Good workbenches, such as the one below, are available commercially. If you construct your own, you can buy plans and the hardware for shoulder and tail vises through a woodworking specialty outlet. Or, install a woodworker's vise on a heavy-duty worktable. The most durable dogs and stops are metal, but you can make your own by drilling holes to fit hardwood dowels.

As a backup for a workbench, every shop should have a pair of sawhorses, useful for cutting with hand or portable power saws, sanding, and even finishing large pieces.

THE WORKHORSE OF THE WORKSHOP

Bench dog
Insert in dog hole in bench and vise; vise adjusts to hold workpiece.

Tool tray
Keeps tools at hand, but off the bench surface.

Tail vise
Clamps workpiece in vertical position or, with adjustable dog raised, works with corresponding bench dogs or stops to provide two-point clamping for stock of almost any size or shape.

Shoulder vise
Holds stock vertically or on edge for tasks such as sawing, planing, and drilling. Long pieces need additional support at other end. Wooden jaws won't damage workpiece.

BENCH ACCESSORIES

Bench hold-down
Clamps pieces to bench. Fits onto bolt in mortise in bench surface; easily removable. Several bolts can be placed in different locations on workbench.

Bench dogs
Used with tail or shoulder vise to clamp pieces flat on bench. Integral spring holds dog in place, yet allows for easy removal.

Bench stop
Middle-of-the-bench clamping point, used in conjunction with bench dog in tail or shoulder vise. Installed in mortise in bench so that it remains flush with surface when not in use.

Bench hook
Used to hold stock steady for small cross-cutting tasks, usually with backsaw (page 44). Angled slots for miter cuts. Lower lip hugs bench edge; cutting mark lines up with upper lip. Usually shop-built; make sure top lip is perfectly square with base.

Woodworker's vise
Secures work vertically or on edge. Look for adjustable dog (to secure work flat on bench) and quick-release lever, as shown; metal jaws need protective pads. Can be installed on worktable.

MEASURING AND MARKING TOOLS

All successful woodworking projects begin with the same three procedures: accurate measurement, layout, and marking. Though hundreds of tools are available for these crucial first steps, basic woodworking requires only a small collection. You can go a long way with just a tape measure, combination square, pencil, and compass. Add more specialized tools—such as a marking gauge or trammel points—as you need them.

Because the quality of any project depends on precise dimensions, invest in the best layout tools you can afford. As well as woodworking and hardware suppliers, try drafting, engineering, and art supply stores for the precision instruments that a woodworker requires.

Measuring tools: Although a rigid bench rule is adequate for measuring distances of a foot or two, you'll need other tools for accurate gauging beyond that, or for measuring cylindrical objects. A kit of standard measuring tools is shown at right.

Layout tools: Squares are the primary tools used to lay out cutting lines. Most squares indicate 90° angles; some also show 45° angles. A selection of these and other helpful layout tools are shown on page 7.

Marking tools: The trusty 2H pencil will see you through most straight-line marking tasks, but for curves or for more precise results, the tools shown on page 7 will come in handy. To draw large circles, you can also use an improvised beam compass (*page 38*).

TOOLS THAT ALWAYS MEASURE UP

Folding wooden rule
Generally 6' long; made from several 6" or 8" sections hinged together. Extends easily without support at the far end. Sliding extension helps accurate inside measurements; add length of extension to exposed rule body's length.

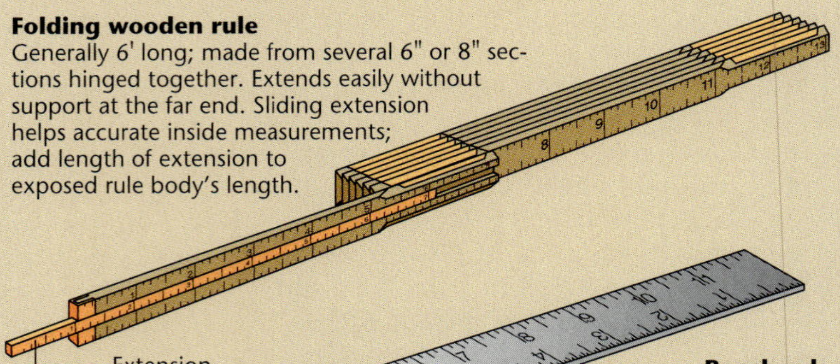

Extension

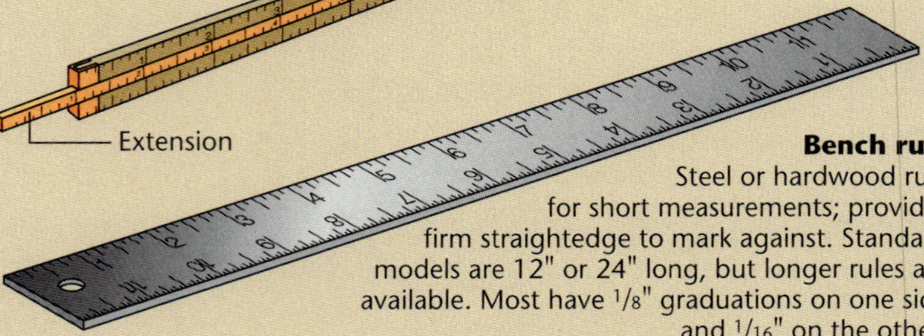

Bench rule
Steel or hardwood rule for short measurements; provides firm straightedge to mark against. Standard models are 12" or 24" long, but longer rules are available. Most have 1/8" graduations on one side and 1/16" on the other.

Tape measure
For all-round utility, use 3/4" wide, 16' long flexible steel tape with 1/16" graduations. Locking button keeps tape from retracting. End hook should be loosely riveted to adjust for precise inside and outside readings. Cases are often an even 2" or 3" in length, aiding inside measurements.

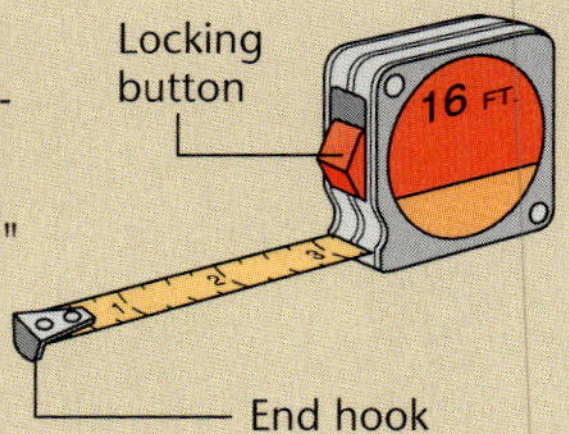

Locking button

16 FT.

End hook

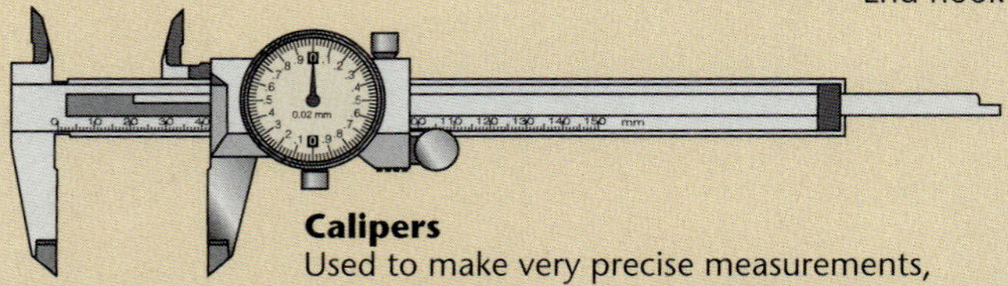

Calipers
Used to make very precise measurements, to transfer measurements, and to measure inside and outside dimensions of cylindrical objects. Model shown gives reading on dial.

🔴 ASK A PRO

HOW DO I KNOW IF A SQUARE IS PERFECTLY SQUARE?
To test a square for accuracy, hold the handle snugly against a straight-edged board and draw a line along the blade. Then flop the square over and repeat the procedure. The two lines should match exactly. A faulty carpenter's square can be repaired, but an off-kilter try or combination square will have to be discarded.

To fix a carpenter's square whose body and tongue form an angle less than 90°, hit the inside corner of the heel with a punch and a ball-peen hammer. Hit the outside corner to correct a square at an angle larger than 90°. Repeat the test and procedure until the tool is square.

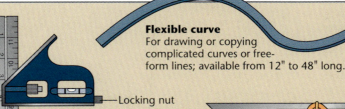

TOOLS FOR ACCURATE LAYOUTS

Try square
Traditional tool for laying out and checking 90° angles; some models include bevel on handle for laying out short miters. Typical blade sizes are 6", 8", and 12"; larger ones are best for general work.

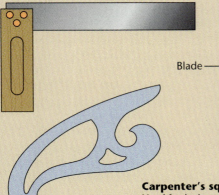

French curves
For laying out irregular curves and arcs, tracing smooth arc between two points.

Combination square
Used for laying out and checking 45° and 90° angles. Sliding handle tightens anywhere along blade for use as depth gauge; blade can be removed and used as bench rule. Spirit level in handle can spot-check level and plumb. Some models have removable scribe to mark fine lines. Make sure there is no play between handle and blade.

Locking nut

Blade

Carpenter's square
Used for laying out lines and checking square when try or combination square is too small. Standard model has 1¹/₂"x16" tongue and 2"x24" body, which meet at exact 90° angle at heel. Steel squares are most durable.

Flexible curve
For drawing or copying complicated curves or free-form lines; available from 12" to 48" long.

Adjustable T bevel
For transferring and checking angles; handy for miters and bevels. Set pivoting blade at any angle between 0° and 180° with protractor, or match existing angle.

Protractor
Used to mark or measure angles.

Body   Heel   Tongue

TOOLS THAT MAKE THEIR MARK

Compass
Essential for drawing circles and arcs with radii up to about 5"; can also be used to "step off" equal measurements.

Pencil lead

Marking gauge
Accurately scribes lines parallel to any straight edge. Adjustable fence guides scribed line. Some models include graduated scale on beam for quick reference.

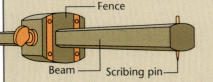

Fence

Beam   Scribing pin

Scratch awl and marking knife
Mark finer lines than pencil when precision really counts; however, unlike pencil mark, this line can't be erased.

Trammel points
To mark circles and arcs with radii greater than a compass can handle. Clamp points—one with pencil lead—to wooden beam or yardstick.

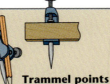

Dovetail square
Marks correct angle of dovetail pins and tails; available in different slopes for joints made in hardwood and softwood.

Wind-up crank

Chalk line
Marks long cutting or layout lines; ideal for dividing up large sheet materials. Long, spool-wound cord is housed within chalk-filled case; end hook wraps around board's edge.

ASK A PRO

HOW CAN I USE MY COMBINATION SQUARE AS A MARKING GAUGE?
By setting your combination square to the proper width or thickness it can serve as an improvised marking gauge. Hold a pencil in the notch at the end of the rule and run the handle down the board's edge.

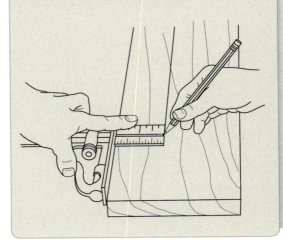

CUTTING TOOLS

Accurate, consistent cutting is essential to strong, square joints and furniture assemblies. In fact, the key to basic woodworking is the combination of precise measuring and careful cutting. Woodworking saws range from handsaws and portable power saws to the more costly stationary power saws. Truth be known, you could make most cuts with a few handsaws only—a crosscut saw, rip saw, backsaw, and coping saw—but a portable circular saw and saber saw will make your work much easier. It is best to learn with basic saws, then move up to a stationary tool *(page 10)* as your needs, budget, and inclinations dictate.

Handsaws: A collection of handsaws is illustrated below. The basic saws are: a crosscut saw for cutting lumber to length, a backsaw for joinery, and a coping saw for cutting curves. A saw's function is a product of its shape, its blade size, and the position and number of teeth along the blade. The term "point" indicates both tooth size and number of teeth per inch (often abbreviated as tpi). An 8-point saw actually has 7 teeth per inch, since the points at both ends of that inch are included. In general, the fewer the teeth, the rougher and faster the cut. For instance, an 8-point crosscut saw would be used for rough, fast cutting, while a 10-point model would cut more slowly, but yield smoother results.

Cutting characteristics are also affected by the amount of set. Saw teeth are bent outward to produce a cut wider than the blade; without this set, the saw would bind in the cut, or kerf. A wider set produces a faster but rougher cut; the smaller the set, the finer the kerf.

Japanese saws are becoming increasingly popular. They cut on the pull stroke, unlike other saws, which cut on the push stroke. Although the blade is thinner—leaving a smaller kerf—it will not buckle from pressure.

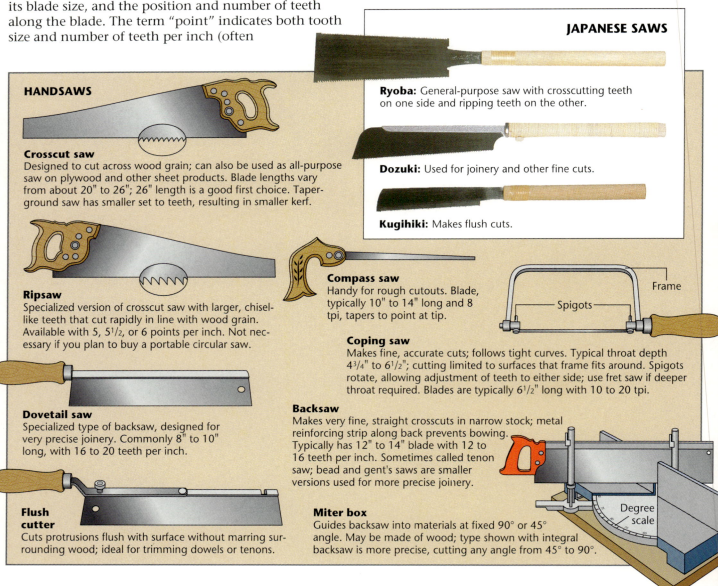

JAPANESE SAWS

Ryoba: General-purpose saw with crosscutting teeth on one side and ripping teeth on the other.

Dozuki: Used for joinery and other fine cuts.

Kugihiki: Makes flush cuts.

HANDSAWS

Crosscut saw
Designed to cut across wood grain; can also be used as all-purpose saw on plywood and other sheet products. Blade lengths vary from about 20" to 26"; 26" length is a good first choice. Taper-ground saw has smaller set to teeth, resulting in smaller kerf.

Ripsaw
Specialized version of crosscut saw with larger, chisel-like teeth that cut rapidly in line with wood grain. Available with 5, 5 1/2, or 6 points per inch. Not necessary if you plan to buy a portable circular saw.

Dovetail saw
Specialized type of backsaw, designed for very precise joinery. Commonly 8" to 10" long, with 16 to 20 teeth per inch.

Flush cutter
Cuts protrusions flush with surface without marring surrounding wood; ideal for trimming dowels or tenons.

Compass saw
Handy for rough cutouts. Blade, typically 10" to 14" long and 8 tpi, tapers to point at tip.

Coping saw
Makes fine, accurate cuts; follows tight curves. Typical throat depth 4 3/4" to 6 1/2"; cutting limited to surfaces that frame fits around. Spigots rotate, allowing adjustment of teeth to either side; use fret saw if deeper throat required. Blades are typically 6 1/2" long with 10 to 20 tpi.

Backsaw
Makes very fine, straight crosscuts in narrow stock; metal reinforcing strip along back prevents bowing. Typically has 12" to 14" blade with 12 to 16 teeth per inch. Sometimes called tenon saw; bead and gent's saws are smaller versions used for more precise joinery.

Miter box
Guides backsaw into materials at fixed 90° or 45° angle. May be made of wood; type shown with integral backsaw is more precise, cutting any angle from 45° to 90°.

Frame

Spigots

Degree scale

Portable power saws: In the realm of portable power tools, the standard saws for today's woodworker are the circular saw and the saber saw (or jigsaw). A circular saw with the correct blade *(page 10)* will cut 10 times faster than is possible with a crosscut saw, and it is your best choice for rip cuts. Circular saws range in size from $5^1/_2$ to $8^1/_4$ inches (referring to the largest diameter of blade the saw can accommodate). The popular $7^1/_4$-inch saw cuts through surfaced 2-by lumber at any angle from 45° to 90°.

The saber saw's specialty is curves, circles, and cutouts, but it also makes straight cuts, miters, and bevels. Its high-speed motor drives interchangeable blades in an up-and-down (reciprocating) motion; an orbital-action saw features a blade that advances as it goes up, retracts as it comes down.

The plate, or biscuit joiner, makes reinforced butt joints quickly and easily. Its circular blade plunges into the edge or face of the stock to cut semicircular grooves in each of the mating pieces, which are then attached by gluing oval wooden "biscuits" in the slots.

CIRCULAR SAW

ON/OFF trigger

Gunsight notch
Indicates where blade will cut; line up with cutting mark on stock. When different blade is installed, check that notch still lines up with outer cutting edge of blade.

Upper blade guard
Fixed in place.

Base plate

Ripping fence slot
For accessory fence; attached to guide straight cuts near edge of stock.

Angle adjustment lock
For bevel cuts; sets blade at angle in relation to base plate.

Lower blade guard
Spring-action guard retracts to expose blade as you cut, then returns to closed position.

SABER SAW (JIGSAW)

Blade-locking screw
Tightened to hold blade in place; ensure tang (shank) of blade fits your saw's locking device.

Blade
Use 4 to 7 tpi blade for rough, fast cuts in wood; 8 to 12 tpi for fine work, tight curves, and scrollwork.

Ripping fence slot
For accessory fence that ensures straight rip cuts; most models become circle guides when turned upside down with end of arm pinned to center of circle.

Locking button
Maintains motor speed without depressing trigger.

Variable-speed trigger
Saw motor accelerates when squeezed; allows fine control when cutting tight curves or different materials.

Base plate
Adjusts to 45° for bevel cuts.

PLATE JOINER

Faceplate
Contains blade slot; pressed against surface to be cut.

Center guide

ON/OFF switch or trigger
May have locking button to free hand during cuts.

Fence
Rests on piece to be cut; adjustable to 45° for beveled edges. Top part rests on stock's face for edge cuts; height set for correct location of groove on edge.

Center guide

Return spring
Retracts blade behind faceplate.

Depth stop
Set to correct blade depth for different size biscuits.

Base plate

Stationary power saws: Though far more costly than either hand or portable power tools, stationary saws offer the ultimate in speed and precision to the woodworker with a lot of fine cutting to do. The table saw is the cabinetmaker's old standby for straight, clean cuts; the radial-arm saw, originally a contractor's framing tool, is a popular alternative, especially for crosscutting lumber. Both saws accommodate a variety of blades for special tasks and materials *(below)*. The band saw is the tool of choice for cutting tight curves or thick materials.

Excellent for accurate rip cuts and for cutting sheet materials, the **table saw** is essentially a circular saw mounted in a table. However, instead of moving the blade through the wood, you feed the wood into the blade. The key to this tool's accuracy is the integrity of its arbor and trunnions, and rip fence and miter gauge; the latter two present the stock perfectly parallel or perpendicular to the blade, for rip cuts and crosscuts, respectively.

Table saws are sized by the maximum diameter blade that they can accept. For all-round work, you should look for a 9- or 10-inch model equipped with at least a 1-horsepower motor. The less expensive 8-inch saws, especially "tabletop" versions, often have a limited ripping capacity and may be underpowered.

TABLE SAW

Miter gauge slot
Carefully machined to be parallel to blade; track for miter gauge, tenoning jigs and other accessories.

Blade guard
Clear plastic; stays in contact with stock.

Rip fence
Guides stock for rip cuts.

Splitter
Prevents stock from binding around blade and kicking back into operator. May also hold antikickback pawls.

Table

Front fence rail
Track for rip fence to slide along.

On/off switch

Miter gauge
Guides stock for crosscuts; head angle adjusts for miter cuts.

Blade tilt control
Angles blade for beveling.

Extension table
Typically included; for safer handling of wide boards and awkward sheet materials.

Blade height control

WHICH BLADE?
Carbide-tipped saw blades are recommended; although more costly than standard steel, they stay sharp much longer.

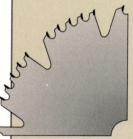

Combination blade
General-purpose blade; normally comes with saw. Used for crosscuts, miter cuts, and rips, but without speed and precision of specialized blade. Typically with 40 to 60 teeth on 10" blade.

Rip blade
Features wide, chisel-like teeth for fast cuts with grain. Has fewer teeth than crosscut blade; typically 24 to 40 teeth on 10" blade.

Plywood blade
Resists abrasion from plywood glues; fine teeth won't splinter plywood, thin veneers, or paneling. Typically with 100 to 120 teeth on 10" blade.

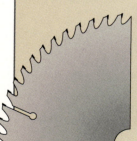

Crosscut blade
Also known as cutoff; finer teeth than combination blades for smooth cuts across grain. Typically with 80 to 100 teeth on 10" blade.

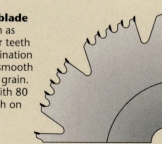

Master combination planer blade
Makes smoother cross, miter, and rip cuts than standard combination blade. Typically hollow-ground with 40 to 60 teeth on 10" blade.

Stacking dado head
Makes cuts in variety of widths in one pass. Type shown has chippers sandwiched between two blades; adjust number of chippers for desired width of cut. Not for use on portable circular saw.

Though the **radial-arm saw** uses the same blade types as the table saw, it works very differently. The wood is positioned on the table, and the motor and blade slide along the arm into the wood. The blade is kept in the straight position for crosscuts, swiveled to one side for miters, or tilted for bevels. For a rip cut, you rotate the yoke assembly 90° and push the stock into the blade, which remains in place. The advantages of this saw are that it crosscuts long boards handily, and, because the blade cuts from above, you can see what you're cutting. But it's awkward to rip—or even crosscut—wide sheet materials, and is very hard to keep in fine adjustment. Follow the manufacturer's instructions to fine-tune the saw for accuracy.

Home workshop radial-arm saws are available in 8¾- to 12-inch versions; a 10-inch saw with a 1½-horsepower motor is a common choice. It should be able to crosscut 24 inches. Some newer models have a safety device that controls sudden blade advance, also improving the precision of cut.

Noted for its ability to cut tight curves and irregular shapes, the **band saw** will also make straight cuts and is considered safer for ripping boards than the table saw or radial-arm saw. Better models will handle materials thicker than 6 inches, which makes them well-suited to resawing boards to the thickness you need. This saw is basically a long, continuous blade looped around a lower, motor-driven wheel and an upper, adjustable wheel. Band saws are sized by wheel diameter, which corresponds to throat depth, meaning the largest radius or width of material you can cut. Band saws for home shops range from about 10 to 14 inches.

RADIAL-ARM SAW

Elevating crank
Raises or lowers arm on column to set depth of cut.

Arm
Supports motor and blade assembly. Swiveled into angled position for miter cuts.

On/off switch

Column

Yoke
Motor and blade assembly; with handle to pull blade into stock. Holds blade perpendicular to fence for crosscuts, or parallel for rip cuts.

Blade guard
Includes clear plastic lower guard.

Bevel lock
Holds motor in vertical or horizontal position, or on angle for bevel cuts.

Blade

Bevel angle scale

Fence
Blade cuts through for crosscuts or miters; replaceable.

Table
Surface in front of fence; add ¼" hardboard for protection, replacing it when badly cut up.

Splitter
Lowered to ride in kerf when ripping to prevent wood from binding around blade; has integral antikickback fingers.

BAND SAW

Blade tension knob
Adjusted to keep blade to correct tightness; when pushed laterally, blade should only move ¼".

Miter gauge slot
Allows use of miter gauge to guide stock.

Blade guard

Blade
Can be from about ⅛" to ½" wide; wide blades are for straight cuts, narrow blades for tight curves.

Table
May have track on either side to attach rip fence.

Bevel scale

Table tilt clamp
Holds table at angle for bevel cuts.

Motor

ON/OFF switch

Dust chute

Lower blade guide
Keeps blade from moving from side to side. Second set located above table.

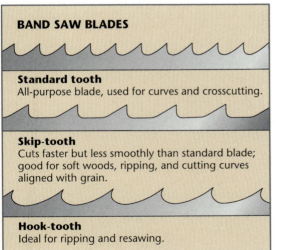

BAND SAW BLADES

Standard tooth
All-purpose blade, used for curves and crosscutting.

Skip-tooth
Cuts faster but less smoothly than standard blade; good for soft woods, ripping, and cutting curves aligned with grain.

Hook-tooth
Ideal for ripping and resawing.

HAND SHAPING TOOLS

After pieces have been sawn, they may require additional cutting, shaping, and smoothing before they can be assembled. The basic hand tools used for these tasks are shown below and on page 13. Chisels and planes must be kept sharp to do their jobs properly; sharpening techniques are shown on page 14. The power tools used for shaping begin on page 15, and tools used to smooth wood, or to remove material, in preparation for finishing are found on pages 20 and 21.

Planes: Jobs such as leveling surfaces, squaring up boards, and adjusting joints call for a plane. The types of planes commonly used in woodworking fall into two categories: block and bench planes. Block planes smooth end grain and bench planes square and smooth wood in line with the grain. They include the jack plane and the jointer plane (both shown below), and the smoothing plane, about 10 inches long and used when extremely smooth results are desired. If you're working strictly with hand tools, you'll also want to consider some of the specialty planes shown below. These are available through mail-order sources or woodworking specialty shops.

Files and rasps: These tools can be used to shape and smooth wood in situations where planes or sanding tools are not practical, such as curves or interior cuts. In general, files shape both metal and wood, while rasps are used for wood only. To choose the file or rasp for the job at hand, consider the pattern and coarseness of the teeth, as well as the length and shape of the tool. File tooth patterns include single- and double-cut, and the coarseness ratings, from rough to smooth, are called bastard, second cut, and smooth cut. Rasps may be classified the same way as files, or they may be rated using terms such as wood rasp (the coarsest) and cabinet rasp (the finest). A longer file or rasp is coarser than a shorter file of the same type, since the teeth on the longer tool are relatively larger. Common shapes include flat, half-round, and round (or rat-tail); the half-round file or rasp is the best general-purpose tool. When you purchase a new file, also buy a handle. Slip the handle's ferrule over the tang, then rap the handle end on a hard surface to drive it on.

Chisels: These are the tools of choice to pare notches and grooves, dig out deep mortises or shave hinge mortises, cut joints, smooth small areas, and clean up surfaces worked with other tools. The basic set of bench chisels includes $1/4$-, $1/2$-, $3/4$-, and 1-inch sizes; otherwise, buy sizes appropriate for the tasks to be performed.

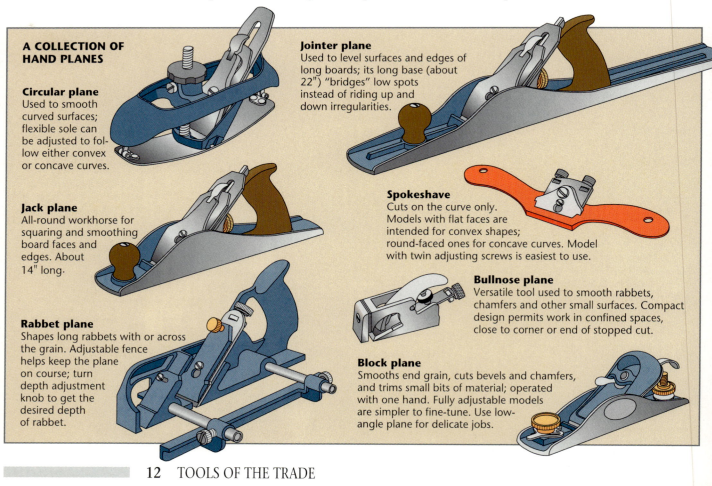

A COLLECTION OF HAND PLANES

Circular plane
Used to smooth curved surfaces; flexible sole can be adjusted to follow either convex or concave curves.

Jack plane
All-round workhorse for squaring and smoothing board faces and edges. About 14" long.

Rabbet plane
Shapes long rabbets with or across the grain. Adjustable fence helps keep the plane on course; turn depth adjustment knob to get the desired depth of rabbet.

Jointer plane
Used to level surfaces and edges of long boards; its long base (about 22") "bridges" low spots instead of riding up and down irregularities.

Spokeshave
Cuts on the curve only. Models with flat faces are intended for convex shapes; round-faced ones for concave curves. Model with twin adjusting screws is easiest to use.

Bullnose plane
Versatile tool used to smooth rabbets, chamfers and other small surfaces. Compact design permits work in confined spaces, close to corner or end of stopped cut.

Block plane
Smooths end grain, cuts bevels and chamfers, and trims small bits of material; operated with one hand. Fully adjustable models are simpler to fine-tune. Use low-angle plane for delicate jobs.

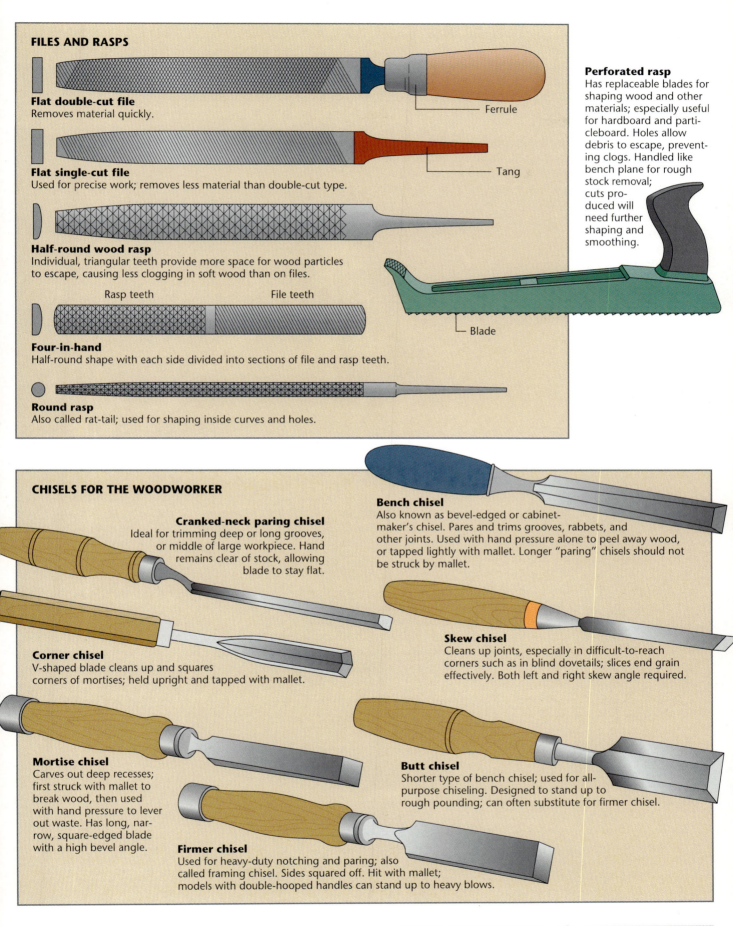

FILES AND RASPS

Flat double-cut file
Removes material quickly.

Ferrule

Flat single-cut file
Used for precise work; removes less material than double-cut type.

Tang

Half-round wood rasp
Individual, triangular teeth provide more space for wood particles to escape, causing less clogging in soft wood than on files.

Rasp teeth   File teeth

Four-in-hand
Half-round shape with each side divided into sections of file and rasp teeth.

Blade

Round rasp
Also called rat-tail; used for shaping inside curves and holes.

Perforated rasp
Has replaceable blades for shaping wood and other materials; especially useful for hardboard and particleboard. Holes allow debris to escape, preventing clogs. Handled like bench plane for rough stock removal; cuts produced will need further shaping and smoothing.

CHISELS FOR THE WOODWORKER

Cranked-neck paring chisel
Ideal for trimming deep or long grooves, or middle of large workpiece. Hand remains clear of stock, allowing blade to stay flat.

Bench chisel
Also known as bevel-edged or cabinet-maker's chisel. Pares and trims grooves, rabbets, and other joints. Used with hand pressure alone to peel away wood, or tapped lightly with mallet. Longer "paring" chisels should not be struck by mallet.

Corner chisel
V-shaped blade cleans up and squares corners of mortises; held upright and tapped with mallet.

Skew chisel
Cleans up joints, especially in difficult-to-reach corners such as in blind dovetails; slices end grain effectively. Both left and right skew angle required.

Mortise chisel
Carves out deep recesses; first struck with mallet to break wood, then used with hand pressure to lever out waste. Has long, narrow, square-edged blade with a high bevel angle.

Firmer chisel
Used for heavy-duty notching and paring; also called framing chisel. Sides squared off. Hit with mallet; models with double-hooped handles can stand up to heavy blows.

Butt chisel
Shorter type of bench chisel; used for all-purpose chiseling. Designed to stand up to rough pounding; can often substitute for firmer chisel.

SHARPENING CHISELS AND PLANE IRONS

When your chisel or plane iron tears and crushes the wood fibers instead of cutting them, it's time to practice the technique that gives steel its edge.

The edge on a chisel or iron is formed by a bevel of about 25° ground into the face of the tool's tip. Grinding produces hundreds of tiny gouges and scratches that have to be removed. Honing—polishing the bevel on progressively finer abrasives until the tip is smooth—actually sharpens the tool. If the edge is badly nicked or if the bevel is worn down, grind a new bevel; otherwise, just hone the tool.

Choose a type of benchstone to use for honing. Oilstones, either natural or manufactured, require light oil as a lubricant. Prized among oilstones are natural Arkansas stones, sawn from novaculite. The preferred alternative to an oilstone is a manufactured waterstone, lubricated with water. Fast, smooth-cutting, more consistent in texture, they are much cheaper than Arkansas stones.

Grinding and honing chisels and plane irons

TOOLKIT
- Bench grinder with a 36- to 60-grit abrasive wheel OR
- Benchstones: coarse and fine

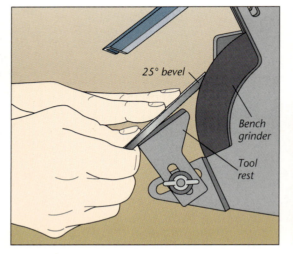

Grinding a bevel
Wear safety goggles. With the grinder unplugged, place your index finger against the front edge of the tool rest. Rest the chisel or iron on this finger so its bevel rides flat on the grinding wheel. Clamp down on the back of the tool with your thumb to complete the grip; rest the fingers of your other hand on the back also. Practice moving your hands steadily back and forth as a unit, applying slight pressure at the tip of the tool as it contacts the wheel. Plug the grinder in and make several passes in this way; then, keeping the same grip on the tool, dip its end in water. Alternate between grinding and cooling. After half a dozen repetitions, examine the bevel. Hone the tool when the edge is square and the entire bevel reflects light uniformly.

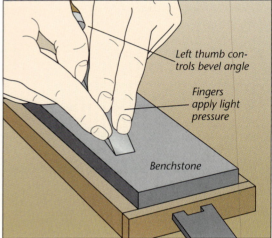

Honing the bevel
Lubricate the stone; keep it wet during honing. Hold the tool's bevel flat against the coarse stone. Rest the upper portion of the tool on your thumb, with your fingers pressing down lightly on the upturned back of the tool near its tip. Your other hand determines the direction of the stroke and does the pushing; stroke lightly and consistently up and down or in a figure-eight motion. When a wire edge, or burr, forms at the tip (typically after 5 to 10 strokes), take a few strokes on the stone with the tool's back pressed flat against it (called "backing off"). Now resume honing the bevel. To check your progress, examine the tool under bright light. When the bevel gleams as a single surface, move on to the finer stone and repeat the honing process.

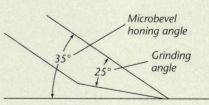

ASK A PRO

HOW CAN I MAKE HONING FASTER AND LESS TIRING?
The procedure will be more manageable if you create a microbevel by sharpening only the narrow band of steel at the very tip instead of the entire bevel. To do this, hone the tool at a 35° angle, as shown. An edge formed with this steeper angle will last longer, and the subsequent sharpening will be much easier.

POWER SHAPING TOOLS

The router produces grooves, rabbets, and mortises, as well as cutting dovetails and shaping edges, while the jointer is key in the preparation of stock for a project.

Router: This stand-up motor rotates a bit at speeds up to 28,000 rpm, making fast, clean cuts. Buy a router with at least a 1-horsepower motor; if you plan to use large bits or cut deep mortises, buy a router that accepts $1/2$-inch-diameter bit shanks rather than the smaller $1/4$-inch shanks. If you plan to use a router table *(page 62)*, make sure the router motor can be separated from its housing. A plunge router facilitates making mortises and other stopped cuts—those that start on the interior of the stock.

Carbide-tipped bits, which stay sharp much longer than steel, are recommended, although costly. High-speed steel bits are sufficient for occasional use. Edge-cutting bits with a ball-bearing pilot are preferable to the fixed type, which may burn the stock. The basic router bits are illustrated below.

Jointer: This stationary tool is simply two tables on either side of a cutterhead that rotates to shave a small amount of wood off the face or edge of the stock. This renders these surfaces even and square with each other, essential for the accuracy of subsequent cuts and joinery. The machine is also used to "joint," or level, the edges of two pieces to be edge-joined, ensuring a perfect fit. Although this can be done with a hand jointer plane, the power jointer is much more efficient.

ROUTER

The plunge router, right, works by pressing down on the handles to drive the bit straight into the wood.

Motor
Raised or lowered to set bit's cutting depth.

Depth indicator

Clamping device
Loosened to move motor up or down.

Depth adjuster
Ring or knob used to set bit depth.

Collet
Holds bit's shank.

Wrench
Turns collet to change bit. Model shown has button to lock shaft, requiring only one wrench for collet nut.

ON/OFF trigger
On handle for easy access.

Housing

Base plate

JOINTER

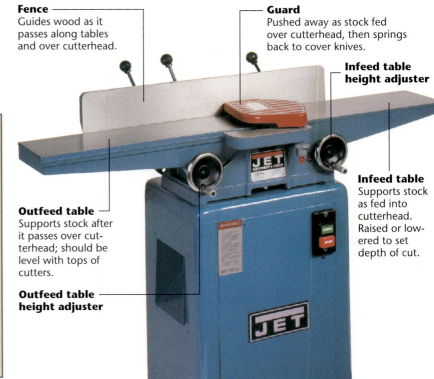

Fence
Guides wood as it passes along tables and over cutterhead.

Guard
Pushed away as stock fed over cutterhead, then springs back to cover knives.

Infeed table height adjuster

Infeed table
Supports stock as fed into cutterhead. Raised or lowered to set depth of cut.

Outfeed table
Supports stock after it passes over cutterhead; should be level with tops of cutters.

Outfeed table height adjuster

WHICH ROUTER BIT?

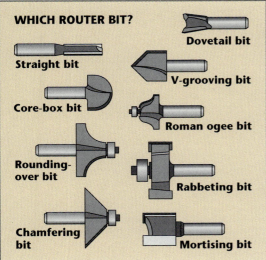

Straight bit

Core-box bit

Rounding-over bit

Chamfering bit

Dovetail bit

V-grooving bit

Roman ogee bit

Rabbeting bit

Mortising bit

DRILLING TOOLS

Woodworkers need to drill holes for screws, bolts, dowels, and hardware; as well, most screws are driven by a drill fitted with a screwdriver bit. The electric drill now is most prevalent, although many woodworkers still find room in their shops for traditional hand drills. They can be operated as slowly as you like, giving complete control when you're starting a hole or driving a screw. Also, it may be simpler to reach for a hand tool than to set up a power drill. A third option, the drill press, is found in many shops, being relatively inexpensive and very handy for precision work.

Hand drills: The hand brace makes large holes (up to 3 inches in diameter); use the hand drill for screw holes up to 1/4 inch in diameter. Operating a hand brace is like turning a crank with a bit attached. Its sweep varies from 6 to 14 inches; a 10-inch brace is a good choice. Some braces have a ratchet, which permits you to bore holes in tight places without having to make a full sweep of the brace's handle. Many ratcheted braces are reversible as well. The hand ("eggbeater") drill is used for holes up to 1/4 inch in diameter. Simply aim and crank the handle. These drills typically have a 1/4-inch chuck capacity and are often used with standard twist bits *(page 17)* or the two-winged drill points that may be found stored in the handle.

Electric drill: Classified by the maximum-size bit shank accommodated in its chuck, the common sizes are 1/4, 3/8, and 1/2 inch. As the chuck size increases, so does power output, or torque; however, the higher the torque, the slower the speed. For most woodworking, the 3/8-inch drill offers the best compromise between power and speed; it also handles a wide range of bits and accessories. For basic woodworking, a medium-duty drill is fine; choose a heavy-duty model for daily use or for long, continuous sessions. Single- and variable-speed drills are available; the latter lets you suit the speed to the job—very handy when starting holes or driving screws. Reversible gears help you remove screws and stuck bits. The common bits for electric drills are shown opposite.

The cordless electric drill, powered by a rechargeable battery pack, is a popular alternative. Buy a second battery pack for long periods of use, so that one can recharge while you work with the other.

Drill press: For accurate drilling, this stationary machine is the tool of choice, as you are guaranteed a perfectly vertical hole. A variety of speeds ensures the correct choice for the bit diameter and stock density. However, extra supports must be set up for large pieces of stock. The typical size for the home workshop would be 11 to 16 inches (from the chuck to the column). A 1/4- to 3/4-horsepower motor is usually adequate. The drill press uses the same bits as an electric drill and then some *(page 17)*, as well as other accessories, such as sanding drums.

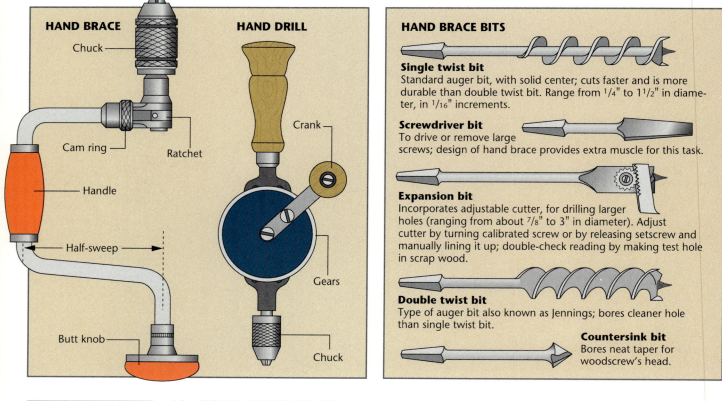

HAND BRACE
- Chuck
- Cam ring
- Ratchet
- Handle
- Half-sweep
- Butt knob

HAND DRILL
- Crank
- Gears
- Chuck

HAND BRACE BITS

Single twist bit
Standard auger bit, with solid center; cuts faster and is more durable than double twist bit. Range from 1/4" to 1 1/2" in diameter, in 1/16" increments.

Screwdriver bit
To drive or remove large screws; design of hand brace provides extra muscle for this task.

Expansion bit
Incorporates adjustable cutter, for drilling larger holes (ranging from about 7/8" to 3" in diameter). Adjust cutter by turning calibrated screw or by releasing setscrew and manually lining it up; double-check reading by making test hole in scrap wood.

Double twist bit
Type of auger bit also known as Jennings; bores cleaner hole than single twist bit.

Countersink bit
Bores neat taper for woodscrew's head.

ELECTRIC DRILL

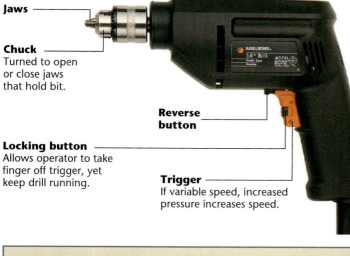

Jaws

Chuck
Turned to open or close jaws that hold bit.

Reverse button

Locking button
Allows operator to take finger off trigger, yet keep drill running.

Trigger
If variable speed, increased pressure increases speed.

CORDLESS DRILL

Rechargeable battery pack

BITS AND CUTTERS FOR YOUR ELECTRIC DRILL AND DRILL PRESS

Expansion bit
Adjustable cutter makes holes from $7/8$" to 3" in diameter. Not for use in electric drill.

Spade bit
For larger holes, from $3/8$" to $1\,1/2$"; center spur prevents the skating common with twist bits. Leaves fairly ragged holes; do not use for holes to be visible or fitted with hardware, plugs, or tenons.

Twist bit
Originally designed for drilling metal. Sizes run from $1/16$" to $1/2$"; sets are graduated by 32nds or 64ths. For durability, choose high-speed steel bits.

Brad-point bit
Makes cleaner holes than twist or spade bits, but more costly; high-speed steel type best. Center spur prevents skating. Available from $1/8$" to an oversize $1/2$".

Pilot bit
Drills pilot hole for screw's threads, larger hole for shank, countersink for head, and counterbore hole for plug to conceal screw's head—all in one operation. Buy individual bits to match screw size; adjust stop collar for correct depth.

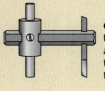

Circle cutter
Use only in drill press, at slow speed; adjusts to cut holes from $7/8$" to 8" diameter.

Plug and tenon cutter
Cuts cylindrical shape; severed for plug or short dowel, left intact for tenon. For use with drill press.

Hole saw
For cutting holes up to 4". Kit comprises mandrel (arbor) with pilot bit, and individual cutters of different sizes that fit onto mandrel.

Screwdriver bit
Transforms variable-speed electric drill into power screwdriver; Phillips and square drive also. Start and end screw slowly to avoid stripping.

Multispur bit
For very clean holes, bored at any angle. Available from $3/8$" to 4" diameter; ideal for drill press.

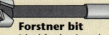

Forstner bit
Ideal for boring clean, flat-bottomed holes. Bores holes in any direction; center spur prevents skating. Range in size from $1/4$" to 2".

DRILL PRESS

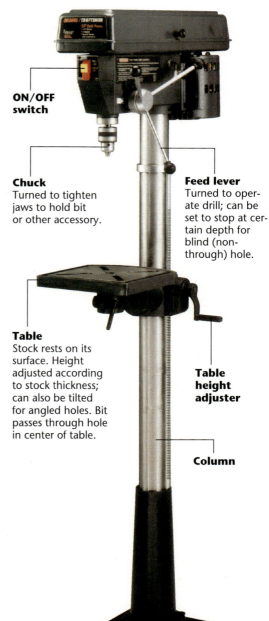

ON/OFF switch

Chuck
Turned to tighten jaws to hold bit or other accessory.

Table
Stock rests on its surface. Height adjusted according to stock thickness; can also be tilted for angled holes. Bit passes through hole in center of table.

Feed lever
Turned to operate drill; can be set to stop at certain depth for blind (non-through) hole.

Table height adjuster

Column

FASTENING TOOLS

A HANDFUL OF HAMMERS AND STRIKING TOOLS

Nailset
Conceals head of finishing nail or brad by driving it below wood's surface; hit with hammer. Match to size of nail head; kit with three nailsets (tip sizes varying from 1/32" to 3/32") handles most fasteners.

Claw hammer
Curved claw offers leverage for nail pulling and allows room to swing in tight spots. Face flat or slightly convex; convex, or bell-faced, type allows you to drive nail flush without marring wood's surface. For general woodworking, 13- or 16-ounce head weight is good. Steel or fiberglass handles are stronger than wood (commonly hickory or ash).

Framing hammer
Has fairly straight ripping claw; designed to pull pieces apart. Common with mesh-type faces for nailing when rough framing; not to be used for fine work where pattern will show.

Cross-peen hammer
Traditional cabinetmaker's hammer; also known as Warrington. Use wedge-shaped cross peen to start small brads and finishing nails without bashing your fingers; use other end for standard nailing. For general work use 6- to 12-ounce models; 3 1/2-ounce "pin hammer" is good for delicate jobs.

Dead-blow hammer
Used for tapping joints together and for disassembly work. Metal shot in head prevents rebound, increasing force of hit; convenient in constricted area.

Mallet
Used to assemble or disassemble stubborn joints, tap dowels into holes, and drive firmer and mortise chisels; head is made of hardwood, plastic, rawhide, or rubber and will not damage wood.

Though hammers and screwdrivers are the basic fastening tools, wrenches also have a place in the woodworker's shop, and no project could be undertaken without clamps. The illustrations below and on page 19 will help you to select the right fastening tools for first-rate results. To choose the correct fasteners to complement these tools, turn to pages 29 to 31.

Hammers: While everyone is familiar with the trusty claw hammer, various other shapes, weights, and compositions of the head must be considered for specific woodworking tasks.

Screwdrivers: There are three main categories of the basic screwdriver, which match the common screw types:

A SELECTION OF SCREWDRIVERS

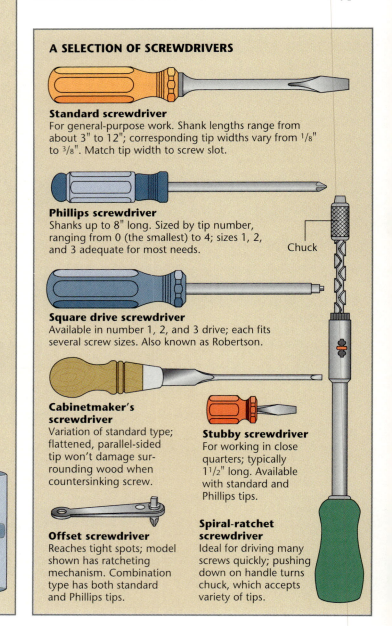

Standard screwdriver
For general-purpose work. Shank lengths range from about 3" to 12"; corresponding tip widths vary from 1/8" to 3/8". Match tip width to screw slot.

Phillips screwdriver
Shanks up to 8" long. Sized by tip number, ranging from 0 (the smallest) to 4; sizes 1, 2, and 3 adequate for most needs.

Chuck

Square drive screwdriver
Available in number 1, 2, and 3 drive; each fits several screw sizes. Also known as Robertson.

Cabinetmaker's screwdriver
Variation of standard type; flattened, parallel-sided tip won't damage surrounding wood when countersinking screw.

Stubby screwdriver
For working in close quarters; typically 1 1/2" long. Available with standard and Phillips tips.

Offset screwdriver
Reaches tight spots; model shown has ratcheting mechanism. Combination type has both standard and Phillips tips.

Spiral-ratchet screwdriver
Ideal for driving many screws quickly; pushing down on handle turns chuck, which accepts variety of tips.

standard, Phillips, and square (or Robertson). Other specialty screwdrivers can save labor and help you reach awkward spots. Within each main category, shank length and tip width—the tip must fit the screw head perfectly—determine the most efficient driver for the task at hand. A long screwdriver lets you apply more force than a shorter one, but the long shank may not leave you much room to maneuver. Screwdriver bits for either an electric drill or a hand brace (*pages 16-17*) are great time- and energy-savers; the reverse gears on an electric drill will also back screws out.

Wrenches: While not used for every woodworking project, wrenches tackle another group of fasteners: bolts and lag screws.

Clamps: These keep the pressure on joints while glue sets; they are also indispensable for holding workpieces firmly for fastening, cutting, shaping, and drilling.

WRENCHES FOR WOODWORKING

Ratchet and socket set
Necessary for countersinking bolt heads and nuts; 3/8" drive is most versatile. Buy range of sockets from 3/8" to 13/16".

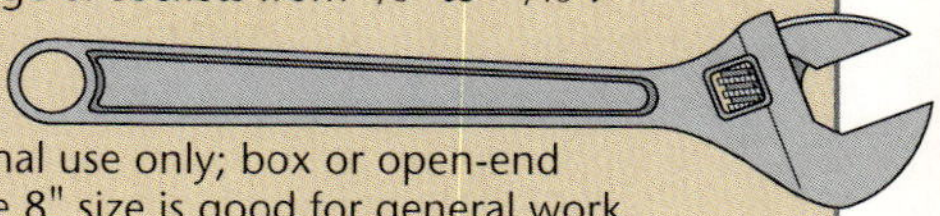

Adjustable wrench
Good for variety of bolt or nut sizes. For occasional use only; box or open-end wrenches are better. The 8" size is good for general work.

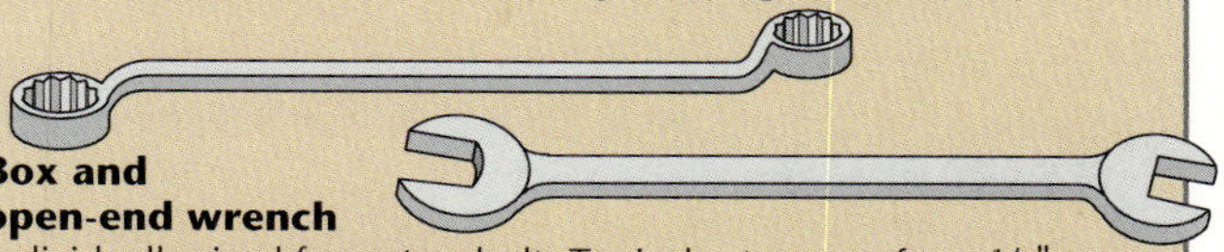

Box and open-end wrench
Individually sized for nut or bolt. Typical set ranges from 1/4" to 1 1/4". Box type is shown above, open-end below; combination wrench has both box and open-end heads.

CONNECTING WITH CLAMPS

Hand screw
General-purpose clamp, ideal for angled, round, or odd-shaped assemblies; non-marring wooden jaws adjust for both depth and angle. Jaws range from 4" to 24" in length, opening from 2" to 17".

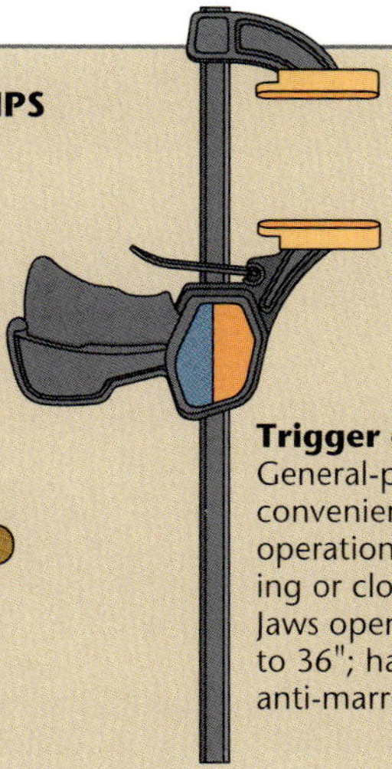

Trigger clamp
General-purpose tool; convenient one-hand operation for opening or closing jaws. Jaws open from 6" to 36"; has built-in anti-marring pads.

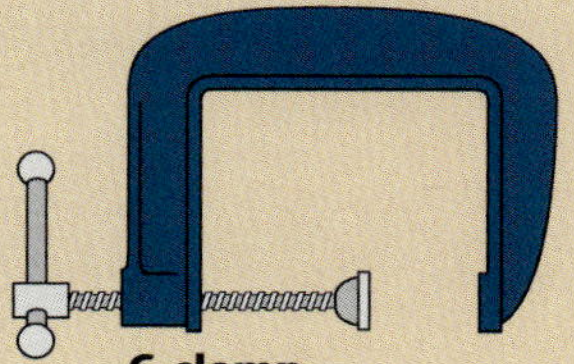

C-clamp
Standard for small jobs—clamping localized areas, holding work to bench or sawhorse, and attaching straightedge guides for cutting or routing. Common jaw openings are 4", 6", and 8"; use wood pads to protect stock.

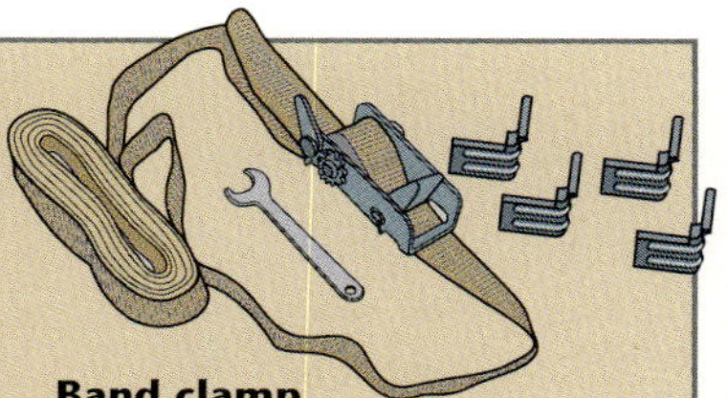

Band clamp
Clamps round, irregular, or square workpieces; comes with corner clips for beveled corners. Nylon or canvas band (1" wide and about 15' long) is drawn securely around object, then tightened with wrench.

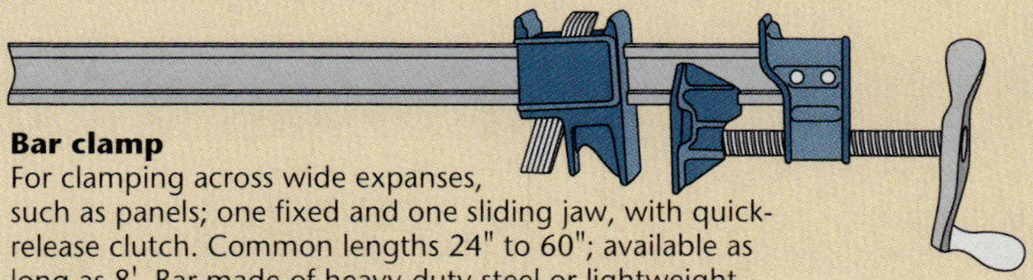

Toggle clamp
Indispensable for holding wood in place on shop-built jigs. Lever raises and lowers padded bolt.

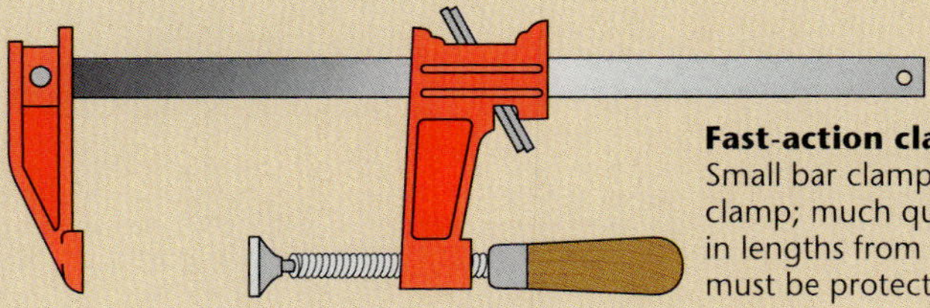

Bar clamp
For clamping across wide expanses, such as panels; one fixed and one sliding jaw, with quick-release clutch. Common lengths 24" to 60"; available as long as 8'. Bar made of heavy-duty steel or lightweight aluminum. Use wood pads to prevent marring.

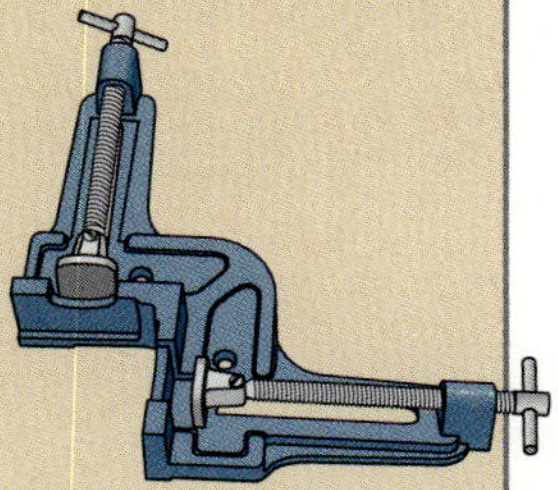

Fast-action clamp
Small bar clamp can be substituted for C-clamp; much quicker to operate. Available in lengths from 6" to 36". Stock to be clamped must be protected with wood pads.

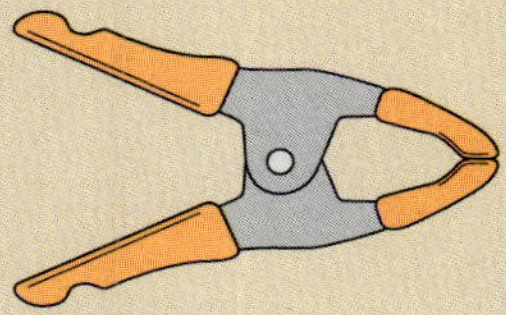

Corner clamp
For 90° miter or butt joints; available for stock up to 3" to 4" wide. Attached to work surface.

Spring clamp
For quick clamping where only light pressure required. With jaw capacities from 1" to 3"; 3" size is most versatile. Usually has protective plastic tips.

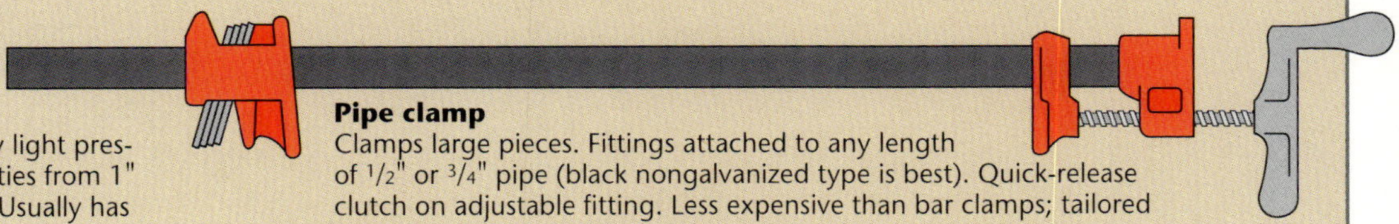

Pipe clamp
Clamps large pieces. Fittings attached to any length of 1/2" or 3/4" pipe (black nongalvanized type is best). Quick-release clutch on adjustable fitting. Less expensive than bar clamps; tailored to suit job. Use protective wood scraps.

FINISHING TOOLS

Woodworking projects require careful smoothing, possibly some repairing, and then finishing before they're ready to be presented to the world. Smoothing means sanding or scraping. Sanding, the most common smoothing technique, can be done with muscle or electric power. Hand-sanding produces good results, and in tight spots or on contoured surfaces, it's the only feasible method. On the other hand, power sanders save time, particularly in the preparatory stages. Three types of power sanders are shown on page 21. Belt sanders abrade wood quickly—they're best for rough leveling over large areas. Finishing sanders, usually with circular action, work at very high speeds (up to 12,000 orbits per minute), giving a polishing effect, but often leaving swirl marks that have to be removed by hand. The random orbit sander produces a very smooth surface, without swirls, and is capable of removing material rapidly. To apply most finishes, you'll need a good brush, roller, or pad; the basic tools are shown on page 21. For details on repairing and finishing wood, turn to page 115.

Use progressively finer sandpaper grades to prepare wood for its finish; steel wool provides the final polish. Scraping is an alternative to sanding—many woodworkers feel that the resulting surface is smoother and

SOME TOOLS FOR HAND SMOOTHING

Sanding block
Provides flat surface for sandpaper. Commercially available *(left)* or homemade *(right)* by wrapping sandpaper around 2x4 wood block faced with ¹/₂" thick felt or sponge rubber pad.

Hook

Steel wool
Mild abrasive, in pad form. Grades 2/0 and 3/0 finely textured; often used for final surface polishing before finish application. Grade 4/0 very finely textured; perfect for smoothing between finish coats.

Hand scraper
Pushed or pulled in line with wood grain; hooked edge produces fine shavings, smoothing surface. Curved shapes for contoured surfaces. Sharpening instructions below.

Sandpaper
Back contains information: type of abrasive, grit number (very coarse 50 to very fine 220 is common range), backing weight (from A, the thinnest, to E), particle spacing (closed-coat has more particles to cut faster, but clogs in soft materials; open coat is better for rough sanding).

Cabinet scraper
Scraper held in frame with two handles; makes scraping less fatiguing and more consistent.

How to sharpen a scraper

TOOLKIT
- Flat file
- Benchstone
- Burnisher

◀ 1 Flattening
Secure the scraper in a vise. File the edge of the scraper to smooth out any nicks or scratches, holding the file flat while moving it along the scraper's edge.

◀ 2 Polishing
(For straight-edged scrapers only, not for curved type.) Lubricate the benchstone and rub each face of the scraper on the stone. Then hold the scraper vertically and run the filed edge back and forth.

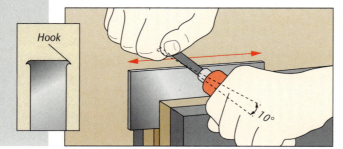

Hook

10°

◀ 3 Forming the hook
Draw a burnisher straight down the edge. Then lower the burnisher's angle to 10° and repeat, first in one direction then in the other, to shape the hook, or burr *(inset)*.

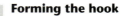

takes finishes better. Choosing the correct material and type of sandpaper—actually not even made with sand—depends on the results you want to achieve. Flint paper, beige in color, offers the least expensive option, but it also is the least durable and effective. Garnet paper, reddish to golden brown, provides excellent results for hand-sanding, especially in the final stages. Aluminum oxide, light gray to grayish brown, is a very tough synthetic material; choose it for rough to medium hand-sanding and for a power sander's belt or pad. Silicon carbide, blue-gray to charcoal, is often called wet-or-dry because its waterproof backing allows you to use it wet, thus eliminating the tendency of its tiny grains to clog. Try it as a final "polish" on wood, or to cut excess gloss between finish coats.

BELT SANDER

Dust collector

Front roller
Freewheeling; rear roller drives sanding belt.

Sanding belt
Sander's size based on belt size that fits it; popular sizes are 3 x 21, 3 x 24, and 4 x 24 inches (width by length). With grit numbers like those on sandpaper sheets; commonly from 36 to 120.

Platen
Flat metal plate for belt to ride over.

Tracking control knob
Centers sanding belt on rollers.

RANDOM ORBIT SANDER

Sanding pad
Commonly 5" or 6" in diameter. Standard pad used for general sanding on flat surface; also available in softer material for sanding contours. Lamb's wool cover can be added for buffing finish.

ON/OFF switch
May be variable speed.

Dust collector
Some models have holes in sanding pad (and paper) for sanding dust to rise through.

Sandpaper
Attached to pad; self-adhesive or with hook-and-loop system. Commonly available grits 80 to 220.

AN ARRAY OF FINISH APPLICATORS

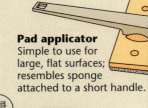

Roller
Paint roller (3" wide) lays on enamels quickly and smoothly.

Pad applicator
Simple to use for large, flat surfaces; resembles sponge attached to a short handle.

Paintbrush
Use 1" brush for edges and delicate trim; 3" type for large, flat surfaces. Use natural bristles (animal hair, commonly Chinese boar) to apply oil-base finishes; synthetic bristles (nylon or polyester) are best for water-base products. Look for "flagged" (split) bristle tips and soft, springy bristles that don't fall out when fanned.

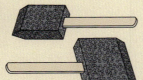

Foam brush
Disposable; produces similar results to pad applicator. Available in different sizes. Not for use with lacquer or shellac.

ORBITAL FINISHING SANDER

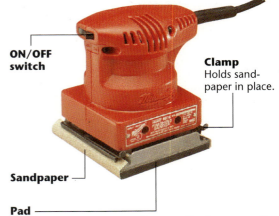

ON/OFF switch

Clamp
Holds sandpaper in place.

Sandpaper

Pad
Base for sandpaper; shape allows sanding in corners. Size of sander indicated by pad size, commonly fitting $1/4$, $1/3$, or $1/2$ sheet of sandpaper. Palm-grip model shown accepts $1/4$ sheet; designed to be held in one hand for ease of use.

THE WOODWORKER'S STOCKROOM

The materials you use in a woodworking project are just as important to the success of the finished product as the workmanship that goes into building it. This chapter covers the basic woodworking materials—lumber, sheet products, and fasteners—and explains the terms associated with each one. Use this information as a guide in determining what you'll need; it will also help you navigate your way through the local lumberyard and hardware store when you are ready to buy.

Lumberyards, home centers, and wholesale yards are good sources for common softwoods, manufactured boards, and fasteners. Fine hardwoods and exotic species are not as readily available at these outlets; try hardwood lumberyards, woodworking specialty shops (often mail-order), rare wood shops, marine stores, or professional woodworkers. If you are having trouble locating what you need, check the Yellow Pages. You'll find lumberyards that specialize in plywoods and other sheet products under "Plywoods & Veneers" and retailers who carry hardwoods listed under "Hardwoods."

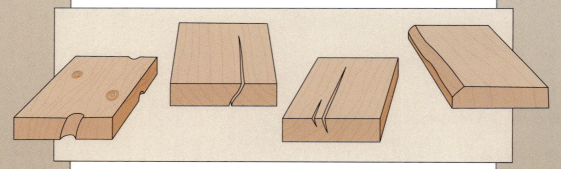

The boards shown above have obvious defects. Though some defective boards can be salvaged, others may have to be scrapped. In this chapter you'll learn what to look for—and what to avoid—when choosing lumber for your project.

SELECTING STOCK

Wood is the starting point for any woodworking project. However, you can't just go to a lumberyard and take the first board you see; size, species, and grade must be taken into account. Make sure you understand these basic terms, and do your homework first. Determine the kind of wood you want to buy, then calculate the exact size of every piece required for your project—adding some for the inevitable wastage. The more careful and complete your planning, the easier it will be to find and buy exactly what you need. If manufactured boards are what you're after, turn to page 25.

Softwood and hardwood: Solid lumber is divided into softwoods—from conifers—and hardwoods—from deciduous trees. Though hardwoods are usually harder, some softwoods, such as Douglas-fir and southern pine, are actually harder than hardwoods such as poplar, aspen, or lauan. As a rule, softwoods are less expensive, easier to work with, and more readily available, but the more durable hardwoods have greater richness and diversity of color, grain, and texture. The characteristics and uses of a variety of wood species are given on pages 27 and 28.

HOW LUMBER IS SOLD

Once you've drawn up the plans for your project, you should know about board measure, nominal size, and moisture content before heading out to buy the stock.

Board measure: Softwoods are sold either by the lineal foot or by the board foot; hardwoods are sold by the lineal foot, by the board foot, or for very dense or expensive types, by the pound. The lineal foot, commonly used for small orders, considers only the piece's length. For example, you might ask for five 1x10s, each 8 feet long, or 40 lineal feet of 1x10.

The board foot—the equivalent of a board 1 inch thick and 1 foot long and wide—is the most common unit for volume orders. To compute board feet, use this formula: (thickness in inches) $\times$ (width in inches $\div$ 12) $\times$ (length in feet). For example, a 1x6 board 10 feet long would be computed: $1" \times 6" \div 12 \times 10' = 5$ board feet.

Nominal and surfaced (actual) sizes: A common mistake is assuming that a 2x4 board is actually 2 inches thick and 4 inches wide. Such numbers give the nominal size of the lumber—its size when sliced from the log. When the piece is dried and surfaced (planed), it's reduced in size, as shown in the chart at right. Available lengths range from 6 to 20 feet, in increments of two feet. Most softwood lumber is surfaced on four sides (designated S4S), but some species are also sold rough, or unsurfaced, remaining close to the nominal dimensions.

Buying hardwoods can be tricky, because they come in random widths and lengths, seemingly odd thicknesses, and often with rough edges. For boards 1 inch or more thick you may see the term four quarter or 4/4;

like 1-by or 2-by, this represents the nominal thickness of a board. A 4/4 board is about 1 inch thick, a 5/4 board about $1\frac{1}{4}$ inches thick, and so on. Hardwoods are normally surfaced thicker than softwoods; see the chart below. Standard lengths range from 4 to 16 feet, in increments of one foot.

The designations S1S, S2S, S3S, and S4S mean surfaced one side, two sides, etc. Hardwoods are often sold S2S, with both faces planed. S1E indicates that the board has been surfaced on one edge; S2E means both edges. These designations can combine to result in something like S1S1E (surfaced one side and one edge). Unless you

STANDARD THICKNESSES OF HARDWOODS	
Rough	Surfaced 2 Sides
$\frac{3}{8}$"	$\frac{3}{16}$"
$\frac{1}{2}$"	$\frac{5}{16}$"
$\frac{5}{8}$"	$\frac{7}{16}$"
$\frac{3}{4}$"	$\frac{9}{16}$"
1"	$\frac{13}{16}$"
$1\frac{1}{4}$"	$1\frac{1}{16}$"
$1\frac{1}{2}$"	$1\frac{5}{16}$"
$1\frac{3}{4}$"	$1\frac{1}{2}$"
2"	$1\frac{3}{4}$"
$2\frac{1}{2}$"	$2\frac{1}{4}$"
3"	$2\frac{3}{4}$"

STANDARD DIMENSIONS OF SOFTWOODS	
Nominal size	Surfaced dry (actual) size
1x2	$\frac{3}{4}$"x$1\frac{1}{2}$"
1x3	$\frac{3}{4}$"x$2\frac{1}{2}$"
1x4	$\frac{3}{4}$"x$3\frac{1}{2}$"
1x6	$\frac{3}{4}$"x$5\frac{1}{2}$"
1x8	$\frac{3}{4}$"x$7\frac{1}{4}$"
1x10	$\frac{3}{4}$"x$9\frac{1}{4}$"
2x2	$1\frac{1}{2}$"x$1\frac{1}{2}$"
2x4	$1\frac{1}{2}$"x$3\frac{1}{2}$"
2x6	$1\frac{1}{2}$"x$5\frac{1}{2}$"
2x8	$1\frac{1}{2}$"x$7\frac{1}{4}$"
2x10	$1\frac{1}{2}$"x$9\frac{1}{4}$"

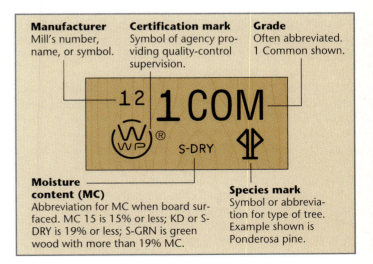

Manufacturer Mill's number, name, or symbol.

Certification mark Symbol of agency providing quality-control supervision.

Grade Often abbreviated. 1 Common shown.

Moisture content (MC) Abbreviation for MC when board surfaced. MC 15 is 15% or less; KD or S-DRY is 19% or less; S-GRN is green wood with more than 19% MC.

Species mark Symbol or abbreviation for type of tree. Example shown is Ponderosa pine.

Reading a grade stamp

The above marking is an example of a grade stamp used by the Western Wood Products Association. If a stamp is applied to appearance grades of lumber, it will be on the back or edge.

have a planer, ask the yard to mill the boards to the exact thickness. For minor resawing jobs—to achieve the desired thickness—a band saw is the tool of choice.

Moisture content (MC): When wood is sawn, it's still "green"—that is, unseasoned; the best lumber is then dried, either by air or kiln. Kiln-drying, the more expensive process, reduces the moisture content to any desired level. For interior woodworking projects, buy "dry" lumber whenever possible. Almost all hardwoods are kiln-dried (KD); softwoods come either air- or kiln-dried, or green. Look for wood stamped "MC 15," which indicates a moisture content not exceeding 15%, although "S-DRY" or "KD," with a maximum MC of 19% is usually stable enough. Green wood will most likely split, warp, or shrink unless you dry it properly.

HOW LUMBER IS GRADED

At the mill, lumber of the same species and size is sorted into grades, then identified with a stamp or inventoried by species and grade. Lumberyards may refer to these grades by different names, so look for a grading stamp or ask for help. Grade distinctions are based on defects; the most economical approach is to decide what you can live with and buy the lowest acceptable grade.

Softwood grades: The two basic categories are dimension lumber (graded for strength) and appearance boards; use the latter for woodworking projects. The most common grading system, employed by the Western Wood Products Association, comprises four main categories for boards, each made up of a number of grades. The Select and Finish grades are those used when appearance counts. Common grades generally sport a knotty look. Alternate board grades (Select Merchantable, Construction, Standard, Utility, and Economy) should be avoided unless intended for a hidden part of the project. High-grade dimension lumber can be used when extra strength or thickness is required.

Select grades comprise B&BTR (the best appearance; often completely clear), C-Select (very good appearance; for items requiring a fine finish), and D-Select (good appearance; for items where the finish isn't as important). **Finish** grades include Superior (the highest grade, including boards that are completely clear), Prime (very good appearance), and E (boards with defects that can be cut off). **Common** grades range from 1 to 5. For woodworking, use 2&Better Common (a combination of 1 and 2 Common; boards with a good, knotty appearance), and 3 Common; avoid 4 and 5 Common.

To complicate the issue, certain lumber species have their own grading systems. For instance, the Idaho white pine (IWP) grades are Supreme, Choice, Quality, Colonial, Sterling, Standard, Utility and Industrial.

For a perfect, natural finish, buy top lumber; the best boards are "clear," with no defects. Buy a lower grade if the board won't be visible, or if you plan to paint and thus hide any defects. Number 2 and 3 Common boards are economical choices, but you must be selective. If only

COMMON LUMBER DEFECTS

Defect	Description	What to do
Crook	Warp along the edge line; also known as crown.	Straighten the edge on a jointer or on a table saw with a jig (page 47).
Bow	Warp on the face of a board from end to end.	Cut the piece into smaller, unbowed pieces, or remove the bow by face-jointing on a jointer.
Cup	Hollow across the face of a board.	Dry the piece until both faces have equal moisture content, or cut the piece to eliminate the cupped part.
Twist	Multiple bends in a board.	Cut off the twisted part, or face-joint to remove the twist.
Knot or knothole	A tight knot is not usually a problem; a loose or dead knot, surrounded by a dark ring, may fall out later, or may already have left a hole.	Cut off the part with a knot or knothole; remove any loose knots before machining the lumber. Sound knots may be kept if a knotty look is desired.
Check	Crack along the wood's annual growth rings, not passing through the entire thickness of the wood.	Cut off or fill (page 117) the checked portion.
Split	Crack going all the way through the piece of wood, commonly at the ends.	Cut off the split part of the board.
Shake	Separation of grain between the growth rings, often extending along the board's face, and sometimes below its surface.	Cut off the shake.
Wane	Missing wood or untrimmed bark along the edge or corner of the piece.	Edge-joint or cut off the affected part.

one side will show, a lower-grade board with one defect-free face may suit your purpose.

Hardwood grades: Hardwoods are graded by the number of defects in a given length and width of board; you can often get by with a lower grade, depending on where the board will be used. The grades used by the National Hardwood Lumber Association include Firsts, Seconds, Selects, No. 1 Common, No. 2A Common, No. 3A Common, and No. 3B Common. The best grades are Firsts, Seconds, and a mix of the two called FAS or 1S & 2S, with the clearest boards, at least 8 feet long and 6 inches wide. Select has defects on the back. Grades lower than No. 1 and No. 2 Common may be unusable. Look for subgrades, with a lower grade on the back than on the face.

OTHER CHARACTERISTICS OF LUMBER

Even within the same grade of lumber, individual pieces may differ. When possible, sort through the stacks yourself; most yards will allow this if you repile stacks.

Vertical and flat grain: Depending on how the board is cut from the log, there will be either parallel grain lines running the length of the piece (vertical grain) or a marbled appearance (flat grain), as shown at right. Vertical grain results from quarter-sawing—a cut nearly perpendicular to the annual growth rings. Flat grain arises when pieces are flat-sawn, or cut tangential to the growth rings.

Heartwood and sapwood: The wood nearest the center of a living tree is called heartwood. Sapwood, next

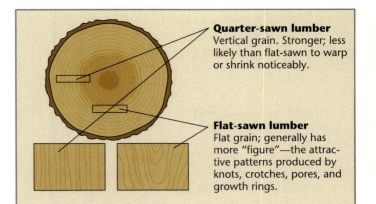

Quarter-sawn lumber
Vertical grain. Stronger; less likely than flat-sawn to warp or shrink noticeably.

Flat-sawn lumber
Flat grain; generally has more "figure"—the attractive patterns produced by knots, crotches, pores, and growth rings.

to the bark, contains the growth cells. The main differences are color and density; heartwood is usually darker, denser, and more decay-resistant than sapwood.

Defects: Lumber may contain defects from weathering or milling *(see chart, page 24)*. Examine each board closely; to test for warping, lift each piece by one end and sight down the face and edges. Pieces with long, gentle bends can sometimes be machined flat, but unless you can work around the defect, reject the board. Also look for general problems such as rotting, staining, insect holes, and pitch pockets (sap reservoirs below the surface). Try to avoid the "bull's-eye pieces" milled from the center of the log; they tend to crack and warp more easily than other pieces.

MANUFACTURED PANELS

Plywood, hardboard, and particleboard offer three main advantages over solid lumber: availability in large sheets, dimensional stability, and economy. Plywood, the most familiar of the sheet products, is used extensively for furniture and doors. The main uses of standard hardboard include cabinet backs and drawer bottoms. Perforated hardboard, known by its tradename, Pegboard, is often combined with hooks for hanging storage. Particleboard is used for shelving, as core stock for pieces to be laminated or veneered, or in other hidden applications.

Plywood: Plywood is manufactured from thin wood veneers peeled from the log with a very sharp cutter, then glued together. The grain of each veneer runs perpendicular to the layers just above and below, making plywood strong in all directions. Standard sheet size is 4 feet by 8 feet; 10-foot-long sheets can be ordered.

There are interior and exterior grades; the difference between them is in the type of glue used to make each one and in the quality of the veneers. Exterior grades require weatherproof glue and higher grade veneers; use these grades for outdoor projects. For most other work, however, use Interior or Exposure 1 plywood, the most common type available. Like solid lumber, plywoods are divided into softwood and hardwood types, according to the face and back veneers only.

Any of 70 different species of wood may be used for **softwood plywood**, but the most common by far are Douglas-fir and southern pine. Species are rated for stiffness and strength and placed in one of five groups, Group 1 being strongest. Panels are also rated by grade, determined by the appearance of the panel's face and back. Although the N grade would be desirable wherever you want a perfect, natural finish, it has to be special-ordered and even so, is rarely available. Generally, pre-sanded A and B grades are the choices where wood will be visible; lower grades are unsuitable for a fine finish. Plywood comes in many face/back grade combinations, though your lumberyard may stock only a few. If both sides of the material will be exposed, choose A/B panels. A/C (exterior) or A/D (interior) panels are economical choices where only one side will be visible. These and other characteristics appear on the stamp imprinted on the back or edge of each panel (shown on page 26). The most important things to look for are the face-back grade and exposure rating; the species group number only shows up for sanded plywood.

Standard softwood plywood commonly is available in thicknesses from 1/4 to 3/4 inch, in 1/8-inch increments.

Though more expensive than softwood types, **hardwood plywood** is an economical—and stable—alternative to solid hardwood for interior projects. This type of plywood is identified by the veneer used on the face side of the panel. Popular domestic faces include ash, birch, black walnut, cherry, maple, and oak. A number of imported woods are also available. Standard panel size is 4 by 8 feet; common thicknesses are $5/32$ inch, $1/4$ inch, $3/8$ inch, $1/2$ inch, and $3/4$ inch.

Hardwood plywood is graded differently than the softwood type. The face grades range from AA to E. AA, the top of the line, is used for high-quality projects. A, with its excellent appearance, is also recommended for furniture-building. For hidden areas, or where the natural appearance is desired, use B (less uniform than A), or the C, D, and E grouping (more color variation and repairs). Back grades are rated from 1 to 4, with 1 being the most sound. You may see a term such as A2, which means the face is grade A and the back is grade 2; the face and back veneers are commonly the same species. All this aside, most panels sold in retail outlets do not have a grade stamp, and the purchaser usually chooses panels individually, by sight.

One of the most popular face species for hardwood plywoods is birch; it's durable and attractive, machines cleanly, and is one of the lowest-priced hardwood plywoods. You can increase your savings by choosing "shop" birch plywood if you can work around the slight defects found on those panels.

Some grades of plywood may have voids in the inner veneers; these can be unsightly if the edges are to be exposed. Where appearance counts, putty the edges or cover them with veneer or molding. Or, buy lumber-core sheets; made of face veneers glued to a solid core (hence the name), this plywood has easily worked edges and holds fasteners better than veneer-core plywood.

If you're planning to clear-finish the edges or you're looking for extra strength in thin sheets, try to obtain some Baltic (which may also be known as Russian), or Finnish plywood, birch panels made up of many very thin, solid veneers. They come in sheets that measure 5x5 or 8x4 feet (the grain runs across the width).

Hardboard: Hardboard is produced by reducing waste wood chips to fibers, then bonding the fibers together under pressure with adhesives. Harder, denser, and cheaper than plywood, hardboard is commonly manufactured in 4x8-foot sheets. It may be smooth on both sides or have a meshlike texture on the back. Of the two main types, standard hardboard can be painted easily, while the tempered type, designed for strength and moisture resistance, is difficult to paint. Hardboard is commonly available in only $1/8$- and $1/4$-inch thicknesses. Though fairly easy to cut and shape, it dulls standard tools rapidly; use carbide-tipped saw blades and router bits. Always drill a pilot hole when fastening.

A similar but less dense product, fiberboard is available in thicker sheets; a common type is medium-density fiberboard, or MDF. It has a smooth, even surface, and can replace solid wood; it machines well, leaving crisp

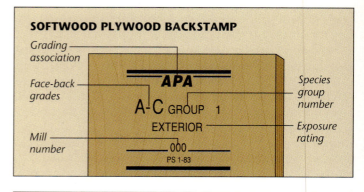

SOFTWOOD PLYWOOD BACKSTAMP

Grading association
Face-back grades
Mill number

APA
A-C GROUP 1
EXTERIOR
000
PS 1-83

Species group number
Exposure rating

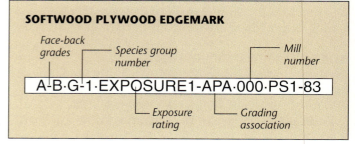

SOFTWOOD PLYWOOD EDGEMARK

Face-back grades
Species group number
Mill number

A·B·G·1·EXPOSURE1·APA·000·PS1-83

Exposure rating
Grading association

Stamps courtesy of the American Plywood Association

edges, which can often be finished without being covered up with edge-banding or molding. To screw into MDF, drill a pilot hole first.

Particleboard: Manufactured from chips and particles of waste wood that are bonded together, particleboard has a speckled appearance. Its advantages are a smooth surface and consistent flatness. Standard sheet size is 4x8 feet; common thicknesses range from $1/4$ inch to 2 inches in $1/16$-inch increments. Several types of particleboard, with different size particles, are available and marketed under different names; some are designed for exterior use. The most common is a single-layer sheet with uniform density and particle size, but whenever possible, choose the triple-layer type with a denser, smoother face and back.

Particleboard is heavy; for shelves or any other horizontal surface, support it at close intervals. You can cut and shape particleboard with standard tools, but equip power tools with carbide-tipped saw blades and router bits. Drill a pilot hole for fasteners. Avoid using water-base finishing products; the water soaks in, causing some of the particles to swell. Any visible edges are commonly covered by edgebanding or molding.

PLAY IT SAFE

WORKING WITH SHEET MATERIALS
When you're cutting sheet products, always wear respiratory protection and work in a well-ventilated shop with no sparks or open flames. Buy MDF and particleboard that is certified to be low in formaldehyde emissions.

A GUIDE TO WOOD SPECIES

Expand your wood-working horizons with the beauty and variety of wood species shown at left and described in the charts.

COMMON SOFTWOODS	
Species	**Characteristics**
Cedar, Alaska yellow	Pale yellow; heavy, strong, more stable than other cedars. Very resistant to decay and splintering. Easily worked; has slightly unpleasant odor when cut. Limited availability; expensive.
Cedar, eastern red	Noted for ivory sapwood and dark red heartwood. Also known as aromatic cedar; used in cedar chests and closet linings. Defect-prone but easily worked.
Cedar, western red	Handsome grain, wide color variation (ivory to pink, russet, red), decay-resistant. Soft and weak, but versatile. Works easily; takes glue, finishes well. Stable when dry. Widely available.
Cypress	Typically straight-grain; yellow to amber tones. Hard, strong, moderately heavy; oily texture; good decay resistance. Machines easily, shrinks little. Holds nails reasonably well. Often used in high-moisture areas (saunas, greenhouses) as well as for millwork. Good for water containers and utensils; doesn't impart taste, odor, or color. Available largely in its native Southeast.
Douglas-fir/western larch	Straight-grain, orange-colored; pronounced stripes. Resinous; exceptionally strong and stiff. Often sold together, fir being predominant. Quarter-sawn boards produce beautiful vertical grain suitable for cabinets and millwork; also highly valued for structural uses. Both work fairly well with sharp tools; avoid using heavily pigmented stains due to differences in grain density.
Hemlock, eastern/balsam fir	Similar to western types. Coarse texture, strong (balsam fir less so), and resin-free.
Hemlock, western/true firs	Cream-colored, bland woods generally sold together as "Hem-fir" (the firs include several western species). Light, moderately strong; shrinkage and warping can be serious problem unless wood is bone dry. Easily worked. Accepts glue, nails, and paint moderately well.
Pine, eastern white/western (Idaho white, lodgepole, Ponderosa, sugar)	Very white to russet. Soft and relatively weak; ideal for shaping. Smooth and uniform; knots and pitch pockets common. Little checking or warping. Hold fasteners moderately well with little splitting. Eastern white, Idaho white (western white), and sugar known for satiny surface and workability. Lodgepole is stable, straight-grain wood found in narrow widths; unlike other pines, knots won't bleed through paint. Ponderosa ("knotty pine") is versatile and popular.
Pine, southern yellow (pitch, shortleaf, longleaf, loblolly)	White to yellowish woods; hard, strong, and moderately heavy. Generally coarse in texture and full of resin. Work and finish relatively well, with excellent nail-holding ability.
Redwood	Red to russet and pink heartwood; creamy white sapwood. Heartwood highly resistant to decay and insects. Lightweight and fine-textured. Quite soft; scratches, splinters, and dents easily. Produces wide, often clear, resin-free lumber. Works easily; finishes beautifully. Holds fasteners only moderately well; prone to splitting. Expensive outside the West.
Spruce, eastern	Nondescript, whitish wood; uniform in grain. Relatively soft; strong for its weight; stable. Works easily, resists splitting; takes paint and fasteners well.
Spruce, Sitka	Creamy to pinkish brown; wide, clear lumber with straight grain. Very strong for its weight. Works easily; planes to silky sheen. Resists splintering.

HARDWOODS, BOTH DOMESTIC AND EXOTIC

Domestic species	Characteristics
Alder, red	Pinkish brown with little figure. Easy to work. Often substituted for birch, but less hard and strong. Inexpensive.
Ash, white	Creamy to grayish brown; tough, strong, wide-grain wood, but with poor durability. Versatile; works easily; accepts finishes well. Moderately priced.
Basswood	Nondescript, creamy white to russet "woodcarver's wood." Lightweight, soft, and uniform in grain; very fine-textured. Accepts glue and paint well; stable. Moderately priced.
Beech	Tan to reddish in color; conspicuous rays. Heavy and hard; prone to checking and warping. Works fairly well. Moderately priced.
Birch, yellow	Light reddish brown with pleasing grain. Hard, heavy, and strong. Versatile; machines easily and accepts finishes well. Moderately priced.
Cherry, black	Uniform, reddish brown color with some figure. Stable, strong, and hard, but not heavy; nondurable. Works well; takes satiny finish. Darkens with age. Moderately priced.
Hickory/pecan	White to reddish brown; fairly uniform grain. Strong, hard woods; often sold together. Must be seasoned carefully. Very tough and elastic; more difficult to work. Moderately priced.
Maple, hard	White to reddish tan; great variety of grain, including curly and bird's-eye. Heavy, hard, but non-durable. Difficult to work but accepts finishes well; takes abuse. Moderately priced.
Oak, red	Very popular pinkish wood; fairly straight-grained with large pores. Heavy, hard, and moderately durable. Machines and finishes well. Moderately priced.
Oak, white	Yellowish brown in color with distinctive quarter-sawn rays and closed pores. Dense, strong, and very durable. Machines and finishes well. Moderately expensive.
Poplar, yellow	Yellowish brown to olive green heartwood; bland, uniform grain. Light and moderately soft. Works easily and shows no grain through paint; stable. Inexpensive.
Walnut, black	Chocolate brown wood; handsome grain and great figure variety. Durable and strong, with good shock-resistance. Works well, takes high polish; very stable. Expensive.

Exotic species	Characteristics
Bocote	Brown to black wood with yellow lines; sometimes called Mexican rosewood. Straight to wavy grain. Heavy, hard, and oily. Expensive.
Cocobolo	Central American wood; russet- to orange-colored with black markings. Wavy grain. Very hard, beautiful wood with spicy aroma; may cause rash when worked. Expensive.
Ebony (African, East Indian, and Macassar)	Indian/African: deep black with little figure. Macassar: brown to black with lighter streaks. Extremely hard and heavy woods; difficult to work. Quite rare; expensive.
Koa	Golden brown Hawaiian wood with some fiddleback figure. Hard, strong, difficult to work, but finishes to lustrous sheen. Becoming rare and expensive.
Lauan	Tan to reddish "Philippine mahogany"; large pores and much ribbon grain. Coarser, stringier, and less stable than true mahoganies; doesn't machine as well. Moderately priced.
Lignum vitae	Green to brown heartwood with tight, swirling grain. Hard, heavy Caribbean wood; difficult to work, extremely oily, but very durable. Expensive.
Mahogany (African, and Central and South American)	Golden to reddish brown wood with variable grain; much figure. Moderately hard; very strong and durable; exceptionally stable. Works very well. Large, clear pieces available. Moderately expensive.
Padauk	Strong and vivid red in color; uniform, coarse texture; good for contrast. Hard heavy wood; machines well. Expensive.
Purpleheart	Mildly striped wood (properly called amaranth) from American tropics; turns royal purple after cutting. Hard and stringy; difficult to work. Moderately expensive.
Rosewood (Honduras and Indonesian)	Dark brown to violet and black with light and dark streaks. Both are heavy; Honduras tends to be oily, and has finer texture than Indonesian. Both finish beautifully. Very expensive.
Satinwood, Ceylon	Yellow to gold, with beautiful figure. Difficult to work; finishes well. Expensive.
Teak	Golden brown Southeast Asian wood; some similarities to walnut. Oily; very stable, even outdoors. May be hard on saw blades, and may cause skin rash and/or respiratory problems. Expensive.
Tulipwood	Pink to red and yellow South American wood with wavy, marblelike grain; looks painted. Very hard; can be difficult to work. Expensive.
Zebrawood	Golden-hued African wood with pronounced black stripes; large pores. Lustrous when finished. Expensive.

FASTENERS

Nails, screws, adhesives, and bolts are needed, either separately or in some combination, to assemble any woodworking project. The fastest way to join two pieces is to nail them together, but when the project demands extra strength and a fine appearance, use screws or an adhesive, or both. A variety of adhesives is available, each designed to work with different materials. For special problems there are special fasteners—nails for every situation, decorative screws and finishing washers to improve a project's appearance. If strength alone is the issue, turn to oversize lag screws or bolts. To assemble furniture without cutting complex joints, use knock-down hardware.

Nails: Many different types of nails are available; those commonly used for woodworking are shown below. Nail lengths may be indicated by the term "penny" (abbreviated as d). This once referred to the cost of 100 hand-forged nails; 3-penny nails, for instance, were 3 cents per hundred. The illustration below shows the equivalents in inches of the nail sizes most likely to be used in woodworking; bigger nails are also available. For outdoor projects, look for hot-dipped galvanized nails.

Screws: Though more time-consuming to drive than nails, screws make stronger and neater joints, especially when combined with glue. Without glue, screws can be removed to dismantle the joint. The array of different screws available to the woodworker can be bewildering. The types most commonly used with wood are shown on page 30. Drywall screws, originally designed for fastening gypsum wallboard to wall studs and ceiling joists, are becoming popular with woodworkers. These versatile fasteners are a big improvement over traditional wood screws: they're sharper and better machined, and the Phillips heads won't strip as easily.

Screws are sized by length (from $1/4$ to 4 inches), and for thickness, by wire gauge number (0 to 24—about $1/16$ to $3/8$ inch). The higher the gauge number for a given length of screw, the greater its holding ability. To determine the correct length for a particular application, see page 66.

Bolts, nuts, and washers: Unlike the screw's tapered point, which digs into wood, the straight, threaded shaft of a bolt passes completely through the materials being joined; it's fastened down with a nut screwed onto its end. Bolts are stronger than nails or screws because the material is gripped from both sides. Most bolts are made from zinc-plated steel, but brass bolts are also available. Bolts are classified by their diameter ($1/4$ to 1 inch) and length ($3/8$ inch and up). If you can't find a bolt long enough for your job, use a threaded rod (a bolt shaft without a head) cut to length with a hacksaw; then add a nut and washer at each end of the threaded rod. A selection of the bolts, nuts, and washers commonly found in woodworking is shown on page 30.

Knock-down hardware: Factory-built furniture often relies on these metal or nylon devices to join components that meet in simple butt joints. Two types of knock-down (K-D) hardware are available. One type allows you to disassemble the components for storage or transport; the other joins pieces permanently.

Knock-down fittings operate on several different principles, ranging from simple slotted plates and angles to cam fittings that engage a bolt head with the turn of a screwdriver; a selection, with examples in position, is shown on page 31. The fitting that is most widely used

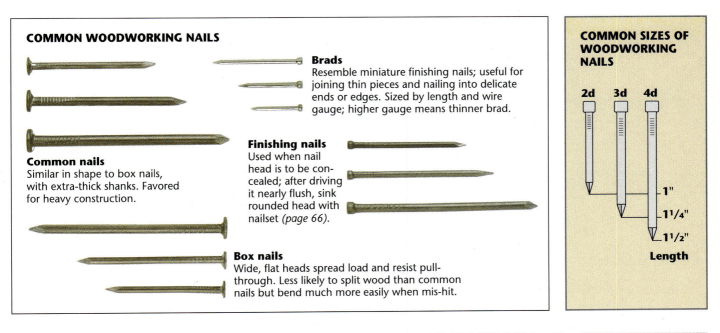

COMMON WOODWORKING NAILS

Brads
Resemble miniature finishing nails; useful for joining thin pieces and nailing into delicate ends or edges. Sized by length and wire gauge; higher gauge means thinner brad.

Common nails
Similar in shape to box nails, with extra-thick shanks. Favored for heavy construction.

Finishing nails
Used when nail head is to be concealed; after driving it nearly flush, sink rounded head with nailset (page 66).

Box nails
Wide, flat heads spread load and resist pull-through. Less likely to split wood than common nails but bend much more easily when mis-hit.

COMMON SIZES OF WOODWORKING NAILS

2d 3d 4d

1"
1 1/4"
1 1/2"

Length

by woodworkers is the threaded insert; one application is shown on page 114. K-D fittings are particularly useful with plywood or particleboard, which don't lend themselves to traditional joinery.

Though components fitted with K-D hardware are typically assembled with no more complicated tools than a mallet, screwdriver, or Allen wrench, the fittings themselves must be placed with great accuracy so the joints lock up tightly and evenly. Knock-down devices are either surface-mounted or mortised in, using a drill bit. If you are having difficulty finding some of these fittings, try mail-order sources specializing in European hardware.

Adhesives: When used correctly, a good adhesive creates a neat, permanent joint that's as strong as—or stronger than—the wood itself. Adhesives vary according to strength, water resistance, ability to fill gaps, and setting time. For general work, most woodworkers reach for white or yellow glue; for outdoor use, waterproof resorcinol is the standard. Other adhesives meet specialized needs; the chart on page 31 will acquaint you with the pros and cons of the adhesives helpful to woodworkers.

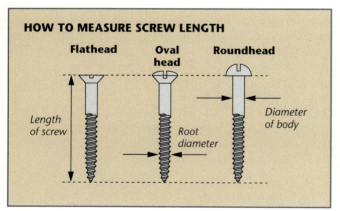

HOW TO MEASURE SCREW LENGTH

Flathead Oval head Roundhead

Length of screw

Root diameter

Diameter of body

Illustration courtesy of *Do-It-Yourself Retailing* magazine

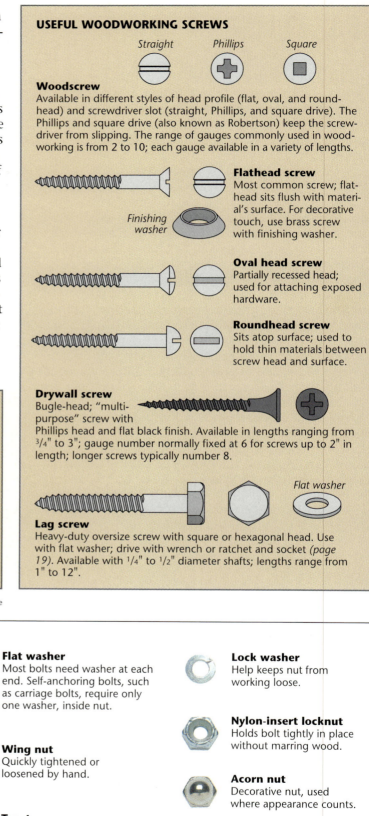

USEFUL WOODWORKING SCREWS

Straight   Phillips   Square

Woodscrew
Available in different styles of head profile (flat, oval, and round-head) and screwdriver slot (straight, Phillips, and square drive). The Phillips and square drive (also known as Robertson) keep the screwdriver from slipping. The range of gauges commonly used in woodworking is from 2 to 10; each gauge available in a variety of lengths.

Flathead screw
Most common screw; flathead sits flush with material's surface. For decorative touch, use brass screw with finishing washer.

Finishing washer

Oval head screw
Partially recessed head; used for attaching exposed hardware.

Roundhead screw
Sits atop surface; used to hold thin materials between screw head and surface.

Drywall screw
Bugle-head; "multipurpose" screw with Phillips head and flat black finish. Available in lengths ranging from $3/4$" to 3"; gauge number normally fixed at 6 for screws up to 2" in length; longer screws typically number 8.

Flat washer

Lag screw
Heavy-duty oversize screw with square or hexagonal head. Use with flat washer; drive with wrench or ratchet and socket *(page 19)*. Available with $1/4$" to $1/2$" diameter shafts; lengths range from 1" to 12".

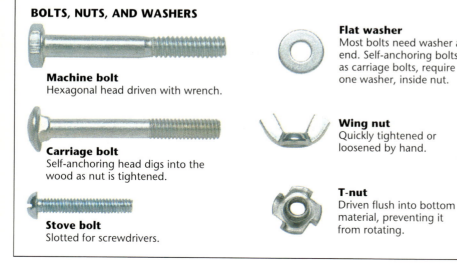

BOLTS, NUTS, AND WASHERS

Machine bolt
Hexagonal head driven with wrench.

Carriage bolt
Self-anchoring head digs into the wood as nut is tightened.

Stove bolt
Slotted for screwdrivers.

Flat washer
Most bolts need washer at each end. Self-anchoring bolts, such as carriage bolts, require only one washer, inside nut.

Wing nut
Quickly tightened or loosened by hand.

T-nut
Driven flush into bottom material, preventing it from rotating.

Lock washer
Help keeps nut from working loose.

Nylon-insert locknut
Holds bolt tightly in place without marring wood.

Acorn nut
Decorative nut, used where appearance counts.

Hex nut
Standard type of nut.

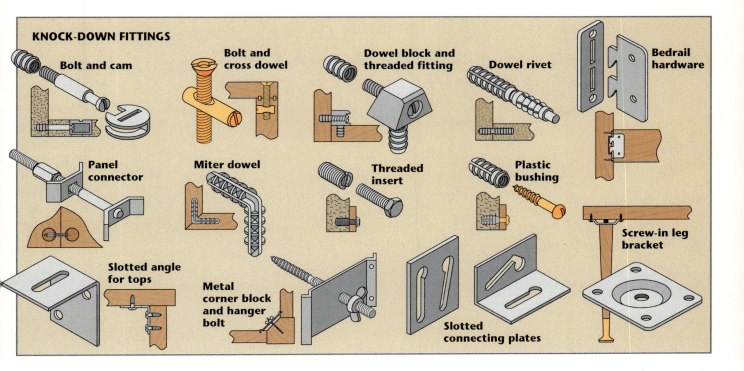

KNOCK-DOWN FITTINGS

Bolt and cam

Bolt and cross dowel

Dowel block and threaded fitting

Dowel rivet

Bedrail hardware

Panel connector

Miter dowel

Threaded insert

Plastic bushing

Screw-in leg bracket

Slotted angle for tops

Metal corner block and hanger bolt

Slotted connecting plates

WOODWORKING ADHESIVES

Type	Characteristics	Uses
White common household glue (polyvinyl acetate)	Rigid bond; difficult to sand (clogs sandpaper); softens above 150°F; not waterproof.	Good for indoor use where heat and moisture are not factors; must be clamped.
Yellow or brown carpenter's or wood glue (aliphatic resin)	Rigid bond; dries clear; heat-resistant (can be sanded); can be applied at temperatures as low as 60°F; more moisture-resistant than white glue.	Best glue for general woodworking; good for indoor use and large assemblies; must be clamped.
Resorcinol glue (marine resin)	Strong, rigid, permanent bond; two components must be mixed; can be sanded; waterproof; dries dark; toxic (releases formaldehyde).	Bonds wood in high-moisture applications; must be clamped; fills gaps between materials.
Plastic resin glue	Strong bond; powder must be mixed with water; can be sanded; water-resistant (not waterproof); urea-formaldehyde base potentially toxic.	Use on wood for a high-strength bond; interior use; must be clamped; provides light-colored, stain-free bond with some water-resistance; fills small gaps between materials.
Liquid hide glue	Strong bond; slow to set, giving long assembly time for complicated set-ups; can be sanded; not waterproof; reversible (with water and heat).	Good for complicated assemblies and musical instruments; must be tightly clamped.
Epoxy resin	Strong, rigid, permanent bond; two components must be mixed; water-resistant to waterproof, depending on type; uncured epoxy is toxic.	Good for indoor/outdoor projects; bonds unlike materials; fills gaps between materials; slow-setting types give generally stronger and more water-resistant bonds than fast-setting types.
Urethane glue	Strong, permanent bond (not as strong as epoxy); single component—no mixing required; waterproof; cures by exposure to moisture.	Good for general repairs; must be clamped; fills small gaps between materials.
Contact cement	Water-resistant; applied to both surfaces, which after drying bond on contact.	Bonds thin materials to a base; use to attach plastic laminate to wood. Choose newer, water-base types, although they may warp thin wood veneers.
Hot-melt glue	Flexible bond; waterproof; applied with electric glue gun; bonds on cooling (glue solidifies).	Fast-setting; bonds awkward-shaped materials that can't be clamped; good for fast repairs; generally lower strength than other glues; fills gaps.
Instant or super glue (cyanoacrylate)	Moisture-curing; fast-setting; strong bond; water-resistant.	Secures materials that can't be clamped; types available to bond nonporous as well as porous materials, such as wood. CAUTION: Bonds quickly to skin.

PLANNING YOUR PROJECT

Once you have the necessary tools on hand and your materials ready to go, the next step is to measure and mark the pieces that will become your project. This chapter takes you through the basic steps of planning and layout.

You'll find a description of the tools and techniques you will need to draw your own plans, allowing you to experiment with your creations—without making expensive mistakes. The common types of shop drawings, and the techniques for making them, are shown, along with information on deciphering the maze of lines, symbols, arrows, and numbers found within.

With your plans in hand, you're ready to mark the materials for cutting. This chapter covers the tried-and-true procedures for marking boards to length, laying out plywood, marking angles, and drawing circles, arcs, and ellipses. Along the way, you'll learn some special tricks, such as how to transfer and enlarge custom designs, and how to connect two perpendicular lines with a smooth arc—indispensable if you want to round the corner of a tabletop.

When tackling any layout job, it's wise to remember the woodworker's adage: "Measure twice, cut once." If you work carefully right from the start, you'll be on your way to fine results.

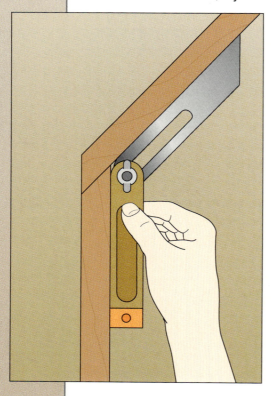

Using a T-bevel to transfer angles is just one of the many handy layout techniques you'll learn how to do in this chapter.

MAKING WORKING DRAWINGS

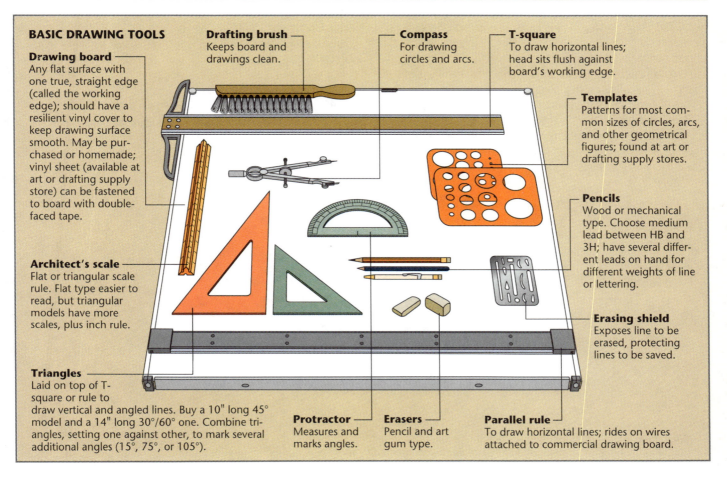

BASIC DRAWING TOOLS

Drawing board
Any flat surface with one true, straight edge (called the working edge); should have a resilient vinyl cover to keep drawing surface smooth. May be purchased or homemade; vinyl sheet (available at art or drafting supply store) can be fastened to board with double-faced tape.

Drafting brush
Keeps board and drawings clean.

Compass
For drawing circles and arcs.

T-square
To draw horizontal lines; head sits flush against board's working edge.

Templates
Patterns for most common sizes of circles, arcs, and other geometrical figures; found at art or drafting supply stores.

Pencils
Wood or mechanical type. Choose medium lead between HB and 3H; have several different leads on hand for different weights of line or lettering.

Erasing shield
Exposes line to be erased, protecting lines to be saved.

Architect's scale
Flat or triangular scale rule. Flat type easier to read, but triangular models have more scales, plus inch rule.

Triangles
Laid on top of T-square or rule to draw vertical and angled lines. Buy a 10" long 45° model and a 14" long 30°/60° one. Combine triangles, setting one against other, to mark several additional angles (15°, 75°, or 105°).

Protractor
Measures and marks angles.

Erasers
Pencil and art gum type.

Parallel rule
To draw horizontal lines; rides on wires attached to commercial drawing board.

Drawings are the most efficient way to communicate how a project is to be built. Though they may look complicated at first glance, they're easy to read and draw once you learn the basic terms and conventions. In woodworking, there are two common types of drawings: pictorial and orthographic (also known as multiview). Either type gives you a good idea of what the finished project will look like, and serves as a guide for building. Pictorial drawings, which show the finished project more or less as the human eye would see it, fall into two categories: isometric *(page 34)* and perspective drawings. A perspective drawing shows the finished project much the same way as a photo does; distant objects appear smaller than closer objects, regardless of relative size. These are not to scale, and therefore are not used to draw out a planned project, although you may want to translate a furniture piece depicted this way into an actual piece. An orthographic drawing *(page 34)*, done to scale, is composed of a group of two-dimensional views, connected by projection lines.

With the right equipment and some practice, making your own working drawings can be uncomplicated and

STANDARD LINES AND SYMBOLS

Element	Use
Visible line	Outlines object and shows important visible features.
Hidden or invisible line	Shows hidden edges and/or contours; also used to show exploded element.
Center line	Indicates center of object (used particularly for circles and arcs); sometimes identified by symbol ℄.
Dimension line	Indicates section being measured; may be solid line or broken in center for numerals. Arrows end at extension lines.
Extension lines	Light extensions of drawing lines beginning about 1/16" from outline. Used with dimension lines to indicate extent of section being measured. If space is limited, dimension lines and/or measurement may be placed outside.
Break lines	Used to indicate break in object too large to be shown in entirety. Zigzag line used for long breaks, wavy line for short ones.

rewarding. The tools you need to make drawing and laying out easier and more accurate are illustrated on page 33; others, such as French and flexible curves are shown on page 7. Use any paper that is easy to draw on—and that is erasable; vellum is a good choice and is available with a blue-line (nonreproducing) grid. Graph paper can be used for laying out both preliminary drafts and final plans. Tape the paper to your drawing board. Use inexpensive tracing paper over drawings so you can test different ideas without redoing an entire drawing.

Standard terms and notations: Orthographic drawings and some lines on pictorial drawings are done to scale; that is, every line shown on the drawing is in exact proportion to the corresponding dimension on the finished object. The scale used is always indicated on the drawing. A full-scale drawing (1:1) is the same size as the actual project. Reduced-scale drawings are more practical; frequently used scales are 3 inches, $1\frac{1}{2}$ inches, 1 inch, $\frac{3}{4}$ inch, $\frac{3}{8}$ inch, and $\frac{1}{4}$ inch—all equaling one foot. For a detail drawing, the scale may even be enlarged; for example, 1 inch on the scale could equal $\frac{1}{2}$ inch on the actual object.

Lines of various types and weights indicate the outline of the finished project, its visible and hidden components, and all important dimensions. The symbols used in woodworking plans are standardized; the chart on page 33 explains the lines and symbols you are likely to encounter.

Drawing out a planned project

Making an isometric drawing

An isometric drawing *(right)* is made so the three lines representing the three planes, or axes, are each 120° apart *(inset)*. Lines depicting the project are drawn in relation to the three axes. The axes and all lines parallel to them are drawn to scale; any other lines are not. First draw the axes representing the three planes of the drawing. Work from the bottom up, drawing one vertical line and two lines at 30° angles to the horizon. You can also use isometric graph paper (from art and engineering suppliers) with lines already drawn at these angles. Calculate and mark the object's overall height, width, and depth on the axes. Next, mark and draw to scale all lines parallel to these three axes. Then add any connecting, nonparallel lines; these won't be true to scale. Fill in any details, then darken all final lines.

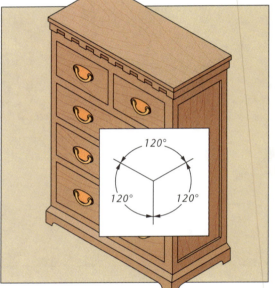

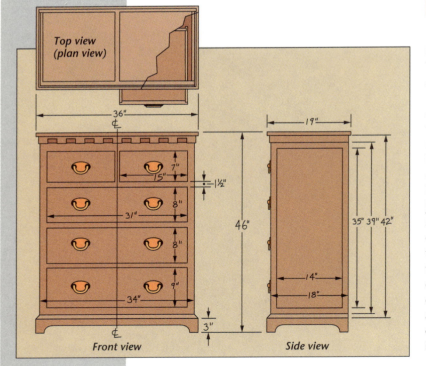

Top view (plan view)

Front view   Side view

Making an orthographic drawing

This consists of three two-dimensional views, each drawn separately and all shown on the same plane *(left)*. Usually only the front, right side, and top view are shown. The front view is the most prominent; the others are connected by thin projection lines. Begin with the outline of the front view by measuring, marking, and drawing all horizontal and vertical lines to scale. Fill in nonparallel lines; add hidden lines and center line; note all dimensions. Add projection lines indicating the overall height and width so they can later connect the front view with the other views (these also serve as extension lines). Draw the other views the same way; the right-side view to the right and the top (plan) view, above. Additional drawing may be included to show other views or details. For interior details, an imaginary cut is made and a section drawing shown. To depict a small or complicated component, do a detail drawing, larger in scale. Darken all final lines.

LAYING OUT STRAIGHT LINES

Whether you're marking cutoff lines, dividing up a sheet of plywood, laying out angles, marking a board's width or its thickness, straight lines will be key.

Marking cutoff lines—length lines on solid boards, or length and width lines on sheet materials—is a primary task. The procedure is shown on page 36. Before beginning any layout work on sheet products, check both the squareness and the dimensions of the sheet. A plywood sheet may not measure exactly 4x8 feet and may be out of square, throwing off subsequent layout marks. (The techniques for marking angles, width and thickness are shown on page 37).

Next, consider which side of the board will be visible on the finished piece. Since wood tends to splinter where saw teeth exit, work with the visible side up if you'll be cutting with a handsaw or table saw, or crosscutting with a radial-arm saw. For a portable power saw or rip cuts with a radial-arm saw, place the good side down and mark on the back.

Follow these tried-and-true techniques to ensure the accuracy of any layout procedure:

• Hold a rule on edge to make a measurement. Because of the rule's thickness, get the graduation marks down against the surface.
• To lay out short dimensions, start measuring from the 1-inch line on your rule. It's much easier than aligning with the end of the rule, and that goes double for the tape measure's loose end-hook. (Don't forget to subtract an inch from your final measurement.)
• Measure following an edge. Angling your rule or tape even slightly can result in work coming out short.
• Use the same measuring tools for the entire project, to ensure that all your measurements are consistent.
• Work with a sharp, hard-leaded pencil or scribing tool. Mark the correct distance carefully with a straight line, or draw a "crow's foot" or caret (V-mark) that points right to the graduation.
• Use existing pieces as patterns, but do not transfer dimensions along the entire length of the piece. For instance, mark the length and width of a mortise using the tenon that will fit into it, but to continue any lines use a straightedge or square.

Using a tape measure effectively

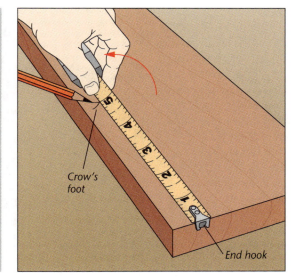

Crow's foot

End hook

Measuring with a steel tape
Pull the tape's end hook tight against the end of the board, and twist the tape to sight it. The hook is loosely riveted to compensate for the thickness of the bent tab at the end for interior and exterior measurements; pulling it tight will ensure that your tape starts at the board's end. Twisting the tape gets the graduation marks right down on the work. Remember, the tape has a cupped surface, so if the graduation point you want to mark is above the surface, it may appear to be at different locations when sighted from various angles (this is called the parallax effect).

ASK A PRO

HOW CAN I DIVIDE A BOARD INTO EQUAL SECTIONS?
Lay a bench rule across the board diagonally with the 1-inch graduation on one edge and the graduation line representing the appropriate number of intervals on the other edge. For instance, to divide a board less than 5 inches wide into six equal pieces, place the 7-inch line on the other edge. For a wider board, use bigger intervals. (Remember to allow for the width of the saw kerfs.) Mark points where the intervening inch lines fall on the board. Repeat at the other end of the board, then connect marks with straight lines.

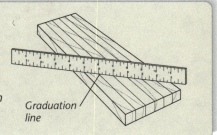

Graduation line

Marking length lines on lumber

TOOLKIT
- Sharp pencil or scribing tool
- Combination or try square
- Measuring tape

Using a square

To mark a cutoff line, start by squaring the board. At one end, well beyond any visible defects, square a line across the face. To draw this line, hold your pencil on the dimension mark or crow's foot and slide the square up to meet it *(below)*. Hold the square's handle firmly against the edge of the board and incline your pencil at a 60° angle to mark *(right)*; angle scribing tools slightly, too. Cut the board along this line. Measure the desired cutoff distance from the new end, mark the point, and draw a second line through this point.

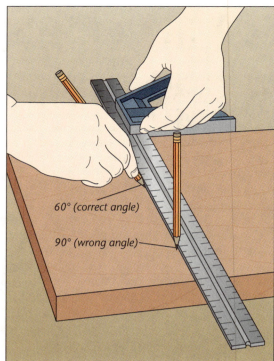

60° (correct angle)

90° (wrong angle)

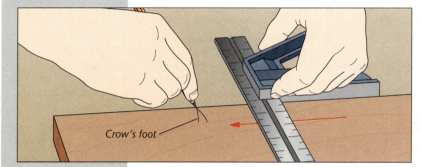

Crow's foot

Marking sheet products

TOOLKIT
- Measuring tape
- Sharp pencil or scribing tool
- Chalk line or T-square
- Carpenter's square

Snapping a chalk line and using a carpenter's square

A woodworker will often do a rough layout with a chalk line or T-square, just to cut the sheet up into more manageable pieces. To use a chalk line, pull the chalk-covered cord from the case and stretch it taut between the two measured and marked points, making sure that the end hook is sitting snugly over one edge. Lift the cord straight up near the other edge and release it quickly so it snaps down sharply, leaving a long, straight line of chalk.

For marking finish cuts, use a carpenter's square, holding the square's tongue or body against the edge of the material and mark along the other side. For longer cutting lines, first measure along both edges of the piece, mark the dimensions, then use a long straightedge to draw a line connecting them.

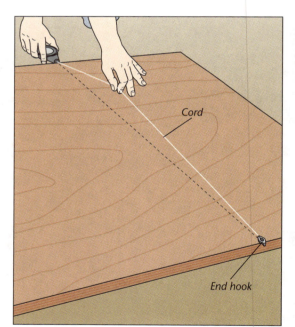

Cord

End hook

ASK A PRO

DO I HAVE TO WORRY ABOUT THE WIDTH OF THE SAW BLADE KERF?

When dividing up a sheet of plywood, you should take into account the width of the kerf made by the blade you're going to use. Lay out and cut the pieces one by one, making each new cut on the waste side of the lines. If you want to lay out the entire sheet at once, draw double lines on the stock to indicate the kerfs.

Marking angles

TOOLKIT
- Protractor
- T-bevel
- Sharp pencil or scribing tool

OR
- Measuring tape
- Sharp pencil or scribing tool
- Protractor
- Straightedge

Using an adjustable T-bevel

To mark an angle with a T-bevel, set it to the desired angle with the help of a protractor and then use the T-bevel as your working guide. Duplicating an angle from an existing piece is simple with this tool. Just hold the T-bevel's handle against the surface that defines one side of the angle and swivel the blade into line with the other (near right). Tighten the wing nut and use a pencil or scribing tool to transfer the set angle to the new stock (far right).

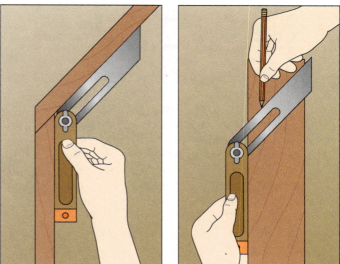

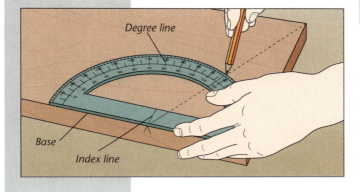

Degree line

Base

Index line

Using a protractor

A protractor is the best tool to use when laying out an angle of known size. Measure and mark the starting point on the stock's edge. With the protractor's base along the edge, align its index line with the mark. Then mark the stock above the appropriate degree line (left), and use a straightedge to connect the two marks and extend the line.

ASK A PRO

HOW DO YOU LAY OUT 45° ANGLES?

For most applications, the combination square is the tool of choice. However, for larger stock or sheet materials, use a carpenter's square. Simply align the graduation marks for matching figures on the two inside scales (one on the tongue, the other on the body) with the edge of the stock; this places both the tongue and body at 45° to the edge. Draw along the square's tongue or body, as shown.

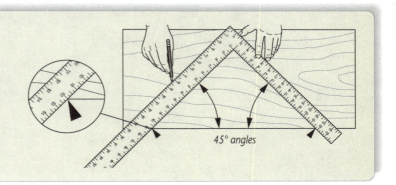

45° angles

Marking width and thickness

TOOLKIT
- Measuring tape
- Marking gauge

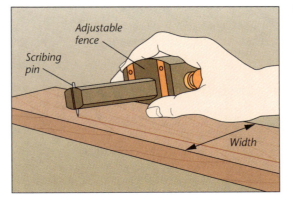

Adjustable fence

Scribing pin

Width

Using a marking gauge

The simplest and most accurate way to lay out width and thickness dimensions is with a marking gauge. But before you can use the gauge, make sure that at least one face and one edge are perfectly flat and square. (See truing techniques on pages 54 to 56 and 62.) To scribe a width line, set the gauge's adjustable fence to the correct distance, position the tool at the angle shown, and push the gauge away from you down the board's face. To lay out thickness, set the fence as required and push the gauge down the edge of the board.

LAYING OUT CURVES

Drawing aesthetically pleasing curves calls for some simple drafting techniques and a little geometry. Follow the same rules as for straight lines (page 35). To hide any splintering, work with the good side of the material up if you're using a hand or band saw, and with the good side down when operating a saber saw. When it isn't worth the effort of laying out a complex shape in its mirror image, you can cut with the good side up, but go slowly and keep extra saber saw blades on hand.

Draw small circles and arcs with a circle template or a compass. Set the distance between the compass legs to the radius you need, plant the pointed leg and rotate the other to scribe the circle; keep the tool upright. For larger layouts, a set of trammel points is ideal; they work the same way, but you can mount them on a beam of any length. For freeform curves and irregular lines, sketch the line first. Then move a French curve around the design to find segments where the tool's outline coincides. Trace the outline of the curve, stopping a bit short of the points where the design and curve diverge. Bend a flexible curve to the contours you need, then lay it on the stock and trace the contours.

Striking an arc

TOOLKIT
• Compass

Rounding a square corner

A design may call for an arc tangent to, or touching, a set of perpendicular lines. Decide on the radius you want for the arc and set your compass; keep the same span for the entire procedure. With the compass point on A, mark an arc at B and C. Then, with the compass point on B, mark an arc at D; repeat with the compass on C. Finally, with the compass point on the intersection at D, strike the arc connecting B to C.

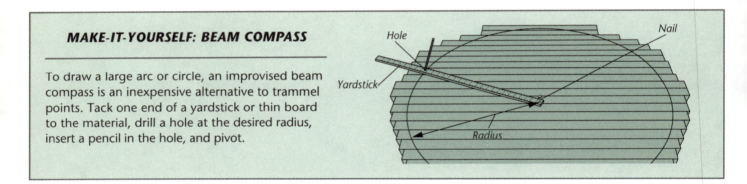

MAKE-IT-YOURSELF: BEAM COMPASS

To draw a large arc or circle, an improvised beam compass is an inexpensive alternative to trammel points. Tack one end of a yardstick or thin board to the material, drill a hole at the desired radius, insert a pencil in the hole, and pivot.

Drawing an ellipse

TOOLKIT
• Measuring tape
• Sharp pencil
• Compass

1 ▶ Defining the major axes
The ellipse is a flattened circle whose widest and narrowest points define its major and minor axes. The first step in laying one out is to decide how long each of the axes should be. Then draw two lines at right angles to each other and label their end points to make axes AB and CD. After setting your compass to span the distance between the intersection of the axes (point X) and A, place the compass point at C and strike an arc that crosses the major axis (AB) at two points; label them Y and Z.

◀ 2 Completing the figure
Insert pins or small brads at Y, Z, and C. Stretch a piece of nonelastic string taut between Y and Z, going around the pin at C; attach the ends to the pins at Y and Z. Then remove the pin at C, replace it with a pencil, and draw half of the ellipse by pulling the pencil 180° from A to B, holding the string taut all the way. Repeat this on the other side of the axis to complete the ellipse.

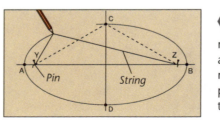

ENLARGING A DRAWING

The planning process often entails enlarging a design from a small-scale drawing to a full-size layout, which is either drawn on a template (a pattern) or directly onto the stock. The best way to execute this is to transfer the design from a grid of small squares onto a grid of larger squares that are at the desired scale for your particular project. This can be done quite simply, even for a com-

plex design. Each square is identified with letters and numbers, and the original drawing is transferred one square at a time, as illustrated below. A ruler will improve your accuracy for any straight sections, and a French or flexible curve is indispensable for contours. (Information on using French curves and flexible curves can be found on page 38.)

Using a grid to enlarge a figure

TOOLKIT
- Sharp pencil
- Graph or tracing paper
- Stiff paper (optional)
- T-square (or chalk line to mark grid right on stock)
- Ruler
- French or flexible curve

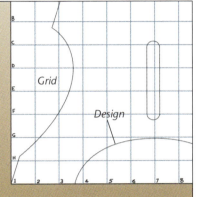

Grid

Design

2 ▶ Laying out a larger grid
To make a grid of larger squares, use graph paper, which comes with squares up to 1" across; or, you can use a T-square to lay out your own grid on stiff paper or directly on the stock. Very large designs can be transferred directly to plywood that has 2" to 4" squares laid out with a chalk line. Label the coordinates identically to the smaller grid.

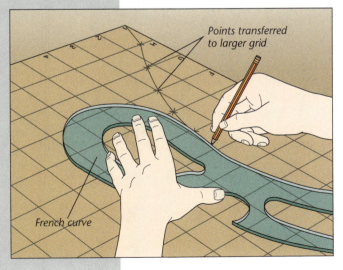

Points transferred to larger grid

French curve

1 ◀ Laying a grid over the original design
Often, scale drawings will already be printed on a grid of small squares. If not, you can trace the design onto graph paper or onto a grid you've laid out on tracing paper; use $1/8$" to $1/4$" squares for these tracings. Label the lines running in one direction with letters and those running in the other direction with numbers, as shown. If the design is already printed on a grid, label the horizontal and vertical lines (called the coordinates) the same way.

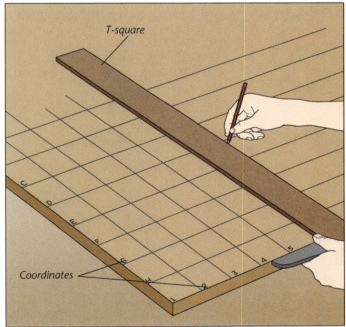

T-square

Coordinates

3 ◀ Plotting the drawing
Choose a point on the original drawing where a line of the design crosses a line of the grid and note its position within the coordinate system. Mark the corresponding point on the larger grid. Repeat, transferring the points for the entire design onto the large grid. Then connect the points, using a ruler for any straight segments, pressing lightly with the pencil when you draw the curved lines; check the shape against the original as you go. When you're satisfied with the general contours, use a flexible or French curve to outline the curved lines more heavily.

WORKING WITH WOOD

Cutting, shaping, drilling, fastening, and smoothing—the steps basic to any woodworking project—are the subject of this chapter. Reading the chapter from start to finish will give you a solid overview of classic woodworking techniques, but if you're looking for specific information on how to make a straight or curved cut with a certain hand or power saw, how to rout a groove, drill a hole, plane the edge of a board, or how to do other common woodworking techniques, turn directly to the appropriate section. Other, more task-specific techniques are shown in the joinery chapter, beginning on page 70. For any of these woodworking procedures, plan your work carefully (previous chapter) and keep your measuring and marking tools handy.

Proficiency with woodworking tools comes with practice. The best advice is to practice on scrap materials. You may also want to look for local woodworking classes in order to acquire some hands-on experience. Then, armed with the skills you need, you'll be ready to tackle your first bookcase or table.

Fine woodworking depends on sharp, reliable tools, some of which have fast-moving parts. Before you begin any work using these tools, take careful note of the safety guidelines on pages 41 and 42.

CAUTION: Though for clarity's sake we may show the table saw and radial-arm saw without the blade guards in place, use the guard whenever possible.

The router—an indispensable woodworking tool—is designed for a variety of tasks ranging from the structural to the decorative; from cutting a dado in the side of a bookcase as a shelf support, to shaping the edge of a tabletop, as shown. This chapter will teach you how to get the most out of your woodworking tools, safely and efficiently.

WORKING SAFELY

Minimizing or eliminating the risks posed by tools and materials should be standard procedure for every woodworker; following are some guidelines for safe work. The accessories illustrated below are designed to protect you from injury and should be considered part of your basic toolbox. Use them without fail.

A SAFE WORKSHOP

A cluttered or poorly lit workshop invites accidents, and certain materials, if allowed to accumulate, produce potentially toxic or combustible fumes, particles, or dust. Clean up as you go; you'll find that a heavy-duty shop vacuum is a worthwhile investment. Organize your tools and materials for maximum working space; use perforated hardboard and hanger systems for visible, hands-on storage. Individual wall racks are good for small tools, such as chisels and screwdrivers, and—although they are less accessible—closed cabinets and drawers protect tools from dust and curious youngsters. Fasteners of all types can be found easily inside labeled minidrawers. Store finishing supplies on high shelves, or, preferably, in a noncombustible metal cabinet.

Good lighting, both natural and artificial, is essential in a workshop. Overhead fluorescent lights are the most efficient; one 4-foot double-tube shop unit lights up about 40 square feet. Place individual, adjustable spotlights where direct lighting is needed. Paint the workshop walls and ceiling white to amplify light.

OUTFIT YOURSELF SAFELY

Respiratory protection
Keeps you from inhaling harmful vapors, dust, or fibers. For vapors or fine particles, use respirator with interchangeable filters designed for specific applications. Disposable painter's masks are sufficient for heavy sawdust.

Hearing protection
Crucial for work with power tools. Earmuff protectors and lightweight foam earplugs filter excess noise, but still allow you to hear.

Hand protection
Wear all-leather or leather-reinforced cotton work gloves when handling rough lumber. Use disposable rubber or plastic gloves for work with solvents, finishes, or adhesives.

Eye protection
Wear full-face shield, glasses, or goggles when operating power tools or high-impact hand tools, such as hammers. Look for comfortable-fitting, fog-free type made of scratch-resistant, shatterproof plastic.

PLAY IT SAFE

SHOP-BUILT HELPERS

Make your own push block or stick, and featherboard to use with stationary power tools; drill a hole to hang them nearby. Use a push block to press down on the workpiece as you push it forward. Glue the lip on (in use, it shouldn't touch the table), and countersink the screws used to attach the handle. Use a band saw or saber saw to cut a push stick to the shape shown (for radial-arm saw ripping, the handle should be at a lower angle). The stock will be held in the notch; the base should be above the table surface when resting on the stock. For a featherboard (shown in use on page 47), cut a 45° miter on one end, draw a parallel line several inches in from the end, then form $1/8$-inch-wide feathers by making cuts up to this line. The notch will house a support board clamped to the table at 90° to the featherboard.

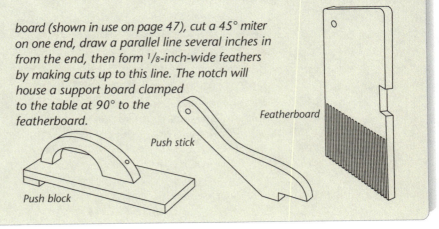

Push block

Push stick

Featherboard

Some woodworking materials can pose health hazards: oil-base enamels, varnish, lacquer, and the solvents associated with them; adhesives (especially resorcinol, epoxy, and contact cement); the waste from some particleboard and hardboard; and even common sawdust. Minimize the risks by following these rules:

• Maintain good ventilation to allow particles and fumes to escape from the workplace.
• Vacuum or wet-mop the area regularly.
• Read and follow all precautions printed on packaging.
• Wash skin and work clothes regularly—and separately from other laundry—to remove toxic materials.
• Wear protective gear *(page 41)* to prevent contact with harmful materials.

SAFETY WITH POWER TOOLS

Power tools are fast and precise, but they can cause serious injury. If handled with respect, these tools are generally quite safe to operate. Try to establish these habits:

• Know your tools' capabilities and limitations before you start. Your owner's manuals are the best source of information—read them carefully.
• Before you turn on a tool, support or clamp the workpiece as necessary.
• When operating a stationary power tool, use whatever jig or device is called for to keep your fingers away from the blade or cutter (shop-built devices are shown on page 41). Ripping on both the table saw and radial-arm saw calls for extra caution; never rip short, narrow, or twisted wood. Always cut a large, unmanageable piece into smaller pieces; a portable circular saw helps. Take care when using a dado head: the more material being removed, the more prone it is to kick back. Before cutting, check that any jigs, clamps, and guides are tight.
• Leave a saw's blade guard in place whenever possible. Some woodworkers argue that guards block visibility, but the potential price of that visibility is not worth it.
• Don't wear loose-fitting clothing or jewelry that could snag in the tool's mechanism. Wear safety goggles and tie up long hair or tuck it up beneath a tight-fitting cap.
• Keep power tools clean and lubricated according to specifications; make sure the blade or bit is sharp. Be sure to unplug any tool before adjusting it.

• Work without interruptions or distractions; keep all visitors, especially young children, away from the shop.
• Avoid awkward positions while working, and never stand or place your hand in line with a blade or bit.

Working with electricity: Properly grounded tools—or better yet, double-insulated tools—must be used to avoid a serious, or even fatal, shock. To ground a tool, connect its three-prong plug to a three-hole, grounded outlet. Double-insulated tools contain a built-in second barrier of insulation. Such tools have two-prong plugs, are clearly marked, and should not be grounded.

When setting up a workshop, put lighting and power tools on different circuits. A tool circuit should be at least 20 amps; stationary power tools may need a 120/240-volt circuit. When working outdoors, protect outlets with GFCIs (ground fault circuit interrupters) and only use cord marked for exterior use.

If you must use an extension cord, the shorter the better; long cords can overheat, becoming fire hazards. Every power tool's nameplate states its amp requirement. Add these up for all tools to be run off the cord at any one time; the cord's amp capacity must equal or exceed that sum. Consult the chart below to select the gauge required. The larger a cord's load capacity, the bigger its wires, and the lower its gauge number.

RECOMMENDED EXTENSION CORD SIZES FOR PORTABLE POWER TOOLS		
Nameplate ampere rating	25-ft. cord	50-ft. cord
(115V tool)	Wire gauge	Wire gauge
0-5	18	18
5-6	18	16
6-8	18	16
8-10	18	14
10-12	16	14
12-14	16	12
14-16	14	12
16-18	14	12
18-20	14	12

Chart courtesy Delta International Machinery/Porter-Cable

PLAY IT SAFE

INSTALLING A 3- TO 2-PRONG ADAPTER

This adapter allows you to plug a three-prong tool into a two-hole outlet. If the outlet is properly grounded, simply attach the connector to the outlet's cover plate screw, as shown. However, if you are unsure whether or not the outlet is grounded, consult an electrician. Unless the adapter's third wire is itself grounded, you're not protected.

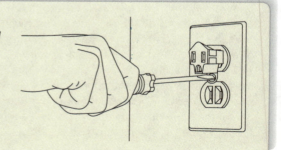

MAKING STRAIGHT CUTS

After marking, cutting is the most important step in the woodworking sequence. The basic straight cuts are crosscuts, rips, miters, and bevels. Crosscuts are made directly across wood grain, to cut a board to length; a rip cut is made with the grain, to reduce the board's width. A miter cut is angled, typically at 45°, across the face. Bevel cuts are angled along the edge or end of the piece. You can make all these basic cuts with a handsaw (below), portable circular saw (page 44), table saw (page 46), or radial-arm saw (page 48).

In general, be sure the entire saw kerf is on the waste side of your cutting line, or the finished piece will be too short. For precise fitting, woodworkers sometimes cut slightly wide of the line, then dress the cut flush with a bench or block plane.

Support the material to be cut securely on a workbench or sawhorses. Cutting across large sheets or crosscutting long boards requires support on both sides of the cut so the waste neither tilts in (binding the saw blade) nor swings out (splintering the cut). Bridge two sawhorses with a pair of scrap 2x4s, lay the piece on top, and cut around the scraps (or into them, with a circular saw); thin sheets may also need support below the cutting line to prevent sagging. Ripping usually requires a pair of sawhorses; when you reach one, either stop sawing and move the workpiece forward and back, or cut right into the sawhorse.

Handsaws: The crosscut saw is the general workhorse; ripsaws are specialty versions intended for cutting with the grain. A backsaw makes the finest cuts of the three, but its reach is limited. With any handsaw, cut with the good side up, or facing you.

Ripping a long board is best done with a power saw, but to rip short pieces, follow the directions for crosscutting (below), holding the blade at a 60° angle.

Circular saw: A portable circular saw cuts much faster than a handsaw and, if the work is set up carefully, can produce accurate finish cuts. Because the blade cuts upward, the material's top surface tends to splinter; place the best side down.

Before you start cutting, set up the saw. CAUTION: Unplug the saw for any adjustment. Start by attaching the correct blade (page 10), using a wrench that fits the saw's arbor nut. (If your model doesn't have a button to freeze the blade, dig the teeth into a piece of scrap wood to stop the blade from rotating.) When installing the blade, be sure the bottom teeth point forward and up. Next, adjust the blade angle; for most cuts, this will be 90°. Loosen the angle adjustment lever, push the base plate into the horizontal position and tighten the lever. To cut a bevel, set the blade with the help of the degree scale on the saw's body, then test the setting on scrap.

Finally, set the correct blade depth. Loosen the depth adjustment lever and set the blade: It should protrude only $1/16$ to $1/8$ inch below the cut. Either measure this with a tape or place the base plate on the material and line the blade up with the marked depth line by eye.

Plate joiner: A relatively new tool on the market, the plate, or biscuit joiner, is essentially a circular saw designed to cut semicircular grooves in the edge or face of the stock. With the faceplate pressed against the stock, the tool's barrel is pushed to plunge the blade into the wood (page 45). Special wooden biscuits are glued into the grooves in the mating pieces, forming a solid joint.

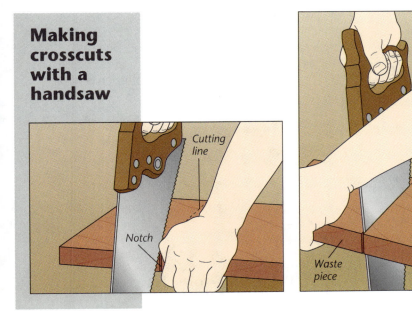

Making crosscuts with a handsaw

Cutting line

Notch

Waste piece

Crosscutting

To start, hold the saw nearly vertical and slowly draw the blade up a few times to make a $1/2$" deep notch in the edge of the board; use the thumb of your free hand to guide the saw (far left). This notch will help guide the saw for the rest of the cut. Once the cut is under way, lower the angle of the saw to about 45° (30° for plywood) and progress to full, even strokes; the saw does most of its cutting on the downstroke. Align the saw by sighting down the back from above; keep your forearm and shoulder in line with the saw's teeth. If the blade veers from the cutting line, twist the handle slightly to the opposite side until the blade returns. As you near the end of the cut, reach around the saw and hold the waste piece (near left). Then with the saw in the vertical position, make short, slow strokes to prevent the waste piece from splintering off.

Using a backsaw

TOOLKIT
• Bench hook or miter box

Bench hook

Making a fine cut

To make a precise 90° crosscut or miter, secure the stock in a vise, or use a bench hook (*page 5*). Grip the saw, positioning your arm, shoulder, and hip directly behind the blade. Begin the cut with slightly angled kerfs at both ends, then bring the saw level and take smooth, full strokes. If you are using a bench hook, grasp the stock firmly with your free hand to prevent creeping. You may choose to use a miter box (*page 8*), which guides the saw at a fixed 45° or 90° angle; or, with better models, at any angle between 0° and 45° in both directions. Insert the backsaw into the correct slot or set the degree scale, then align cutting line with the teeth. Hold or clamp work firmly. With a deep miter box, you can set the stock on edge to cut a bevel (an end miter).

Using a portable circular saw

TOOLKIT
• Straightedge guide and clamps
• Ripping fence
• Kerf splitter (long rips)

Basic operation of the saw

To start a cut, rest the saw's base plate on the stock. Line up the blade with the waste side of your cutting line; don't let the blade touch the material yet. Be sure the cord is free of the cutting path, and wear safety glasses. Release the safety button, if the saw has one, and press the trigger. Let the motor reach speed; then carefully begin the cut, either aiming the blade directly from the side or using the gunsight notch on the base plate (test it first). As you near the end of the cut, be sure you're in position to support the saw's weight. If necessary, grip its front handle with your free hand. When crosscutting an unsupported piece, accelerate at the end to avoid splintering. Let the blade stop completely before swinging the saw up or setting it down.

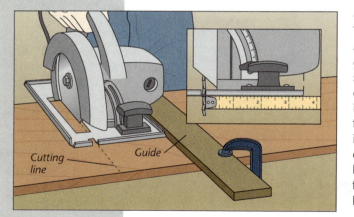

Cutting line

Guide

Crosscutting

The secret to straight crosscuts is to clamp a guide to the material for the saw's base plate to ride against. Use a manufactured guide, a perfectly straight length of scrap lumber (*left*), or build a simple cutoff jig (*page 45*). To position the guide, measure the exact distance between the base plate's edge and a sawtooth set in that direction (*inset*); clamp the guide or jig at that distance from your cutting line. If the saw binds, check that your support is adequate. To cut lumber thicker than the saw's capacity, first extend the cutoff line around all four sides with a square. Set the blade to just over half the depth and cut through one side. Then flip the piece over and cut through the back, carefully matching kerfs. Smooth any unevenness with a block plane or rasp.

Ripping

To rip near a board's edge, set the blade at minimum depth and attach the ripping fence loosely. Line the blade up with the width mark at the board's end—accounting for the kerf. Tighten the fence and set blade depth. For wider rips, clamp a long scrap guide to material, or construct a simple ripping jig (*page 45*). To cut, push the saw slowly away from you, keeping the ripping fence tightly against the edge. When you need to move down the line, back the saw off an inch in the kerf and let the blade stop while you move. On long rips, use a kerf splitter to prevent binding (*right*).

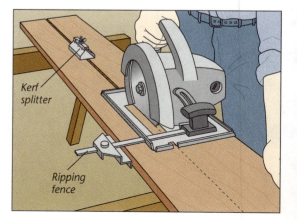

Kerf splitter

Ripping fence

MAKE-IT-YOURSELF: CIRCULAR SAW JIGS

These jigs will help you make more accurate crosscuts and rip cuts with your portable circular saw.

Cutoff jig: This jig guides crosscuts, and allows you to quickly place the blade on the cutting line. Build it with 1x3 hardwood or 3/4-inch plywood. Attach the arm to the head with screws. Customize the jig to your saw and blade by making the head longer than necessary, then cutting it to the exact length by running the saw's base plate along the arm. To use the jig, align the cut edge of the head with the cutting line on the workpiece, and clamp the jig firmly

in place. Keep the saw's base plate pressed firmly against the arm when making the cut.

Ripping jig: To direct a rip cut in a wide panel, make this jig, using 3/4-inch plywood for the base and guide. Cut the base wide, screw on the guide piece, and then run the saw down the jig to trim the base to size. To use the jig, first support the workpiece on sawhorses, then align the edge of the jig base with the cutting line and clamp the jig at both ends. The base plate of the saw must remain against the guide for the entire length of the cut.

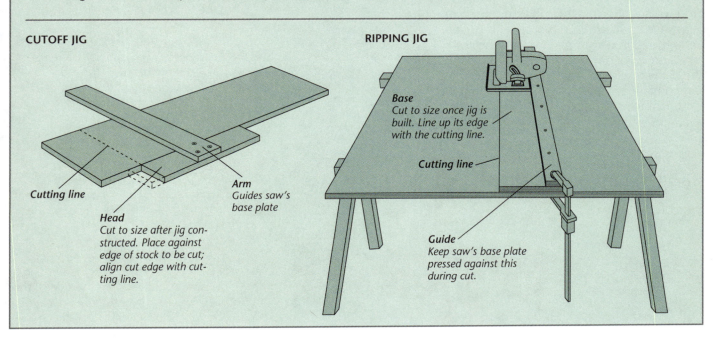

CUTOFF JIG

Cutting line

Head
Cut to size after jig constructed. Place against edge of stock to be cut; align cut edge with cutting line.

Arm
Guides saw's base plate

RIPPING JIG

Base
Cut to size once jig is built. Line up its edge with the cutting line.

Cutting line

Guide
Keep saw's base plate pressed against this during cut.

Using a plate joiner

TOOLKIT
• Clamps

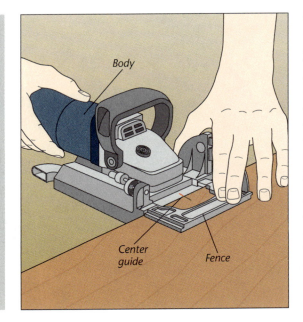

Body

Center guide

Fence

Cutting a slot
Mark the center of the desired slot location on the stock, and clamp the stock down. Adjust the fence: To cut into an edge, set the fence height so that when the fence is on the board face, the blade slot is centered on the edge. For a beveled edge, adjust the angle of the fence so that it rests flush against the adjacent surface. (For a face cut, hold the joiner vertically.) Next, adjust the tool's cutting depth to match the size of biscuit you plan to use. Align the joiner's center guide with the slot location mark, and keeping the faceplate pressed against the stock, turn on the tool. Hold the handle or support the fence with one hand and grip the body with the other. Once the motor has reached full speed, push the body to plunge the blade into the wood *(left)*, and then retract it. Keep your hands clear of the blade slot at all times.

TABLE SAW TECHNIQUES

The table saw is the best power tool for many cutting operations, but it must be set up carefully and used with utmost attention to safety. Before you begin, make sure the blade angle, rip fence, and miter gauge are exactly square to one another (see your owner's manual for instructions). Be sure to read the "Working Safely" section on pages 41-42. Some additional safety pointers are described at right.

To choose the right blade for the job, see page 10. To change a blade, first unplug the saw. Remove the table insert, then hold the arbor with one wrench while you loosen the arbor nut with another. If you are using a dado blade, make sure you install the correct table insert, with a wider opening. Set the blade one tooth's height (for carbide-tipped blades or hollow-ground planers), or 1/8 to 1/4 inch (for high-speed steel blades) above the stock.

Operating a table saw

TOOLKIT

For crosscuts:
• Miter gauge
• Carpenter's square
• Cutoff box (page 48) or roller stand (optional)

For rip cuts:
• Featherboard and clamps
• Push stick
• Roller stand (optional)

For miter cuts:
• Miter gauge
• T-bevel and pro-tractor (or combination square for 45° angles)

For bevel cuts:
• Items for crosscuts, rip cuts, or miter cuts
• T-bevel and pro-tractor

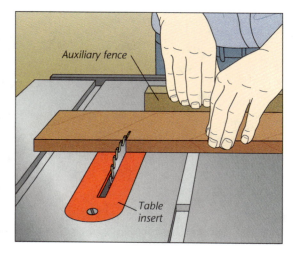

Auxiliary fence

Table insert

Crosscutting

Place miter gauge in either the left- or right-hand table slot. Set the scale for a 90° cut, and check angle. Screw a hardwood auxiliary fence to the gauge to give more bearing surface for a safe, accurate cut. For long pieces, attach a longer fence and cut into its bottom. Hold stock tightly against the gauge or fence with the left hand, as shown, and push the gauge and stock past the blade with the right hand. To cut wide material, turn the gauge around in the slot and push it through with the stock behind. A cutoff box (page 48) is helpful for large stock; it can also be used to improve accuracy for smaller pieces. For long pieces, use a roller stand or a helper to keep the stock level.

ASK A PRO

HOW CAN I MAKE IDENTICAL CROSSCUTS?

For repeated cuts of the same length, clamp a stop block to either the rip fence (far enough from the blade that the stock is away from the block by the time it contacts the blade) or to an extension on the miter gauge (see page 83). This will help align each subsequent workpiece quickly and easily. Never use the rip fence as a stop; the waste will bind between the fence and the blade and kick back.

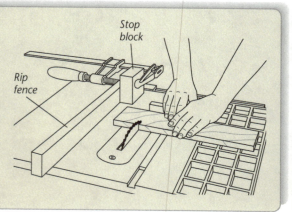

Stop block

Rip fence

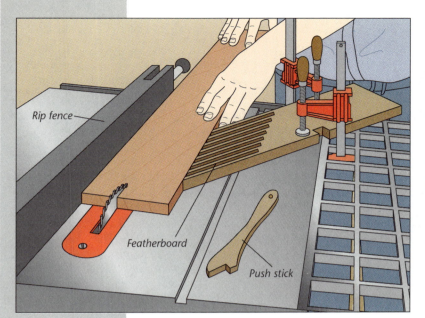

Rip fence

Featherboard

Push stick

Ripping

A rip cut is guided by the rip fence, positioned either to the right or left of the blade. Set the rip fence to the desired width by placing the stock on the table, lining up the cutting mark with the blade, and bringing the rip fence in to butt against the stock; lock the fence in position. Clamp a featherboard (page 41) to the table in line with the front of the blade. When ripping long boards or sheet materials, you'll need a helper or other type of support, such as a roller stand, at the rear of the table. Ripping is prone to kickback, so stand to one side while you're working. Don't rip twisted, badly cupped, or narrow, knotted pieces. Turn the saw on and with the stock flat, hold it firmly against the rip fence with your left hand, as shown, and feed it into the blade with your right hand. As you near the end, use a push stick to keep your hands a safe distance from the blade.

STRAIGHTENING A WAVY BOARD

Never run an uneven edge along the rip fence. Instead, build a jig as shown to rip it safely. Use 3/4-inch plywood for the base and the cleats; cut a notch out of one cleat to serve as a stop for the end of the stock. Attach a toggle clamp to each cleat to hold down the stock. Run the jig and the stock through the blade together, as you would a normal rip cut. If the opposite edge is also wavy, use the newly cut edge against the rip fence to guide the cut.

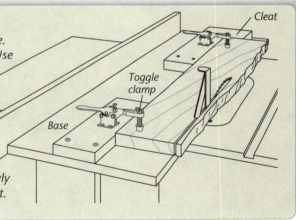

Cleat

Toggle clamp

Base

Making miter and bevel cuts

For a miter cut, attach an auxiliary fence to the miter gauge; glue sandpaper to the fence to avoid slippage. Set miter gauge to the desired angle and make a test cut. If possible, keep the gauge tilted in the direction shown. To cut, grip stock firmly and guide the gauge past the blade (left). You may have to reposition the miter gauge to make matching left- and right-hand miters; to avoid potential error, build a miter jig (page 48). Beveling combines crosscutting, ripping, or mitering techniques with the correct blade tilt; the setup must be precise. Set the blade angle, tilting the blade away from the fence; check by testing on a scrap piece. If you're mitering and beveling at once (a compound miter), be sure the blade will clear both miter gauge and blade guard. Watch your hands; use a push stick and a featherboard when ripping.

Auxiliary fence

Sandpaper strip

Miter gauge

The shop-made jigs shown below not only make using the table saw safer, but also ensure more accurate cuts. The cutoff box helps you make the square crosscuts needed for such things as carcase pieces. The miter jig enables you to make consistent 45° left- and right-hand miters. Both jigs run in the saw table's miter gauge slots; size the bases appropriately for the dimensions of stock you will cut most often. Make the fences from hardwood.

Cutoff box: This jig is, in effect, an enlarged table and miter gauge that provides support and true 90° cuts in wide or bulky workpieces. To assemble, place the runners in the miter gauge slots. Apply a bead of glue down each runner, lay the base on top, and screw it to the runners.

Remove the assembly from the saw table and screw the base to the fences; use a carpenter's square to keep the rear fence perfectly perpendicular to the runners. Cut a kerf through the rear fence, along the base, and through the front fence. To use, hold the stock securely against the rear fence and push the jig into the blade.

Miter jig: To make this jig, fasten the base to the runners as for a cutoff box, then cut the kerf in the base as shown. Position each miter fence at exactly 45° to the kerf, using a square to check that they form a 90° angle where they meet. Attach the rear fence. To use the jig, hold the workpiece firmly against the left or right miter fence and guide the jig into the blade.

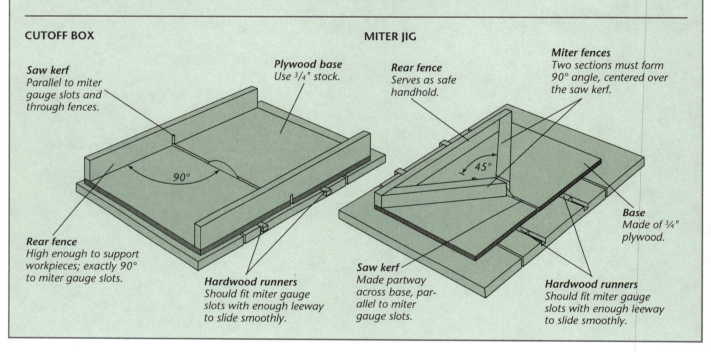

CUTOFF BOX

Saw kerf
Parallel to miter gauge slots and through fences.

Plywood base
Use 3/4" stock.

Rear fence
High enough to support workpieces; exactly 90° to miter gauge slots.

90°

Hardwood runners
Should fit miter gauge slots with enough leeway to slide smoothly.

MITER JIG

Rear fence
Serves as safe handhold.

Miter fences
Two sections must form 90° angle, centered over the saw kerf.

45°

Base
Made of 3/4" plywood.

Saw kerf
Made partway across base, parallel to miter gauge slots.

Hardwood runners
Should fit miter gauge slots with enough leeway to slide smoothly.

RADIAL-ARM SAW TECHNIQUES

This saw's specialty is crosscuts but, used correctly, it is versatile at performing all basic straight cuts. Consult the owner's manual for details on fine-tuning the components. In addition to these adjustments, line the tabletop in front of the fence with 1/4-inch plywood or hardboard, as the blade cuts about 1/8 inch into the surface. Attach it with glue or small nails, ensuring that the nails are out of the blade's path. Prepare this surface prior to use by making a 1/8-inch-deep crosscut kerf, a 45° miter kerf, and a rounded groove with the blade in the rip position. Replace this auxiliary top when it is worn.

For pointers on choosing the right blade for the job, see page 10. To change a blade, first unplug the saw and remove the blade guard. Lock the arbor, or hold it with

a wrench, and use another wrench to remove the nut. Slip the blade off, replace it, teeth pointing down and toward the column, and retighten. Replace the blade guard.

Make sure your stock is supported; if crosscutting long boards or ripping entire plywood sheets, set up extension tables or roller stands on either side of the main table. If possible, use a portable circular saw to rough-cut bulky pieces before ripping them.

Read the safety tips on pages 41-42; wear safety goggles and other protective gear. Keep a 6-inch margin of safety between your hands and blade. Always use the guard, set to just clear the work, and use the antikickback fingers when ripping. Ripping calls for extra precautions. Rotate the saw's yoke 90°, then feed stock to the rotating blade.

Making cuts with a radial-arm saw

TOOLKIT

For crosscuts:
- Clamps (optional)

For rip cuts:
- Featherboard and clamps (optional)
- Push stick or long wood scrap

For miter cuts:
- T-bevel and protractor (or combination square for 45° angles)

For bevel cuts:
- Items for crosscuts, rip cuts, or miter cuts
- T-bevel and protractor

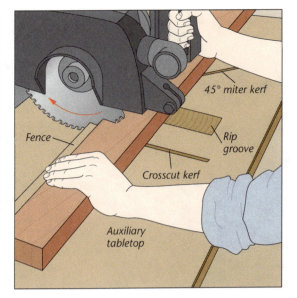

45° miter kerf

Fence

Rip groove

Crosscut kerf

Auxiliary tabletop

Crosscutting

First, set the blade for a 90° cut, and make sure both the miter and bevel scales are at 0°. With the blade behind the fence, use the elevating crank to position the blade about ⅛" below the front table surface. Loosen the rip lock, freeing the motor to slide along the arm. Place the stock against the fence and hold it there tightly with your free hand *(left)*. **CAUTION:** Keep fingers at least 6" away from the blade; clamp the stock to the fence if necessary. Grip the saw's handle with your other hand. Turn on the saw, let the motor reach speed, then pull the blade smoothly through the stock. Hold the handle firmly to control the blade. As soon as the blade completes the cut, push it back through the kerf, returning it to its position behind the fence. Turn off the saw, but do not remove stock until the blade has stopped spinning.

ASK A PRO

IS THERE AN EASY WAY TO CROSSCUT SEVERAL BOARDS?

If you have more than one board to cut, either "gang-cut" them all at once, as shown, or clamp a stop block to the fence to locate each subsequent cut easily and accurately. To cut an extra-wide board or sheet, crosscut as far as possible on the first pass, then turn the stock edge-for-edge, line it up, and finish the cut with a second pass.

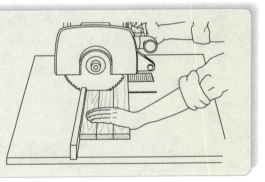

Ripping

Swivel the yoke to bring the blade parallel with the fence; lock in position. For most jobs, the in-rip position (with blade closer to the fence and motor near the table's front) is best. For extra-wide rips, use the out-rip position (motor near the fence). Align the blade for the correct width of cut, then tighten rip lock. Consult the owner's manual to set the splitter, antikickback fingers, and blade guard; on some models the guard's nose will pivot down near the stock's surface. Stock must be fed against the direction of the rotating blade—from right to left for in-rips, the reverse for out-rips. Turn on the saw. With one hand pressing the stock firmly against the fence (or install a featherboard), use the other hand to feed stock slowly into the blade *(left)*. Stand just to one side of the blade, not behind it, in case of kickback. When the board's end is about 6" from the blade, use a push stick—or, for very narrow rips, a long scrap piece. Turn off the saw; wait for the blade to stop before removing the stock.

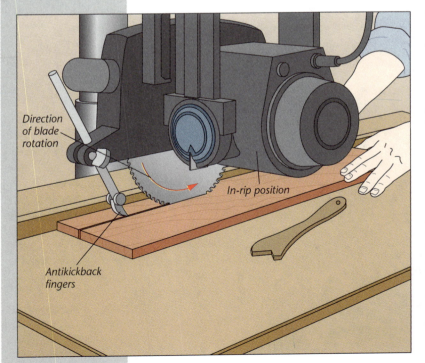

Direction of blade rotation

In-rip position

Antikickback fingers

Mitering

Like crosscutting, mitering is easy work for the radial-arm saw; in fact, the only difference in setup is the angle of the arm. Loosen the miter lock, select the angle by pivoting the arm, and tighten the lock; be sure the bevel angle scale is at 0°. Make a test cut on scrap and measure it with a protractor. To cut a miter, position the stock as you did for crosscutting, and make the cut the same way, pulling the saw across the work (*left*). Exact 45° miters can be tricky to match if you must "mirror" two pieces. You'd either have to cut one piece upside down or swing the arm from one side of 90° to the other, and both leave room for error. Instead, use a miter jig (*below, left*).

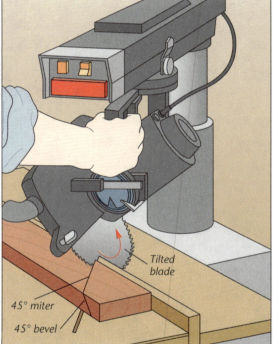

Tilted blade

45° miter
45° bevel

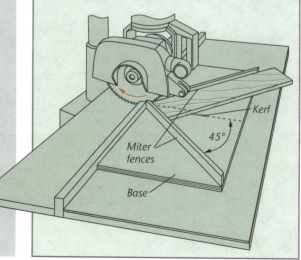
Beveling

To set up the saw to cut a bevel, first raise the blade a few inches above the table, then loosen the bevel lock and tilt the yoke to the desired angle. Tighten the bevel lock, then lower the blade; make a test cut on scrap and double-check the angle. With the blade set in the bevel position, use the crosscutting, ripping, or mitering techniques described above to make the cut. A combination miter and bevel cut, called a compound miter, is shown here. Be very careful to keep your hands well away from the blade when it's angled like this.

MAKING CUTOUTS, CURVES, AND CIRCLES

When it comes to cutting drawer-pull cutouts, scrolling a headboard, or rounding a circular or oval table, you'll need a different collection of tools and techniques than for straight cutting. A curve-cutting saw must have a thin blade and fine teeth to bank around turns. Coping saws and compass saws fit the bill. Portable saber saws bring power to the work and handle large cutouts. For curves in thick stock (up to 6 inches), use a band saw. The trick to fine curves is to cut slowly, just to the waste side of the cutting line. Smooth the edges with a spokeshave, rasp, or sandpaper. Read the safety information for power tools on pages 41 and 42; always wear safety goggles when cutting.

Handsaws: The basic coping and compass saws handle cutouts and curves. The coping saw can cut fine, tight curves, but its reach is limited by the depth of its frame; its cousin, the fret saw, with its deep throat, reaches where the coping saw can't. A compass saw is the choice for large, rough cutouts within a board or panel.

Saber saw: The saber saw makes cutouts, tight curves, and, with the right attachment or jig, perfect circles. You also can cut right in the middle of a panel, or cut straight lines just as with the band saw. Attach a straightedge guide, and keep the saw's base plate pressed against it as you make the cut.

Band saw: The band saw is unmatched for cutting curves along a board's edge; and, because most models can handle material at least 6 inches thick, or high, you can cut curved profiles on edge. The band saw is also good for making straight cuts; use a miter gauge or rip fence for accurate crosscuts and rip cuts, respectively. A straight cut with the piece on edge, to make the board thinner, is called resawing. Information on band saw blades is on page 11.

Using a coping saw

TOOLKIT
- Drill and bit larger than blade (to make cutouts)

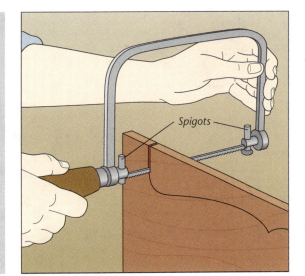

Spigots

Cutting fine curves near an edge

Clamp material in a vise or on a sawhorse. To change a blade, turn the handle counterclockwise; butt the frame end against a solid surface, push, and remove the blade. Slip in a new blade and tighten the handle. For tight curves, choose the finest blade you can. If the material is in a vise, point the teeth toward the handle and cut on the pull stroke; on a sawhorse, point the teeth away from the handle and cut on the push stroke. Cut slowly to prevent snapping the blade. When cutting, rotate the blade to any position by turning the spigots; complicated figures may require you to stop and turn the blade several times. It helps to cut out to the waste at points, then start from another angle to meet the first cut. This saw also makes cutouts near an edge; drill a hole, slip the blade through, then reattach it.

Using a compass saw

TOOLKIT
- Drill and bit larger than saw's tip
- Crosscut saw for long, straight sections

Making a cutout

The compass saw is the choice handsaw for most large cutouts. First, drill a pilot hole in opposite corners of the the waste area for the saw's blade. Hold the saw at a right angle to the stock, and cut slightly inside the marked cutting line. For best control, cut near the handle; for cutting mild curves, you can cut near the tip, but watch that it doesn't bend. Once the cut is under way, switch to a crosscut saw for any long, straight sections.

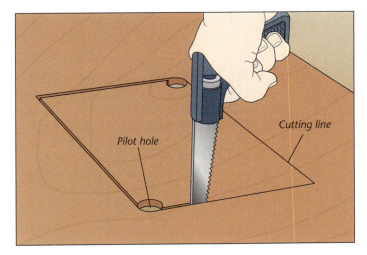

Pilot hole

Cutting line

TOOLKIT
- Drill and bit larger than blade (for cutout)
- Straightedge guide and clamps (for straight cuts)
- Circle guide

Curve-cutting

Use the narrowest blade possible; keep some on hand, as you may snap a few. To replace a blade, loosen the blade-locking screw, slip the old blade out, insert the tang of a new one (with teeth facing forward), and retighten. For a bevel cut, adjust the base plate; otherwise, make sure it is at 90° to the blade. Line up the saw outside the stock, on the waste side of your cutting line. Begin the cut. As you reach tight curves, resist the urge to "steer" the saw by raising the base plate—the angle of the cut will go askew. Instead, slow down; the tighter the curve, the more slowly you cut. If the curve is too tight, cut into the waste area to remove part; then finish the curve. It may be easier to cut inward from both sides of a curve toward the center. If you have a persistent problem keeping the blade on line, it may be dull or bent; replace it.

Making a cutout inside a panel

Drill a pilot hole in the waste area for the blade. With practice, you can also start a cutout by "plunge-cutting" with a rough-cutting blade: With the saw resting on the base plate's front edge, make sure the blade will clear the surface at the end of its down-stroke. Turn the saw on; slowly lower it until the blade tip cuts into the material and the base plate rests flat on the surface. It may help to screw (only if into waste) or clamp a stop block to keep the base plate steady (inset). Now cut the basic outline. To keep a long, straight cut on track, clamp on a scrap guide for the baseplate. For square corners, round them off first, then saw into the corners, as shown by the arrows (left).

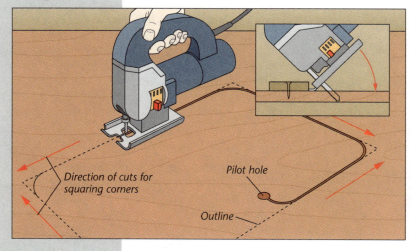

Direction of cuts for squaring corners

Pilot hole

Outline

Cutting a circle

You can execute a perfect circle—or an arc—with a radius up to about 7" with the help of a circle guide. (For larger circles, use a circle-cutting jig as shown below.) A circle guide is usually the accessory ripping fence turned upside-down. Drive the pivot pin, aligned with the front of the blade, into the stock at the circle's center point. Cut the circle as you would any curve (right). For a cutout, drill a pilot hole or make a plunge-cut first, and cut to the circle's outline, then attach the guide and complete the cut.

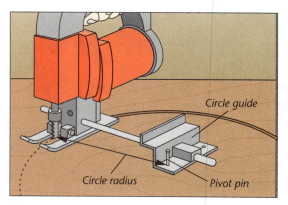

Circle guide

Circle radius

Pivot pin

MAKE-IT-YOURSELF: SABER SAW CIRCLE-CUTTING JIG

To cut large arcs and circles, use hardboard or ¼-inch plywood with a small notch for the blade, a pivot pin (a screw), and some type of attachment to hold your saw's base plate. Try cleats and stove bolts, wing nuts and washers; cut a groove in each cleat if there are ridges on the sides of the base plate. Place a cleat over each side of the base plate; tighten wing nuts. Drive the pivot pin even with the front of the blade: the distance from the pin to the front of the blade equals the circle's radius.

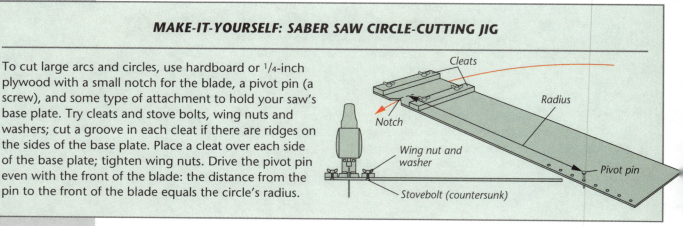

Cleats

Radius

Notch

Wing nut and washer

Stovebolt (countersunk)

Pivot pin

Cutting with a band saw

Setting up the saw

The finer the curve, the narrower the blade; wide blades are best for straight cuts. To change a blade, loosen the upper wheel with the blade tension knob, remove table insert, and slip blade off wheels and through table slot. Loop new blade over wheels, with teeth facing you, and take up the tension so the blade flexes no more than $1/4$". Rotate the blade by hand; if it doesn't stay centered, adjust the tracking knob. Set the upper and lower blade guides so they're just behind the teeth and a paper strip's thickness away. Check that the blade-to-table angle is exactly 90°; for a bevel cut, set the table at the desired angle and make test cut to check angle.

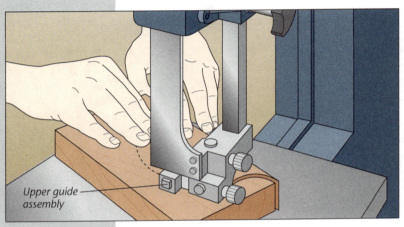

Upper guide assembly

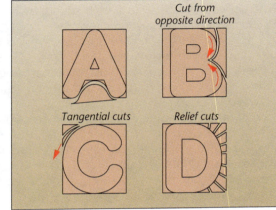

Cut from opposite direction

A B

Tangential cuts   Relief cuts

C D

Cutting curves

Set upper blade guide assembly $1/4$" above work. To cut a simple curve, stand facing, and slightly to one side of the blade. Turn saw on and feed the work smoothly *(above, left)*—too fast and the blade may twist and break; too slowly and the work will burn. Feed the piece with your right hand and guide it with your left. To cut several identical pieces, join them with double-sided tape and cut them at once.

Several tricks are shown *(above, right)* for tight curves. Clear most of the waste first *(A)*, or cut in stages so you can make the second cut from the opposite direction *(B)*. Veer off tangentially through the waste to an edge, then come back and continue the curve *(C)*. Make relief cuts first *(D)*; you can also drill holes just to the waste side of the cutting line so the waste will fall away.

MAKE-IT-YOURSELF: BAND SAW CIRCLE-CUTTING JIG

For best results—especially for large circles—use a jig. Use $3/4$-inch plywood for the base, hardwood stock half that thick for the extension, and 1x2 stock for the cleats. Size the base to fit your band saw table; cleats should hug each side tightly. Rout a groove in the base to slide in the extension flush with the surface; the extension's centerline must line up with the bottom of the blade's gullets (between two teeth). Use a dovetail bit on the edges of the groove; make matching bevel cuts on both edges of the extension. For the pivot pin, drive a countersunk screw from underneath so about $3/8$ inch of the tip protrudes. To use the jig, measure the desired radius between the pin and the edge of the base; slide the extension out the correct amount, then screw it to the base. Make an entrance cut to the outline on the workpiece; fix the center of the desired circle to the pin and install the jig on the saw. Turn the stock to rotate the cutting line through the blade *(right, below)*.

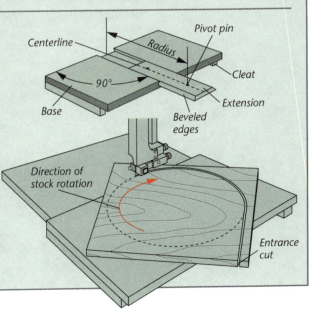

Centerline   Radius   Pivot pin

90°   Cleat

Base   Beveled edges   Extension

Direction of stock rotation

Entrance cut

SHAPING WITH HAND TOOLS

After cutting pieces to rough length and width, check them carefully for square and true them. Traditionally, this is a job for hand planes, although power jointers (*page 62*) will make it easier. You'll need to clean up notched corners and cutouts, smooth curves, and round over sharp profiles, corners, and edges using spokeshaves, files, rasps, and chisels. Use chisels to pare notches and form dadoes, mortises, and other shapes by hand. Page 58 shows these basic techniques. When you're shaping by hand, remove the stock in small increments until you are right down on the marked line.

Hand planes: Bench and block planes are both used for truing boards square, flat, and smooth; end-grain work is the block plane's specialty. To get the most from a plane, it must be finely tuned. See below for instructions on adjusting a bench plane. Block plane adjustments vary according to the model: The fully adjustable type has both lateral and depth adjustment controls, as well as a mouth adjustment lever below. Adjustable block planes may include a depth adjustment nut and/or a locking lever for the cutting iron assembly; loosen the locking lever to adjust the blade angle and blade depth.

To square up a board, follow this five-step sequence, referring to the directions for the planing techniques on pages 55 and 56: **1)** Smooth and level the best face to serve as a reference for the other surfaces; **2)** Square one edge to the good face; **3)** Scribe a thickness line, using the good face as a guide, on both edges; then plane the other face down to the lines; **4)** Scribe a width line from the square edge along both faces, and square the other edge down to these lines; and **5)** Mark the board's ends with a combination square; plane the end grain square.

The specialty planes shown on page 12 come in handy for different situations; the circle plane, as its name suggests, planes curves, and the bullnose plane is perfect for smoothing small or confined areas.

Spokeshave: Flat- and curved-sole models are available for shaping convex and concave curves, respectively. The technique is shown on page 57.

Files and rasps: These provide quick cutting action and good control to shape or smooth curves. Often, they're the only choice for enlarging or adjusting tight curves, inside corners, and notches. For most flat surfaces, planes, chisels, or sanding tools are preferable.

Setting up and adjusting a bench plane

TOOLKIT
• Screwdriver

1 ▶ Honing the cutting iron
Lift up the locking lever, remove the lever cap, and lift off the irons. Loosen the cap iron screw from below the cutting iron, pivot the two irons at 90° to one another, and slide the cutting iron free. Sharpen the cutting iron (*page 14*).

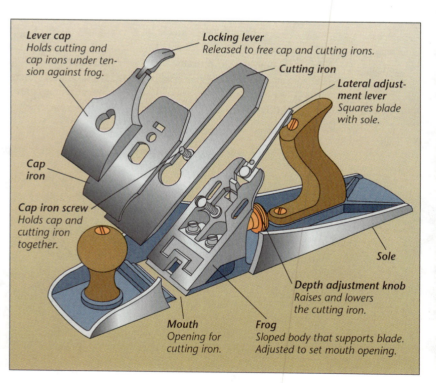

Lever cap
Holds cutting and cap irons under tension against frog.

Locking lever
Released to free cap and cutting irons.

Cutting iron

Lateral adjustment lever
Squares blade with sole.

Cap iron

Cap iron screw
Holds cap and cutting iron together.

Sole

Depth adjustment knob
Raises and lowers the cutting iron.

Mouth
Opening for cutting iron.

Frog
Sloped body that supports blade. Adjusted to set mouth opening.

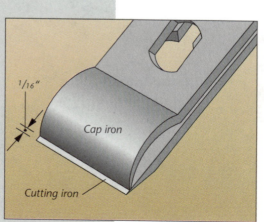

1/16"

Cap iron

Cutting iron

◀ 2 Setting the clearance between the cap and cutting iron
Once the blade is sharp, replace the cap iron and set the clearance between it and the cutting iron—normally 1/16". Tighten the cap iron screw, then reassemble the plane. Press down on the locking lever to hold the iron assembly in place.

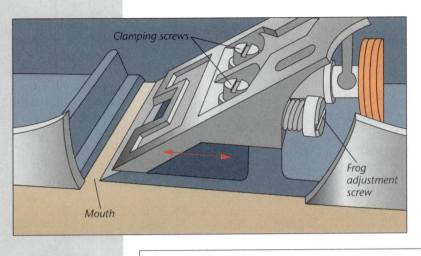

Clamping screws

Frog
adjustment
screw

Mouth

3 Checking the mouth clearance

Loosen the two clamping screws, then turn the frog adjustment screw—clockwise to reduce the opening for fine finish work, or counterclockwise to enlarge it for more aggressive stock removal. Tighten the clamping screws and check the opening with the cutting iron in place; it should be about $1/16"$ for general work, and as small as $1/32"$ for fine work.

4 Setting blade angle and exposure

Turn the plane over and sight down its sole. If the blade is out of square in relation to the sole, push the lateral adjustment lever (shown in step 1) toward the side that's extended the farthest. To adjust blade exposure, turn the depth adjustment knob—clockwise to lower the blade, counterclockwise to raise it—until the blade just protrudes through the mouth. Remove the slack from the knob by turning it in the opposite direction until you feel tension.

Leveling a board face

TOOLKIT
• Jointer, jack, or smoothing plane
• Square
• Winding sticks (perfectly straight 1x2 strips, longer than the stock is wide)

1 Making diagonal passes

Before you begin, clamp the stock securely. Depending on the surface area, you can use a jointer, jack, or smoothing plane. Whichever you opt for, adjust the blade depth for a fine cut. Grip the rear handle with one hand and the front knob with the other. Work diagonally across the board, first in one direction (right), then in the other. If the board is very rough, set the blade for a deeper cut and overlap your passes.

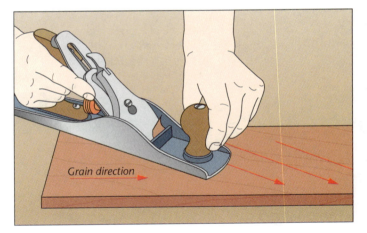

Grain direction

2 Checking your progress

Check the surface with a square (left): Any light that shows beneath the blade indicates a low spot. Shade in the adjacent high spots with a pencil, then plane the penciled areas only, and test again. Check for board twist with a pair of winding sticks by sighting across their top edges (below). They should be perfectly parallel; if not, plane down the high spots and recheck.

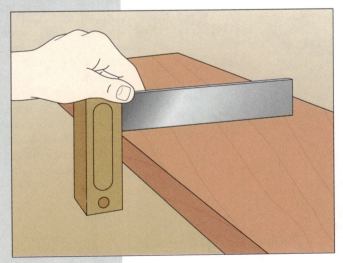

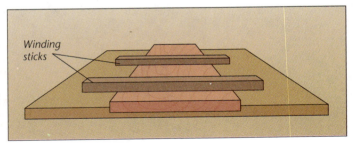

Winding sticks

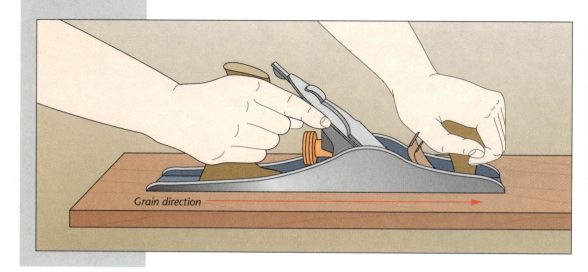

Grain direction

3 Making the final passes

When the board is basically flat, set the plane for a very fine cut and plane directly in line with the grain *(left)*. With slightly overlapping passes, continue until the surface is perfectly flat and smooth.

Truing a board edge

TOOLKIT
• Jointer plane

Planing a long board
Working on the edge of a long board requires a wide, balanced stance and continuous passes. Using a jointer plane, walk with each pass, if necessary *(right)*, and guide the plane by bracing the fingers of your leading hand against the edge of the board *(inset)*.

Squaring up board ends

TOOLKIT
• Block plane

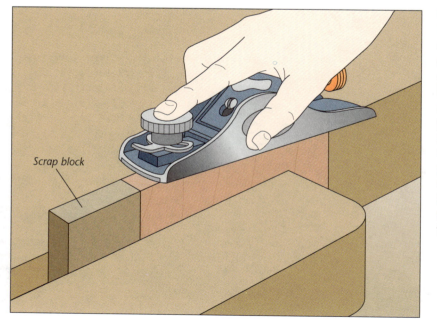

Scrap block

Using a block plane
Hold a sharp plane in one hand, applying pressure with your forefinger as necessary. Holding the plane at a slight angle to the direction you're working, use short, shearing strokes. To prevent splitting the edge, plane inward from both edges, or clamp a scrap block the same thickness as the workpiece to the far edge *(left)*.

MAKE-IT-YOURSELF: SHOOTING BOARDS

To guide a block plane for end-grain work, many wood-workers turn to a shooting board. The 90° and 45° shooting boards shown here help fine-fit board ends for butt or miter joints, respectively. To make either model, use ³/₄-inch plywood. Fasten the fence to the base, and add the lip underneath so you can brace the jig against the edge of the workbench. For the 90° model, screw a stop block onto the fence, flush with the edge of the fence. For the 45° model, add a mitered stop to the fence, as shown, placing the stop even with the fence's edge. To use either type, hold the workpiece against the stop, about ¹/₃₂ inch over the edge of the fence; with the other hand, run a block plane along the fence past the workpiece's end. For larger pieces, use a bench plane rather than a block plane.

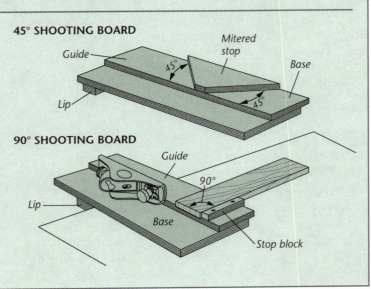

45° SHOOTING BOARD

Guide · Mitered stop · 45° · Base · Lip · 45°

90° SHOOTING BOARD

Guide · 90° · Lip · Base · Stop block

Using a spokeshave

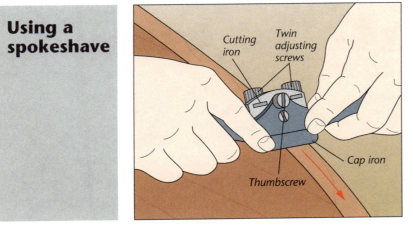

Cutting iron · Twin adjusting screws · Cap iron · Thumbscrew

Planing curves

To smooth a curve in thin stock, first choose the correct spokeshave for the curve. Flat-faced models are designed for convex surfaces; the curved-face type are for concave curves. To adjust the spoke-shave, first loosen the thumbscrew. If your model has twin adjusting screws, use them to set the depth for a fine cut, then tighten the thumbscrew; otherwise, adjust the cutting iron manually. To use a spokeshave, grip the handles, with your thumbs placed behind and your forefingers extended, as shown. Work downhill with the grain, pushing the tool away from you, as shown on a convex curve (left). Always work with the grain.

Shaping a curve with a file or rasp

Quick shaping

Choose a flat file or rasp for convex surfaces; for concave curves a half-round profile is best. With either, cross-file with overlapping passes while moving down the curve. Position the file at about a 30° angle to the stock. Using downward pressure, stroke smoothly and rhythmically away from you along stock. Pick the file up on the return—filing in the opposite direction dulls the teeth. Maintain even pressure and tempo, and check the surface periodi-cally to ensure you're removing stock evenly. To round off square edges, cross-file across the edge with a flat file or rasp. Draw-filing produces smoother results: Hold the tool at a right angle to stock and push straight away from you (right). To enlarge holes or inside curves, use a rat-tail file or rasp; hold it in one hand, extending your forefinger down the blade, and stroke directly away from you.

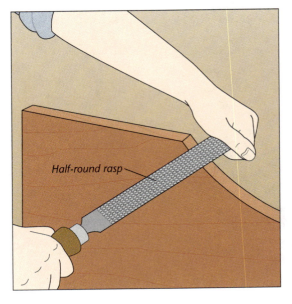

Half-round rasp

CHISELING

The most important rule for using a chisel is to keep it sharp *(page 14)*. Secondly, use the right type and size of chisel for the job. For general cutting and finishing off rough cuts, choose a bevel-edge bench chisel. For heavy-duty mortising, notching, or any job requiring extra strength, select a butt, mortise, or firmer chisel. In general, choose a bench chisel slightly narrower or a mortise chisel the same width as the notch, groove, or mortise you're shaping; to cut along an edge or end, select a chisel that's wider than the work. Most chiseling operations boil down to either horizontal or vertical paring; the correct hand positions are shown below. To drive a butt, firmer, or mortise chisel, you'll probably need to use a mallet, as shown in the basic chiseling steps on page 59.

Hand and body positions for chiseling

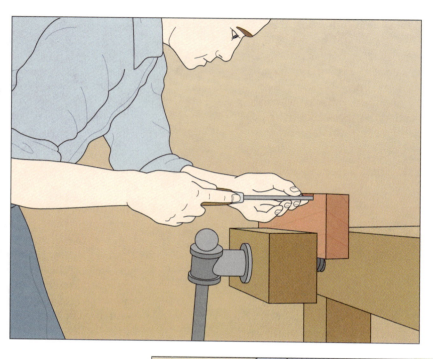

Horizontal paring
Place the palm of your dominant hand against the back of the chisel handle and wrap your hand around the handle to grip the chisel, extending your forefinger along the handle. Align your body directly behind the chisel so your legs, hips, and shoulder can work together. Your other hand guides the blade; brace it with your thumb on top and your forefinger below *(left)*.

Vertical paring
Place the thumb of your dominant hand on top of the handle end and wrap your other fingers around the handle. Cock your arm up so that as you lean down, the chisel is lined up with your shoulder. As for horizontal paring, guide the blade with the thumb and forefinger of your other hand. Push down with your shoulder to drive the chisel.

Basic chiseling technique

TOOLKIT
• Mallet

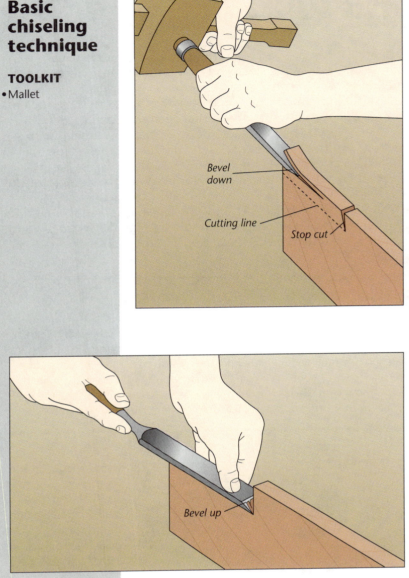

Bevel down

Cutting line

Stop cut

Bevel up

Removing waste

To remove material quickly, work with the bevel down. Clamp down the workpiece and pare horizontally or vertically, as shown opposite. If cutting as shown, make a stop cut to prevent splitting. If you're using a mallet, grasp the chisel with one hand and strike the end of the chisel handle sharply with the mallet *(left)*. Start out with short, light taps and swing harder as required.

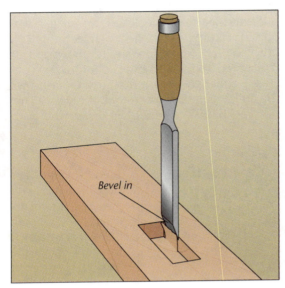

Bevel in

Smoothing to the line

For more controlled work or to finish up rougher cuts, turn the chisel bevel up for a horizontal cut, or in for a vertical cut. First, secure the stock. As you approach the cutting line, nibble small bits, finishing with hand pressure alone. Make the smoothing passes with the chisel flat, with your thumb pressing firmly down on the blade just behind the bevel *(left)*. When notching with the chisel held vertically, keep the bevel facing in toward the waste *(above)*.

ASK A PRO

ARE THERE SPECIAL TRICKS TO CHISELING?
To avoid splintering when you're cutting a dado, don't go all the way through in the same direction; instead, cut in from both sides. Once you are halfway through the dado, reverse the workpiece and cut in from the other side to meet the other cuts, as shown. Use the same principle when you are smoothing the end of a workpiece, for easier chiseling of the stubborn end grain. Start in from one side, working toward the middle; leave some stock intact on the other side. Then turn the workpiece around and cut in from that direction.

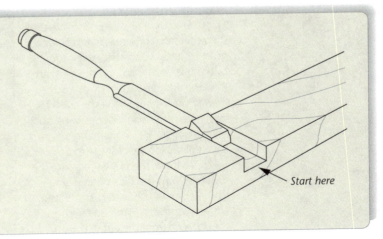

Start here

SHAPING WITH POWER TOOLS

The router shapes edges, decorative grooves, recesses, and woodworking joints. The jointer makes edges and faces flat and square to one another for a joint or as preliminary board preparation; it does the same job as a hand plane, but more quickly and accurately. For either tool, read the safety cautions on pages 41 and 42.

Router: Set up the stock on a workbench with bench dogs or clamps. To shape an edge, hang it over the edge of the bench. Make sure the setup won't interfere with the router. To install a bit, slip it into the collet and tighten the collet with a wrench; use a second wrench above the collet unless you can lock the shaft. The depth-setting mechanism varies from one router to the next. To ensure an accurate setting, mark the desired depth on the side of the stock and lower the bit to this line. Test the setting on a piece of scrap.

Jointer: Check that the knives are correctly secured in the cutterhead, and that the outfeed table is at the same height as a knife at its maximum height. To set the depth of cut, lower the infeed table 1/8 inch below the outfeed table for softwoods, or 1/16 for hardwoods.

If your board came surfaced on two sides, joint the edges only. Otherwise, follow this sequence: **1)** Joint the best face; **2)** Joint one edge square to this face; **3)** Plane the other face parallel; **4)** Rip the board to width using the edge from step 2 as the guide edge.

Operating a router

Standard routing technique

Grip the router securely, lining it up just outside the area to be cut (to make an interior cut, drill a pilot hole or make a plunge cut). Because the bit spins in a clockwise direction, the tool tends to drift or kick back counterclockwise. To compensate, rout from left to right, so the bit's leading edge always bites into new wood. Turn on the router and let the motor reach full speed, then carefully feed the bit into the work. Turn off the motor as soon as the bit is clear of the stock; let the bit stop completely before setting the router down. Never rout without a guide; either the accessory edge guide, a straightedge or circle guide, a template, or a piloted bit.

Guiding straight router cuts

TOOLKIT
• Edge-shaping bit with ball-bearing pilot

OR

• Edge guide for your model router

OR

• Straightedge guide and clamps

Inside edge

Outside edge

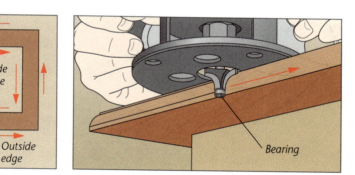

Bearing

Making a groove cut

To guide a cut near an end or edge, use the accessory edge guide available for most routers. Attach the guide loosely to the base plate, line up the bit with a reference line on the stock's edge, then tighten the guide. If the cut is further in from the edge, clamp a straightedge to the stock, to the left of the cutting line, for the base plate to follow (right). To locate the guide, measure the distance from the bit's outside edge to the edge of the base plate; or test cut against the straightedge and check the distance from the cut to the guide.

Using a piloted bit

For edge-shaping, choose a self-piloting router bit; its bearing runs along the edge being shaped, guiding the router (near left). If you're shaping all four sides, begin with the end grain on one side, then continue from left to right, following the path shown (far left) for an outside or inside edge. If you're routing the ends only, work from the edges in, or clamp a wood block flush against the far edge to prevent the end grain from splitting as the bit exits the stock.

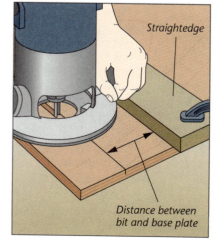

Straightedge

Distance between bit and base plate

HOW FAST SHOULD I FEED MY ROUTER?

It takes some looking and listening to acquire a feel for the correct speed. Examine the cuts you're producing: If the edges are ragged and chipped, you're cutting too fast; if they're burned, *you're moving too slowly. Listen for the sound of the router's motor that corresponds to the smoothest cut, and maintain this speed when feeding the bit into the stock.*

Guiding curved router cuts

TOOLKIT
- Edge guide for your model router, flipped over
OR
- Circle guide (store-bought or shop-made jig)

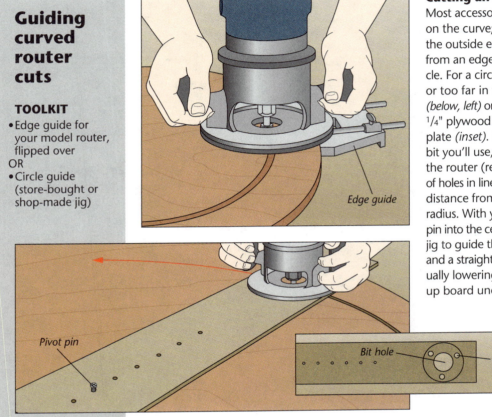

Edge guide

Pivot pin

Cutting an arc or circle

Most accessory edge guides are also designed to cut on the curve; keep the guide pressed firmly against the outside edge of the stock *(left)*. If you can't work from an edge, tack the guide to the center of the circle. For a circle with a radius too large for the guide, or too far in from the edge, construct a circle jig *(below, left)* or buy a trammel guide. Build the jig from $1/4$" plywood cut the width of your router's base plate *(inset)*. Bore a hole to fit the largest diameter bit you'll use, and drill counterbored holes to attach the router (remove base plate first). Make a number of holes in line with the bit for the pivot pin screw; the distance from this pin to the bit equals the circle's radius. With your router installed on the jig, drive the pin into the center of the workpiece's circle and use the jig to guide the cut. Using this jig or a trammel guide and a straight bit, you can cut through stock by gradually lowering the bit between passes; place a back-up board underneath to protect the workbench.

Bit hole

Mounting holes

HOW CAN I CARVE CUSTOM DESIGNS?

Build a template from $1/4$-inch plywood or hardboard. Screw a guide bushing to the base plate so the bit won't cut the template. Be sure to account for the bushing's thickness when making the template, and add an extra $1/4$ inch to the bit's depth. Or, buy a top-piloted bit that rides against the template. To start a cut into the interior, make a plunge cut: Tip the router back on its base plate so the bit is clear of the work, then turn on the motor and lower the router slowly until the bit digs in and the base plate is flat on the work. Follow the template with the guide bushing to make the desired outline, then remove any waste from the center freehand. Square off corners as necessary with a sharp chisel.

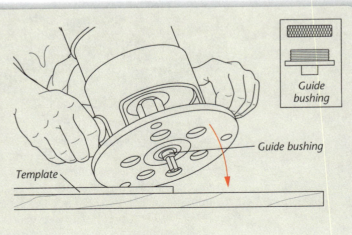

Guide bushing

Guide bushing

Template

MAKE-IT-YOURSELF: ROUTER TABLE

For easier grooving and edge-shaping, buy or build a table to hold your router upside down. Use 3/4-inch plywood for the top, with 1/4-inch hardboard glued on to reduce friction. Drill a hole for the bit, remove the router's base plate, and mount the router upside down using countersunk screws. For bits that aren't self-piloting, make an L-shaped hardwood fence; cut a notch so you can partially recess the bit. Attach one end of the fence with a carriage bolt; clamp the other end in the desired position. There's no incorrect fence alignment—the only critical distance is that between the fence and the bit. Feed the stock from right to left past the bit as shown, keeping it pressed against the fence with one hand (or install a featherboard). Use push sticks or blocks to keep your hands away from the bit.

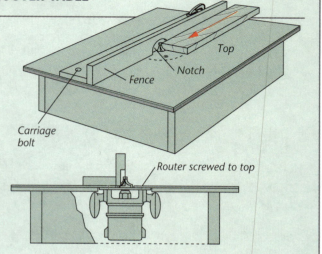

Top

Notch

Fence

Carriage bolt

Router screwed to top

Jointing

TOOLKIT
• Push blocks for face-jointing

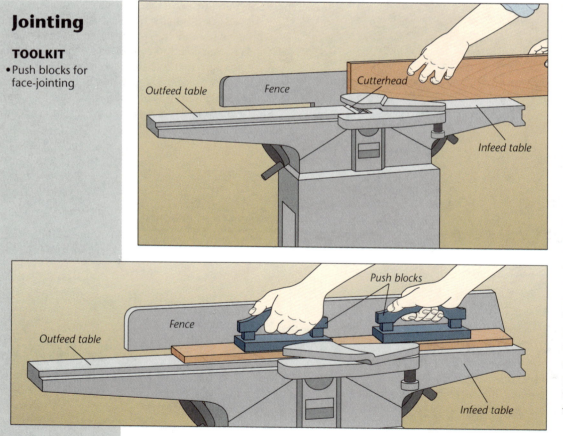

Outfeed table

Fence

Cutterhead

Infeed table

Push blocks

Outfeed table

Fence

Infeed table

Edge-jointing
The stock must be wider than 2" and longer than 1' to be safely jointed. Always cut with the grain; unless it runs parallel to the edges, orient the board so that the grain runs downhill away from the cutterhead, as shown. With the board on the infeed table, push the piece slowly over the cutterhead, using a hand-over-hand method to press the stock against the fence and down on both tables. Keep your hands well away from the cutterhead. If you have to joint end grain, to avoid tearout at the end of the piece, go in partway, then remove the board and finish from other side.

Face-jointing
Face-joint only pieces thicker than 3/8". To face-joint, or surface, a board, place it with the grain going away from the cutterhead, as shown. Keep the board against the fence and flat on the tables as you push it slowly along the infeed table, over the cutterhead and onto the outfeed table. To distance your fingers from the knives, use commercial push blocks as shown, or make your own (*page 41*). For a long piece, bring your leading hand back behind your trailing one to continue applying downward pressure on the board.

DRILLING

Most woodworkers use an electric drill and a variety of drill bits in place of the traditional manual drills (the brace and hand drill). But for those who retain an affection for hand drills, the basic instructions for their operation are shown below. The drill press is known for its ability to bore precise holes, although it also can perform a variety of other woodworking tasks when fitted with the appropriate jigs and accessories. The bits for all three types of drills are shown on pages 16 and 17.

Safety tips for power tools are covered on pages 41 and 42; remember to always wear safety goggles whenever you are drilling.

For a woodworking project, one of the most likely reasons to drill is in preparing the wood to receive a screw without splitting. Information on drilling these pilot holes for woodscrews, as well as holes allowing the screwhead to rest level with the surface—or hidden below it— is presented on page 65.

How to use a hand drill

Operating a brace or hand drill

The brace is basically a bit attached to a crank that is turned. To bore a hole, position the bit's center screw on your mark. Holding the butt knob with one hand, turn the handle clockwise with the other. If you're drilling horizontally, use your body to keep the knob in line. If you're drilling vertically, use your shoulder or chest as support *(right)*; it may take practice to keep the brace steady. If the bit sticks, back it out a few turns to clear the waste.

To use the hand ("egg-beater") drill, just aim the bit and turn the handle with a fast, steady motion. To avoid bending or breaking the small bits, don't bear down on the drill.

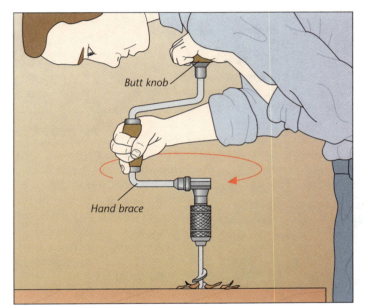

Butt knob

Hand brace

How to use an electric drill

Stop collar   Tape   Pilot bit

Operating an electric or cordless drill

To change a drill bit, insert the chuck key in one of the holes in the chuck and turn it counterclockwise until the bit can be removed. Insert the new bit all the way and tighten the jaws; don't forget to remove the key! When possible, clamp the material before drilling, particularly when using a $1/2$" drill. If your drill allows, match the speed to the job: a higher speed for small bits and softwoods, and a slower speed for large bits and hardwoods or metal. As you drill, apply only light pressure, letting the bit do the work *(left)*. Leave the motor running as you remove the bit from the wood. To drill a large hole in hardwoods—especially with oversized twist bits—first make a small lead hole. Back the larger bit out occasionally to cool it and to clear stock from the hole.

To stop a bit at a specified depth, install a stop collar, wrap tape around the bit at the correct depth, or use a pilot bit *(inset)*.

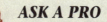
HOW DO I START A HOLE AND DRILL A PERFECTLY STRAIGHT HOLE?

To center the moving bit on its mark when starting a hole, use a pointed tool as a center punch. An awl hole or a couple of taps with a hammer and nail, or punch, will prevent the bit from wandering. When you need to drill a perpendicular—or correctly angled—hole, a simple trick is to line up the drill body or auger bit with the help of a square, as shown at right (use a T-bevel for an angled hole). Commercial accessories are also available: A portable drill press (far right) will hold your drill for big jobs, but an adjustable drill stand that adjusts for angles is more convenient, as it can be held against a vertical surface. A commercial doweling jig increases accuracy when drilling edges and end grain.

How to use a drill press

TOOLKIT
• Clamps or clamping device for workpiece

Boring a hole

The combination of proper drilling speed and feed pressure will help you avoid ragged cuts, damaged bits, and burnt stock. Most drill presses come with a chart to help you choose the proper speed for the job; consult your owner's manual to make adjustments. Determining the right feed pressure may require some practice on an off-cut from the actual stock. To install a bit, loosen the chuck jaws with the chuck key, insert the shank, and tighten by hand; finish with the key, then make sure to remove it. Check that the bit is centered over the table's hole or, for a stopped hole, set the depth-stop as required. For an angled hole, adjust the angle of the table or drill head—depending upon your model—and to protect the table, clamp a board underneath your stock.

To bore a hole, align your mark on the stock with the bit and clamp the piece down; several commercial devices are available to secure irregularly shaped pieces. Turn on the drill and pull the feed lever with a steady downward motion to lower the bit into the stock *(right)*. With thick pieces, raise the bit several times to clean chips out of the hole.

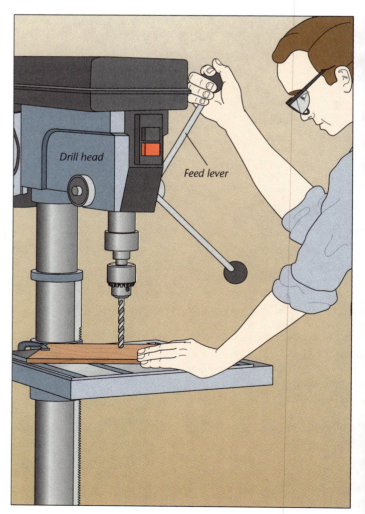

Drill head

Feed lever

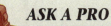
HOW DO I PREVENT THE WOOD FROM SPLITTING WHERE THE BIT EXITS?

There are two ways to keep the back side of the stock from breaking away as the drill bit pierces through. You can clamp a wood scrap to the back of your workpiece and drill through the piece into the scrap (near right), *protecting the stock from the clamp with a wood pad. Or, drill until the bit's point or center spur just breaks through* (far right), *then flip the piece over and finish drilling from the other side. Use the hole made by the bit as your starting point.*

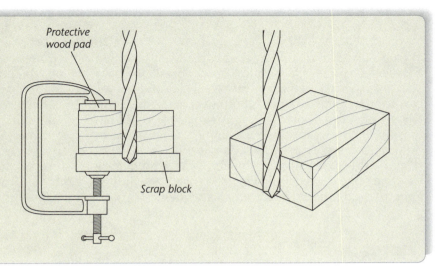

Protective wood pad

Scrap block

DRILLING HOLES FOR WOOD SCREWS

Woodworkers drill a variety of holes for screws, as shown below. Drilling a pilot hole, also known as predrilling, helps prevent the wood from splitting. A screw is usually driven flush with the surface (by drilling a countersink hole) or below the surface (a counterbore hole) so that the screw head can be completely hidden with a wooden plug or putty.

Countersinking and counterboring: Drywall and flathead wood screws are usually countersunk; often the screw is sunk below the surface (countersunk and counterbored) so it can be covered with wood putty or a plug. Choose a special countersink bit, or a pilot bit (which creates body, pilot, countersink, and counterbore holes in one operation). Or, you can use standard bits: For a countersink hole, use a twist bit the same diameter as the screw head; for a counterbore hole, use a bit (such as a Forstner) that will give you a flat-bottomed hole slightly

larger than the screw head. Unless you're using the all-in-one pilot bit, always bore the larger hole first, then add the body and pilot holes in the center.

Machine bolts and lag screws look best when they're counterbored *(below, right)*. Drill the counterbore hole first, using a bit the same diameter as the washer that will go behind the bolt head or nut. Then drill the hole for the shaft down the center.

Drilling body and pilot holes: For a wood screw, pick a drill bit the size of the screw shank diameter at its widest, and bore right through the top piece to be joined. Use a second bit, the same size as the shank's core between the threads, to drill a pilot hole into the lower piece to a depth equal to the length of the screw.

Driving a drywall screw into softwood with an electric drill and screwdriver bit usually doesn't require a pilot hole. In harder wood, make a pilot hole as above.

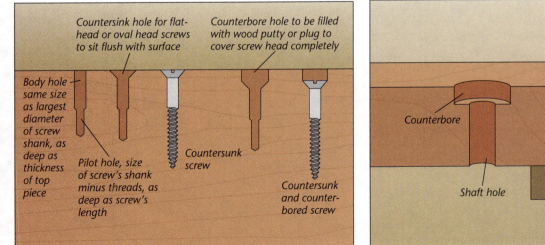

Countersink hole for flathead or oval head screws to sit flush with surface

Counterbore hole to be filled with wood putty or plug to cover screw head completely

Body hole same size as largest diameter of screw shank, as deep as thickness of top piece

Pilot hole, size of screw's shank minus threads, as deep as screw's length

Countersunk screw

Countersunk and counterbored screw

Bolt head

Counterbore

Washer

Shaft hole

FASTENING

Nails, screws, and bolts are the simplest ways to assemble your project. Bolts allow you to break down an assembly for easy moving or storage. Nails and screws, on the other hand, are far less obtrusive, especially if countersunk or counterbored. In many situations you'll have to drill pilot holes for these mechanical fasteners; the drilling techniques are shown on pages 63 to 65. Adhesives are the least visible "fasteners" of all, and require that the pieces be carefully clamped together. Gluing is a methodical process, and it's also a sequential task that requires keeping one eye on the clock. To avoid clamping, you can combine glue with a few well-placed nails or screws.

Directions for all these fastening techniques follow, but before you can assemble the components of a project, you will have to cut and shape the joints. For joinery options and procedures, turn to the following chapter. The basic steps involved in gluing and clamping an assembly are shown on page 67; for specific setups, see the chapter on furniture making *(page 95)*.

Nailing

TOOLKIT
• Drill and bit slightly smaller than nail diameter (optional)
• Nailset for finishing nails

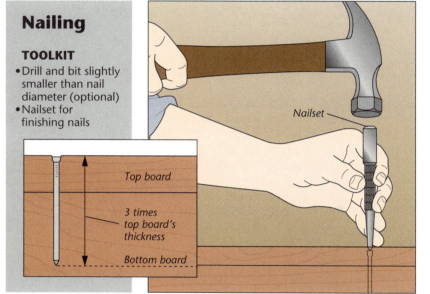

Nailset

Top board

3 times top board's thickness

Bottom board

Basic nailing technique

As a rule, choose a nail that's three times as long as the top piece's thickness *(inset)*. Hardwoods split easily; to avoid this, drill pilot holes first when nailing near an edge; use a bit slightly smaller than the nail. To start a nail, hold it between your thumb and forefinger and give it a few light taps with a hammer. Once it's started, remove your fingers and swing more fully, combining wrist, arm, and shoulder action.

Drive finishing nails to within 1/8" of the surface, beginning with full hammer strokes and ending with short, careful taps. Then tap the nail head below the surface with the point of a nailset *(left)*, and conceal the resulting hole with wood putty.

If you bend a nail, remove it with the hammer's claw—insert a scrap block between the hammer and the wood to protect the surface.

Driving a screw

TOOLKIT
• Drill and bit *(page 65)* for pilot hole
• Screwdriver or variable-speed electric drill with screwdriver bit

Basic screwdriving technique

When screwing through one board into the end grain of another, use a screw that's long enough so that about two-thirds its length will enter the bottom piece *(near right)*. To join boards face to face, the screw should be 1/4" shorter than the combined thicknesses *(far right)*. Screws usually require pilot holes *(page 65)*. If you're driving screws by hand, use the correct size screwdriver; if it's too large or too small for the screw's slot, it can burr the screw head or worse, slide off and gouge the work. If a screw is stubborn, try rubbing paraffin or paste wax on the threads. If it still sticks, drill a larger or longer pilot hole. An electric drill fitted with a screwdriver bit will save an incredible amount of time and labor. Use a variable-speed drill, keeping firm pressure and a two-handed grip on the drill to keep it from twisting or slipping as the screw slows down. To drive a stubborn screw home, turn the drill on and off rapidly while bearing down.

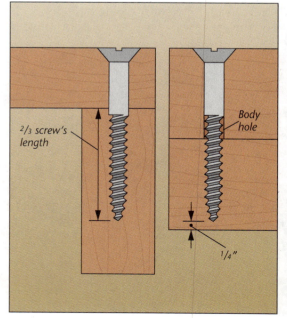

2/3 screw's length

Body hole

1/4"

Driving bolts and lag screws

TOOLKIT
- Drill and bit
- Wrench or ratchet and socket

Using a wrench or ratchet

To drive a lag screw, first drill a pilot hole into the pieces to be joined; this hole should be two-thirds the diameter and length of the screw. Then use a wrench to tighten the lag screw.

To drive a bolt, the bolt should be $1/2$" longer than the combined thicknesses of the pieces being joined, to give the nut a firm bite. If you're countersinking or counterboring the head and/or the nut, subtract these depths from the total. Drill a clearance hole through both pieces to be joined—this hole should be slightly bigger than the bolt's diameter. Tighten the nut; to keep it from spinning, hold the bolt's head with a second wrench or ratchet and socket.

Gluing and clamping an assembly

TOOLKIT
- Brush or paint roller
- Clamps
- Chisel

1 **Dry-fitting**

Always test-fit the assembly before spreading the glue. Not only will you be able to determine if the pieces fit, but this will force you to consider the best sequence, how to deal with any sub-assemblies, what you will need in the way of clamps—and whether or not you need a helper.

2 **Spreading the glue**

White (polyvinyl acetate or PVA) and yellow (aliphatic resin) glues can be applied straight from the bottle, but should be spread out with a small brush or paint roller. Spread glue evenly onto both surfaces to be joined; a plumber's flux brush makes application easy *(right)*. On end grain, apply one coat, then recoat it along with the mating piece.

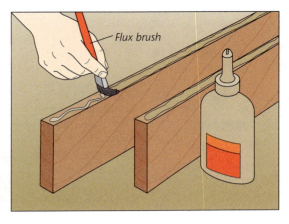
Flux brush

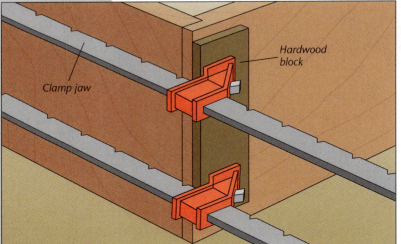
Clamp jaw
Hardwood block

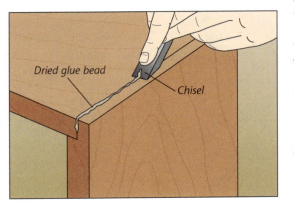
Dried glue bead
Chisel

3 **Clamping**

Work on a large, level surface. Prepare hardwood blocks to spread clamping pressure evenly and protect the wood from the metal clamp jaws; wax paper can also be used to keep the clamp jaws from staining or sticking to the piece. Always center the jaws of your clamps directly over the joint, or the pressure may pull the joint askew. If you're clamping curved surfaces, use wooden handscrews or curved blocks, specially cut for the particular application, to supply the pressure. Before tightening the clamps all the way, check the assembly's alignment carefully for square and make any adjustments that are required *(page 97)*. Once everything is perfectly aligned, tighten the clamps until they're snug but not too tight; you should see a thin bead of glue along the joint.

4 **Removing excess glue**

Let the glue dry, remove the clamps, and then scrape off the excess glue with a sharp chisel *(left)*.

SANDING AND SCRAPING

The choice between sanding or scraping wood smooth is up to you. If, like most woodworkers, you decide to sand, you'll need to divide the procedure into three and sometimes four steps. You should rough-sand before assembling the parts, while you can still reach all the surfaces easily. Basic sanding procedures appear below; for finish-sanding instructions, see page 117. Scraping is like planing on a very fine level. The difference between sanding and scraping can be seen on the wood: Sanded surfaces appear soft and fuzzy from the abrasives, while a scraped surface looks harder and clearer. (Some woodworkers use a very sharp block plane for a similar effect.)

Sanding: You can choose hand-sanding or power tools. A belt sander levels or cleans up a rough surface; a random orbit sander removes stock with coarse paper, and with finer paper gives you a very smooth surface without any swirl marks; a finishing sander is good for intermediate and finish-sanding. To remove minor dents and scratches, lumber stamps, or scribed lines, first rough-sand as required—either by hand, or with a belt or random orbit sander—using 50- to 80-grit paper or a 100- (2/0) or 120-grit (3/0) belt. Once the material is smooth and uniform in color, switch to 120-grit paper on the sanding block or random orbit or finishing sander. Then sand once more with 180- to 220-grit paper. Some materials and finishes may require a fourth pass with even finer paper or 3/0 to 4/0 steel wool. Be careful on end grain; move straight across in only one direction to avoid rounding the edges and clogging the wood pores.

Scraping: Particularly effective on hardwoods, scraping will take some practice to be able to do properly. The key to scraping is a sharp edge on the tool; sharpening instructions are on page 20. You may find a cabinet scraper is easier to use than a hand scraper; with its preset blade angle and thumbscrew that controls the amount of bow, it takes the pressure off your fingers.

Sanding flat surfaces

TOOLKIT
- Sanding block
OR
- Belt sander
- Clamping devices for small pieces
OR
- Finishing or random orbit sander

Sanding by hand
Traditional hand-sanding still produces fine results for rough or fine sanding and, depending on the contour of the wood, may be the only feasible method. To provide a flat surface for the sandpaper, use a sanding block. To cut the sandpaper to size, first fold it, then bend and tear it over a bench edge or cut it with an old utility knife. Keep the sanding block flat and always sand in line with wood grain *(right)*. On end grain, move straight across in one direction only to avoid rounding the edges.

Sanding block

Overlapping passes

Stop block

Operating a belt sander
Use the finest grit that will do the job; a 100-grit belt is sufficient for most rough-sanding. To install a belt, release the lever that slackens the front roller, install the new belt with the arrow on the backing pointing in the clockwise direction, then tighten the lever. Hold the sander up and turn it on; center the belt on the roller with the tracking control knob. Before you start, keep a small board from moving by clamping a stop block on each end, as shown; or, place it between bench dogs or stops. To sand, move the tool forward and back in line with the grain; at the end of each pass, lift it up and repeat, overlapping the previous pass by half. A belt sander can remove a lot of material quickly; always keep it moving when it is in contact with the work. Don't apply pressure—the tool's weight alone is sufficient.

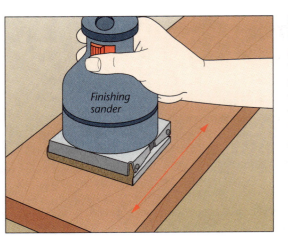

Using a finishing or random orbit sander

Finishing sanders take from $1/4$ to $1/2$ a standard sandpaper sheet. To load your sander, slide one end of the paper under the clamp on one side, stretch the sheet tightly, and clamp the other end. Use a light touch with a finishing sander, moving it back and forth with the grain. Move a random orbit sander in ovals, also following the grain. For both types, always keep the sanding pad flat on the surface.

ASK A PRO

HOW DO I SAND CURVES AND CONTOURS?

Sanding curves or contours is difficult since there's no flat surface for a standard sanding block or power sander's belt or pad. You can use a random orbit sander with a soft sanding pad attached, or, for a curve with a large radius, try replacing the felt pad on the bottom of your finishing sander with a rubber one. Some other tricks are shown here. For sanding curves by hand, make a special sanding block by wrapping sandpaper around a dowel or a contoured wood scrap shaped for the job (below, left); an older, broken-down sandpaper sheet may follow the curves better. To sand outside surfaces, try using a thin strip of sandpaper "shoeshine style" (below, center). A drum sander accessory for your electric drill or drill press will follow wavy or irregular shapes (below, right).

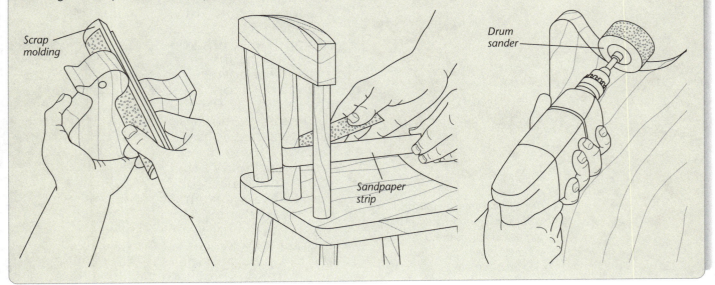

Scrap molding

Sandpaper strip

Drum sander

Scraping a flat surface

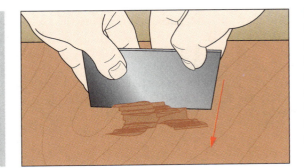

Using a hand scraper

Hold the scraper upright with your fingers behind, as shown. Bow the blade out with finger pressure, angle the scraper toward you slightly, and pull it along the board. The correct tension and angle are a matter of feel; keep trying until you get it right. Check the wood that is being removed; you should see minute shavings. Sawdust tells you that the scraper angle is incorrect, or that the blade is dull.

JOINING WOOD

Whatever woodworking project you take on, whether it's a simple box or a fine table, you'll need to make joints. The quality of the joints will determine whether your piece gives reliable service or comes apart with use. Though hundreds of joints have evolved over time, modern woodworkers can manage with a dozen or so. The most commonly used joints fall into six groups—butt, rabbet, dado and groove, lap, mortise-and-tenon, and dovetail; all are covered in this chapter.

You'll find suggestions for choosing the right joint for the job, tips on layout and marking, and procedures for achieving accurate, predictable results with a variety of hand and power tools.

If you're new at the joinery game, don't try to be too fancy; choose the joint that's the easiest to make, yet meets your requirements for both strength and appearance. For more guidelines on selecting joints for specific applications, turn to pages 95 to 114; the chapter beginning on page 41 contains information on how to use the various tools. Keep the basic measuring and marking tools on your workbench; you'll be using them often.

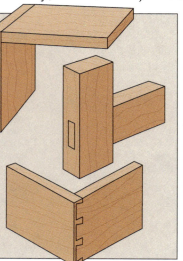

These representative joints, along with their variations, cover the gamut of joints needed for most woodworking projects. Find out more about them in this chapter.

For a properly fitted joint, the dimensions must have an accuracy greater than the graduations on your measuring tools. Achieving this precision may seem impossible, but in practice, it's actually the relative fit of the two pieces that counts. The keys to first-rate joinery are not only patience and practice, but also testing your setup on scrap of the same thickness and width as your stock. When the fit is dead on, cut your actual stock.

CAUTION: Though for the sake of clarity we may show the table saw and radial-arm saw without the blade guards in place, use the guard whenever possible.

BUTT JOINTS

The simplest of all woodworking joints, butt joints are made by butting two pieces of stock together, fastening them with glue or mechanical fasteners—or both—and in some cases reinforcing them with dowels, splines, or glue blocks. Most unreinforced butt joints are inherently weak, due to their minimal gluing surfaces; this weakness is multiplied if the highly absorbent end grain is being glued. An exception to this would be the edge-to-edge and face-to-face joints, which are very strong, since they don't involve end grain. However, precisely made butt joints are acceptable for many applications, and when they're reinforced, they can compete in strength with mortise-and-tenon or dovetail joints. Six commonly used types of butt joints are illustrated below. On the following pages you'll find information on how to cut and reinforce each of the butt joints described. In general, for best results, saw just slightly wide of the cutting line, then check the end with a square. Plane the end dead square or to a perfect 45° angle; homemade devices such as the cutoff box or miter jig *(page 48)*, or the shooting board *(page 57)* can facilitate the process while increasing your accuracy. Instructions on how to glue and clamp are presented on page 67.

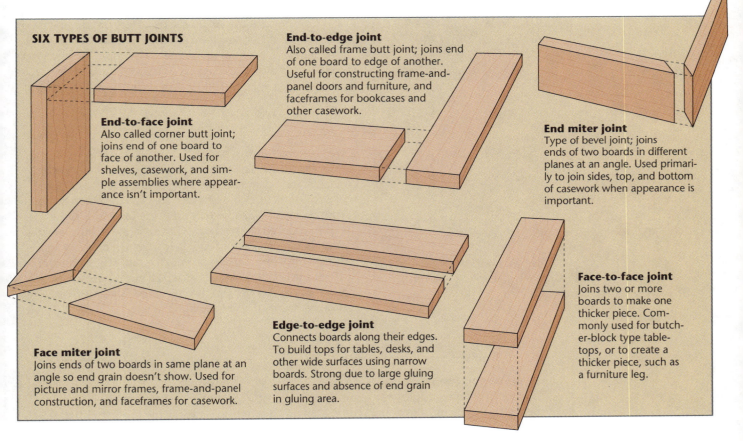

SIX TYPES OF BUTT JOINTS

End-to-face joint
Also called corner butt joint; joins end of one board to face of another. Used for shelves, casework, and simple assemblies where appearance isn't important.

End-to-edge joint
Also called frame butt joint; joins end of one board to edge of another. Useful for constructing frame-and-panel doors and furniture, and faceframes for bookcases and other casework.

End miter joint
Type of bevel joint; joins ends of two boards in different planes at an angle. Used primarily to join sides, top, and bottom of casework when appearance is important.

Face miter joint
Joins ends of two boards in same plane at an angle so end grain doesn't show. Used for picture and mirror frames, frame-and-panel construction, and faceframes for casework.

Edge-to-edge joint
Connects boards along their edges. To build tops for tables, desks, and other wide surfaces using narrow boards. Strong due to large gluing surfaces and absence of end grain in gluing area.

Face-to-face joint
Joins two or more boards to make one thicker piece. Commonly used for butcher-block type tabletops, or to create a thicker piece, such as a furniture leg.

Making end-to-face and end-to-edge joints

Cutting the joints

The procedure for both joints is the same—you need to make crosscuts perfectly square to the board's edge. Use a handsaw, portable circular saw, table saw, or radial-arm saw. If you're using hand tools and your stock is narrow enough, you can cut the wood with a backsaw and miter box. For wider stock, use the backsaw alone, or switch to a crosscut saw. However, the radial-arm saw—used with a fine-cutting blade—is the tool of choice for these cuts. (For detailed instructions on crosscutting, see pages 43 to 50.)

End-to-face and end-to-edge joints must be reinforced *(page 73)*; assemble and glue up the joint, clamping it in a similar way to the carcase shown on page 96.

Making an edge-to-edge joint

TOOLKIT
- Saw
- Hand plane or power jointer
- Try or combination square
- Pipe or bar clamps

1 Arranging the boards
Because the wide surfaces made from edge-joined stock are often highly visible, take extra care in selecting the boards. Avoid cupped or bowed boards, and make sure they have pleasing grain patterns. Select boards at least 2" longer than the finished length, and be sure you have enough boards to allow removal of up to 1/4" from the width of each. Arrange the pieces for appearance on a large surface, alternating the end grain if possible *(see step 3)* to minimize warping; using boards no more than 4" wide also helps. Mark the laid-out boards with a "V" or triangle so you can reassemble them the same way for step 3.

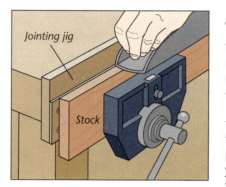

Jointing jig
Stock

2 Jointing the boards' edges
The edges must be straight, smooth, and square to the faces of the boards; no amount of clamping pressure can compensate for uneven or out-of-square edges. To true the edges, use a jointer *(page 62)*, or hand plane (the longest jointing, jack, or smoothing plane you have) with a razor-sharp blade.

Make a jointing jig by attaching a 1/4" thick piece of hardboard to a 1x6 as shown at left. Adjust the plane for fine cuts, then with the side of the plane's sole tight against the jig, make repeated passes along the board until the surface is square. Whatever tool you use, check the edge against the face with a square, and test the boards carefully for fit; if there are any gaps, repeat the jointing.

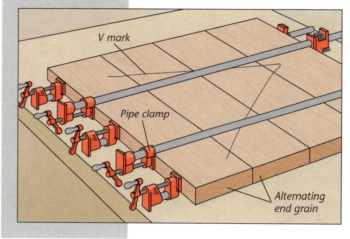

V mark
Pipe clamp
Alternating end grain

3 Clamping the panel
Place your pipe or bar clamps jaws-up on the bench, positioning one clamp about every 18" to 24". Butt one board against the farthest clamp and then stand all the others on edge to spread glue thinly and evenly on all the top edges. Once all the glue is applied, lay the boards down on the clamps, even up their ends and bring the clamps' jaws together, applying light pressure only. Now add clamps from the top, centering them between the bottom clamps. Tighten all the clamps slowly, starting with the lower ones and then the upper ones *(left)*; make certain all the boards stay flat and in alignment.

Making a face-to-face joint

TOOLKIT
- Saw
- Power jointer
- Try or combination square
- Clamps

1 Preparing the stock
Crosscut the boards to their approximate length (at least 1" longer than the final length) and rip to approximate width (at least 1/2" wider than final width). Joint the mating faces of the boards, check for square, then dry-assemble the pieces, positioning them for the most attractive look in terms of color and grain pattern. Turn each successive board so the end grain is facing up on one piece and down on the next.

2 Gluing up
Spread glue evenly on one face of each board (except the top one), then set the pieces on edge and butt them together. Install clamps along the top edge of the joint, using as many clamps as you can fit, with a maximum spacing of 12". Use pipe or bar clamps as shown in step 3 above, or, for a small assembly, use C-clamps or fast-action clamps. Don't tighten the clamps all the way just yet; first flip the joint over to add clamps on the other edge, centering them between the first clamps. Then tighten all the clamps until a thin bead of glue comes out from between the boards.

Making a miter joint

TOOLKIT
- Saw
- Plane (optional)
- Combination square
- Clamps

Cutting miters

The fit between the two pieces of a miter joint is far more important than their absolute dimensions; there should be no gap. To help you achieve tight-fitting joints, set up your saw to cut as closely as possible to the desired angle (45° for a 90° joint), and make test cuts on two pieces of extra stock. Check the fit and angle of the joint and adjust your saw as necessary. Retest and adjust until you achieve a tight fit. Another way to produce tight-fitting face miters is to make your cuts a little proud of the cutting lines, then carefully trim the cut surfaces back with a plane and shooting board (*page 57*). You can cut face miters with a backsaw and miter box, a table saw, or a radial-arm saw. For end miters (bevels), the latter two are best. A power miter saw, a finish carpenter's tool, also cuts crisp miters in stock up to 4" or 5" wide.

Clamping a miter joint can be tricky; for a face miter assembly, use a corner clamp or a special picture frame clamp. For end miters, use a band clamp, or a series of bar or pipe clamps.

REINFORCING BUTT JOINTS

If the butt joints in your project require reinforcement, you have several options, as illustrated at right. Dowels, splines, and biscuits can reinforce any butt joint, but dowels may be a problem for end miters cut in thin stock. Glue blocks reinforce end-to-face and end miter joints. The techniques for reinforcing are described below and on page 74; if you want to use a biscuit joiner, consult the owner's manual for instructions on choosing the correct size and number of biscuits for the particular application.

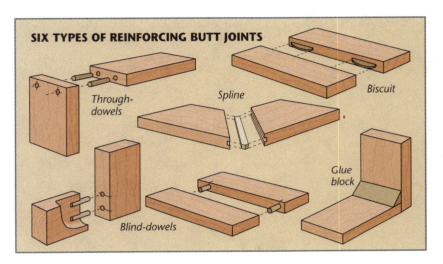

SIX TYPES OF REINFORCING BUTT JOINTS

Through-dowels · Spline · Biscuit · Blind-dowels · Glue block

Reinforcing with dowels

TOOLKIT
- Drill and brad-point bit
- Saw
- Clamps

For through dowels:
- Mallet
- Flush-cutting saw
- Sander

For blind dowels:
- Doweling jig or dowel centers

Selecting the dowels

Whether you use through- or blind dowels depends on the joint; you can't use through-dowels with edge-to-edge joints or face miter joints, for example, although they are a good choice for end-to-face joints. Use at least two dowels in each joint; space blind dowels in edge-to-edge joints 6" apart. Bore dowel holes in the center of stock's thickness; use a brad-point bit with an electric drill. Buy fluted or spiral-groove dowels equal to half the thickness of your stock.

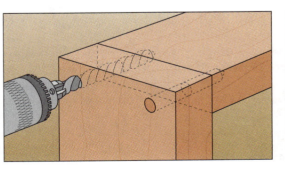

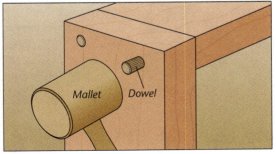

Mallet · Dowel

Through-doweling

Assemble the joint and when the glue is dry, remove the clamps and mark the hole centers. Drill holes extending at least 3/4" into the other piece (*above, left*). Cut the dowels slightly longer than the depth of the holes. Coat the dowels sparingly with glue and tap them into the holes with a mallet (*above, right*); clamp the joint. After the glue is dry, saw off the excess and sand the dowel flush with the surface.

JOINING WOOD   **73**

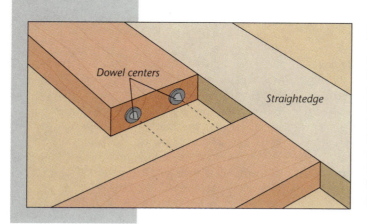

Dowel centers

Straightedge

Blind-doweling

The holes in each piece must line up exactly. A commercial doweling jig makes the task much simpler and helps ensure that the holes are drilled straight; buy a self-centering model if possible. Otherwise, mark the stock with dowel centers: Drill dowel holes in one piece and insert the dowel centers in them. Press the two pieces together using a board as a straightedge guide *(left)*. Drill the holes so they extend at least $3/4$" into the pieces; cut the dowels a bit short to allow $1/16$" to $1/8$" of space in the bottom of each hole for excess glue. Coat the dowels with glue and insert them in the holes of one piece; they should go in with finger pressure. Quickly attach the other piece and clamp the joint.

Reinforcing with splines

TOOLKIT
- Router and straight bit
- Edge guide
OR
- Table saw
- Dado head
- Featherboard or tenoning jig for mitered end

Making a spline

The spline is inserted into grooves cut in the edges of the joint pieces, then glued. Cut splines from hardwood, hardwood plywood, or hardboard; if you use hardwood, make sure the grain runs across the width of the spline. For stock up to $3/4$" thick, the spline should be $3/4$" wide and $1/4$" thick. For thicker wood, the spline should be 1" wide and $3/8$" thick.

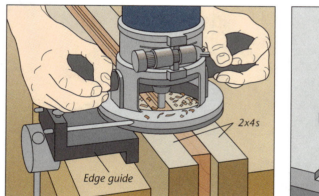

2x4s

Edge guide

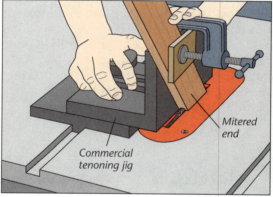

Mitered end

Commercial tenoning jig

Making the grooves

The combined depths of both grooves should be $1/16$" greater than the spline's width; make the grooves wide enough to insert the spline with finger pressure. Cut the grooves with a router or table saw. To give the router a wide, stable surface, clamp the workpiece between 2x4s with the top edges flush. (For a beveled edge, bevel the edges of the 2x4s to the same angle.) Install a straight bit and adjust the router's edge guide to center the cut in the stock *(above, left)*. To cut a groove with a table saw, install a dado head and use a featherboard whenever the setup permits. For the edge of a piece, position the rip fence for a cut right in the middle of the edge, and as you feed the board into the blade, hold its face against the fence. For a mitered end, clamp the piece in a tenoning jig *(above, right, and page 91)*, positioning it for a center cut. To groove a beveled edge, tilt the blade 45° away from the fence, and with the piece flat on the table, set the fence to place the groove about $1/4$" from the inside edge of the bevel. Use the same setup for a beveled end, adding the miter gauge.

Reinforcing with glue blocks

Making and installing glue blocks

You'll need a handsaw, table saw, or radial-arm saw, glue and small finishing nails or brads. Wait until the glue in the joint is completely dry. Then cut square or triangular blocks, as shown on page 73, from molding stock (quarter-round works well) or a 1-by board. Glue the blocks in place, and drive in the finishing nails or brads to secure the blocks until the glue dries.

RABBET JOINTS

A rabbet is an L-shaped recess cut along the edge or end of a piece of wood to accommodate another piece. The rabbet joint has several advantages: It's easy to cut and assemble, it's strong, and it shows less end grain than a butt joint. Rabbets are often used to join the bottom, sides, top, and back in casework, to construct drawers, to form lips on door and drawer fronts, and to house panels in doors.

Before cutting a rabbet, calculate the dimensions for both the cheek and shoulder; the guidelines for the dimen-sions of the three common types of rabbet joints are described below. When you are ready to cut the rabbet, read the procedures for making rabbets with both hand and pow-er tools, illustrated on the following pages. If hand tools are your preference, you can cut a rabbet with a back-saw or with a rabbet plane. If you have both a saw and a plane, use the saw to cut rabbets across the grain and the plane to cut with the grain. Though the rabbet plane works best when cutting with the grain, it also makes cross-grain rabbets.

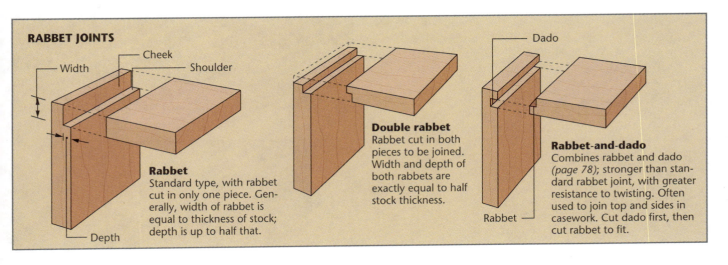

RABBET JOINTS

Rabbet
Standard type, with rabbet cut in only one piece. Gen-erally, width of rabbet is equal to thickness of stock; depth is up to half that.

Double rabbet
Rabbet cut in both pieces to be joined. Width and depth of both rabbets are exactly equal to half stock thickness.

Rabbet-and-dado
Combines rabbet and dado (page 78); stronger than stan-dard rabbet joint, with greater resistance to twisting. Often used to join top and sides in casework. Cut dado first, then cut rabbet to fit.

Cutting a rabbet with a backsaw

TOOLKIT
• Straight edge guide and clamps (optional)
• Chisel (optional)

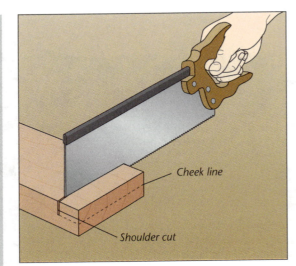
Cheek line
Shoulder cut

2 **Making the cheek cut**
Turn the stock on end and clamp it in place. Make the cheek cut to meet the shoulder with the saw *(right)*, or—if you prefer—remove the waste with a sharp chisel. Smooth the cut surfaces with a chisel if necessary.

1 **Making the shoulder cut**
First, mark the stock and clamp it securely, face-down. To make the shoulder cut, saw to the cheek line (the depth of the rabbet) on the waste side of the shoulder line *(left)*. If you need help keep-ing the saw straight, clamp a straight piece of wood to the stock as a guide.

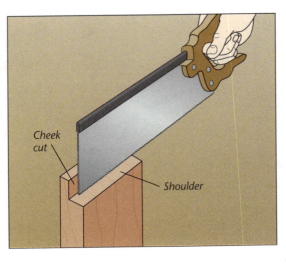
Cheek cut
Shoulder

Using a rabbet plane

Setting up and operating the plane

Be sure the cutting iron is razor sharp, then adjust it for thin cuts; it's easier to make six or seven thin cuts than one or two thick ones. Adjust the fence so the edge of the iron is aligned with the waste side of the shoulder line. Adjust the depth gauge to align it with the waste side of the cheek line. If you're cutting across the grain, adjust the spur to sever the wood fibers in advance of the iron. Then, to cut the rabbet, with the fence tight against the edge of the stock to guide the plane and the sole of the plane flat on the stock, make successive passes *(right)* until the depth gauge touches the face of the stock all along the length of the rabbet.

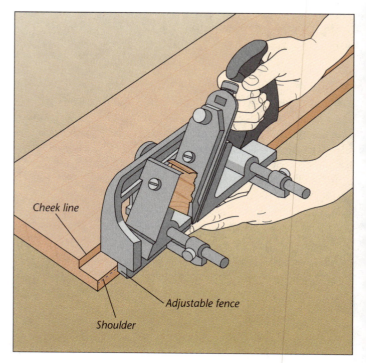

Cheek line

Shoulder

Adjustable fence

Rabbeting with a router

TOOLKIT
- Rabbeting bit with a ball-bearing pilot
OR
- Straight bit
- Edge guide or straightedge and clamps

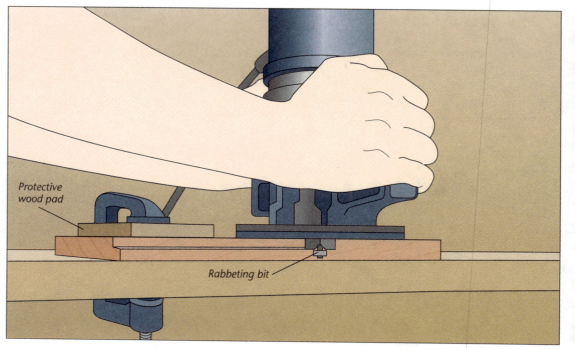

Protective wood pad

Rabbeting bit

Quick and easy rabbet cutting

Install a rabbeting bit with a ball-bearing pilot to guide the router *(above)*; keep the pilot snug against the stock while you're cutting. Or, especially for rabbets wider than ³/₈", use a straight bit and guide the router with the edge guide *(page 79)* or a straightedge *(page 60)*; the bit should cut on the waste side of the shoulder line. When cutting, keep the edge guide tight against the stock, or the router base plate tight against the straightedge. Depending on the router, the rabbet's depth, and the wood's hard-ness, you may have to make several shallow cuts instead of one pass. If the rabbet is wider than your straight bit, cut along the shoulder line first, then remove the rest of the waste. To cut a rabbet on the end of narrow stock, clamp the stock to the bench and fasten a wood scrap of the same thickness on either side of the stock, with the edges flush with the end *(page 82)*. The scraps will support the router's base plate and prevent the bit from rounding or breaking out the corners.

Cutting a rabbet with a table saw

TOOLKIT
• Dado head or standard blade

With a dado head

Equipped with a dado head, a table saw can cut a rabbet in a single pass *(below)*. To prevent the dado head from hitting the rip fence, make an auxiliary fence from a straight 1x4 the same length as the rip fence. Position the rip fence about 1/4" from the dado head and lower the blade beneath the surface. Fasten the auxiliary fence to the rip fence, then turn on the saw and slowly raise the dado head until the resulting cutout is 3/4" to 1" high (don't measure until the blade has completely stopped). Set the blade height to the depth of the rabbet, and align the rip fence so the blade lines up with the waste side of the shoulder line. Install featherboards *(page 41)* as shown, then run the stock through, using a push stick as your hand nears the blade.

When rabbeting across grain in solid lumber, guide the piece with a miter gauge and extension *(page 46)*. If necessary, smooth the cut surfaces with a chisel.

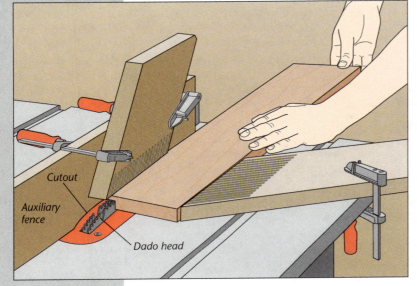

Cutout

Auxiliary fence

Dado head

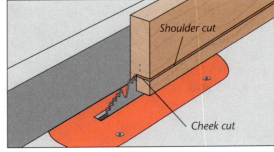

Shoulder cut

Cheek cut

With a standard blade

Make the shoulder cut with the stock placed flat: Set blade height to the depth of the rabbet, and the distance between rip fence and blade to the rabbet's width. Make the cheek cut with the stock on edge *(above)*; set the blade height to the width of the rabbet, and the distance between fence and blade to the rabbet's depth, matching the shoulder cut.

Cutting a rabbet with a radial-arm saw

TOOLKIT
• Dado head
OR
• Standard blade and chisel
For crosscut:
• Clamp
• Chisel to smooth cut surfaces if necessary
For rip cut:
• Push stick
• Chisel to smooth cut surfaces if necessary

With a dado head or a standard blade

A dado head is the simplest to use: Install enough chippers to make a cut slightly wider than the width of the rabbet. Make sure that enough threads are exposed on the shaft to secure the nut. (If you need to make a rabbet wider than the maximum thickness of your dado head, first make the cut on the waste side of the shoulder line, then make more cuts to remove the remaining waste.) Set the height of the dado head to the depth of the rabbet.

To cut across the grain, with the saw in the crosscut position, hold the stock firmly against the fence and move it until the outside edge of the blade touches the waste side of the shoulder line. Clamp a block of scrap wood to the fence at the end of the stock, both to help you hold the stock securely and position additional pieces quickly. Turn on the saw and draw the dado head through the stock.

To cut with the grain, rotate the yoke to the in-rip position, as shown at right. To protect the fence, clamp a length of wood to it as an auxiliary fence. Place the stock firmly against this fence and pull the yoke out until the edge of the dado head is aligned with the waste side of the shoulder line; lock the yoke. Turn on the saw and run the stock through

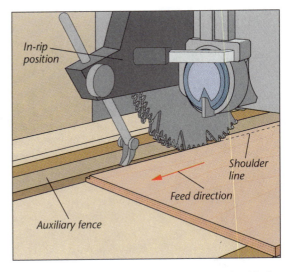

In-rip position

Shoulder line

Feed direction

Auxiliary fence

from right to left. When your hands near the blade, finish the cut with a push stick.

You can use a standard blade instead: Adjust the depth of cut, and, for a cut with the grain, set the yoke to the in-rip position. Make a cut on the waste side of the shoulder line, then a series of cuts to remove the rest of the waste. Overlap these cuts, or remove the waste with a chisel.

DADO AND GROOVE JOINTS

A dado is a recess cut across the grain on the face of a board, while a groove goes with the grain, on either the board's face or edge. A dado can also be combined with a rabbet *(page 75)*.

Strong and easy-to-make, dado joints are self-aligning, simple to square, and are used primarily in casework to join shelves to uprights, partitions to tops and bottoms, and drawer backs to sides. Grooves are used for frame-and-panel assemblies *(page 103)* or as joints, such as the tongue-and-groove. Used for edge-joined pieces making up furniture backs, it is often not glued, to allow for wood movement.

Dadoes and grooves are either through or stopped at one or both ends. For the through type, cut the dado from edge to edge or the groove from end to end; for the stopped type, cut the dado or groove only partway and notch the other piece to fit. The end of a through joint can be covered with a facing or molding to hide the recess; the recess doesn't show in a stopped joint.

The first step in making a dado or groove joint is to measure and mark the location of the outside edges. Then set a marking gauge or combination square for the depth of the recess. Mark the bottom of the cut; for a dado or a face groove, 1/4 to 1/3 the thickness of the board is enough (never exceed one-half). An edge groove is often 1/2 inch deep, and no wider than 1/3 the thickness of the stock. If you're making a stopped cut, draw a line on the face or edge of the board to indicate the end.

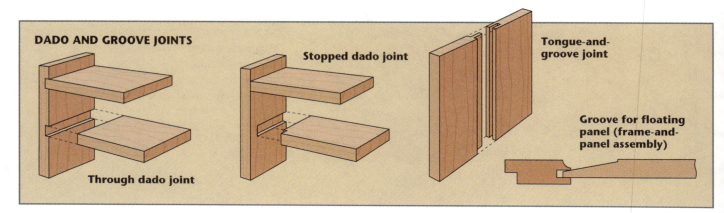

DADO AND GROOVE JOINTS

Through dado joint

Stopped dado joint

Tongue-and-groove joint

Groove for floating panel (frame-and-panel assembly)

Cutting a dado with hand tools

TOOLKIT
- Backsaw
- Straightedge guide and clamps
- Chisel and mallet

1 **Making the saw cuts**
Because of the length of the saw, this technique works for short dadoes only. As a rule, use power tools for dadoes over about 8" long. Secure the board in a vise or clamp it to the bench. Begin by cutting on the waste side of one line to the depth line; clamp a hardwood straightedge to the board to guide your saw. If necessary, clamp a block to the saw to control the depth of cut. Next, cut on the waste side of the other line, then, between the two cuts, making several cuts to the depth mark for easier waste removal.

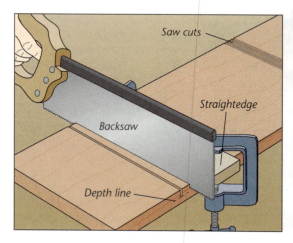

Saw cuts

Straightedge

Backsaw

Depth line

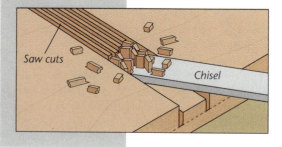

Saw cuts

Chisel

2 **Removing the waste**
Hold a chisel, bevel side down, at a point about half the dado's depth; tap it lightly with a mallet to remove waste. Work toward the center, gradually lowering the depth of your cuts. When you reach the bottom, turn the chisel over and, holding it flat, smooth the dado. Check the fit of the other piece; it should slide in with light hand pressure or a few taps with a mallet. If the fit is too tight, plane or sand the second board rather than making the dado wider.

TOOLKIT
•Straight bit
•Edge guide
•Router table
(optional)
For stopped cut:
•Clamp
•Chisel

Setting up and making the cut

Rout a recess simply and accurately with a straight bit the same size as the dado or groove's width and some sort of guide. Use an adjustable edge guide (available for most router models), a straightedge guide (store-bought or made from a scrap piece of hardwood), or for a wider recess, a shop-built jig.

For grooves or dadoes within about 6" from an edge or end, an edge guide is the most convenient (below); adjust it so the bit lines up exactly with the marked lines. If you're using a straightedge guide instead (page 60), clamp it to the board at the correct distance from the outline. To cut a groove in the edge of a piece, use a router table or set up a wider platform for the router and use the edge guide, as shown on page 74.

Set the router bit for the desired depth of cut, then make a test cut on scrap wood. Make several shallow passes instead of removing all the waste at once; adjust the bit each time until the full depth is reached. To rout the recess, push or pull the router through the stock from left to right, keeping the guide fence tight against the board's edge—or end—or the router's base plate firmly against the clamped-on straightedge.

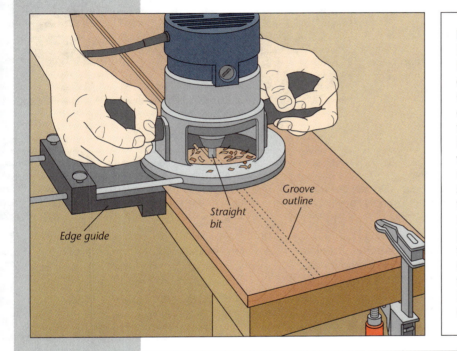

Edge guide

Straight bit

Groove outline

Making a stopped dado or groove

Measure the distance from the edge of the bit to the base plate's edge; then mark that distance beyond the desired length line. Clamp a wood block at this mark. Start the cut as you would a through dado or groove, then, when the base plate contacts the stop block, turn the router off, hold it steady, and wait for the bit to stop spinning before you remove it from the stock. If the recess is stopped on both ends, plunge the bit into the stock to start the cut (page 61). A plunge router is best for stopped cuts; it's simple to plunge into the stock and raise the bit at the end of the cut with the router running. (Consult your owner's manual for instructions on plunging and locking the bit in the lowered position.) Square up the stopped end of the recess with a chisel.

HOW TO ROUT A WIDE DADO OR GROOVE

To cut a dado or groove wider than your straight bit, use two scrap guides—one for each side of the recess—or a jig, as shown. Make the jig of 1x2 stock, fastening the corners with lap joints and screws. To calculate the correct distance between the guide boards, measure the distance from the edge of the bit to the edge of the base plate. Double this and add on the width of the dado or groove.

To use the jig, place the bit just to the waste side of one of the cutting lines, butt one edge guide against the router's base plate, and clamp the jig in place, making sure it's square to the board's edge. First make a pass against each guide board, then go back and remove the waste with freehand passes, always cutting against the direction of bit rotation; the guides will keep the router within the outlines.

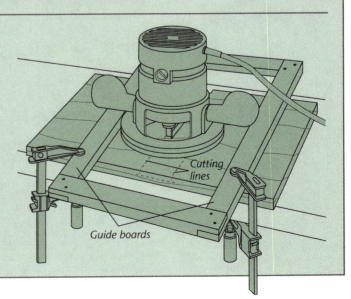

Cutting lines

Guide boards

Using a circular saw

TOOLKIT
- Straightedge guide and clamps or cutoff jig (page 45)
- Chisel (slightly narrower than the width of the dado or groove)

Cutting a dado or groove

Clamp a straightedge guide or cutoff jig (page 45) to a scrap board, make cuts on both sides, and measure the distance from the guide to each cut. Mark these two points on the stock on both sides of the recess; with the guide's edge clamped on a mark, the saw blade should be on the waste side of one cutting line. Set the blade to the depth of the recess and test on a piece of scrap. Cut the length of the recess, holding the base plate tight against the guide. Relocate the guide and cut the other side (right), then make several cuts between the first two until the waste is nearly gone (you can leave the first guide in place to ensure that you stay within the outlines). Clear out the remaining waste with a chisel (page 78).

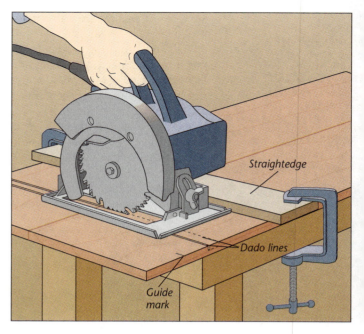

Straightedge

Dado lines

Guide mark

Using a table saw

TOOLKIT
- Dado head
For dado:
- Clamp and miter gauge
For groove:
- Featherboards and clamps

Setting up a dado head

The table saw and the radial-arm saw are the two stationary power tools used to cut dadoes and grooves. Though the table saw wins hands down for cutting accurate grooves, it does have some disadvantages when cutting stopped or short dadoes. Most beginners will find it easier and safer to cut these joints on the radial-arm saw, since you can see the cut. For either type of recess on either tool, a dado head is best, although you can use a standard blade to first cut the outlines; then make several cuts in between and chisel out the waste. Install the dado head on the saw's arbor; use enough chippers to equal the desired width. For minute adjustments, insert washers cut from thick paper or thin cardboard between the chippers. Adjust the depth by raising or lowering the blade; make a test cut on scrap.

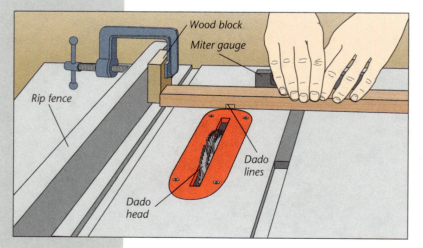

Wood block

Miter gauge

Rip fence

Dado lines

Dado head

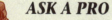

ASK A PRO

HOW DO I GET DADOES IN THE SIDES OF A BOOKCASE TO LINE UP?
When you want shelves to line up in both sides of a bookcase, prepare your setup for the first dado, then make that same cut in the other side. Then reposition the fence for the next set of cuts, and so on.

Cutting a dado

Clamp a wood block to the rip fence (near the end of the fence) to help position the stock and to prevent it from binding against the fence. Align the dado lines on the stock with the dado head, then place the rip fence so the block butts the end of the stock. Turn on the saw, and—keeping the stock tight against the miter gauge—feed the stock into the blades to cut the length of the dado. Then, if necessary, carefully smooth the bottom of the dado with a chisel.

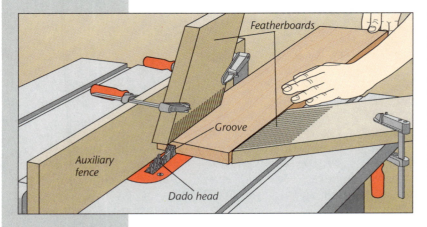

Featherboards

Groove

Auxiliary fence

Dado head

Cutting a groove

Attach a board to the rip fence as an auxiliary fence. Place the edge of the stock against the fence and adjust it so the groove lines on the stock's end line up with the dado head. Install featherboards (*page 41*) on the table and to the auxiliary fence as shown. Turn on the saw and feed the stock into the dado head to cut the length of the groove. Guide the end of a narrow piece with a push stick. If necessary, smooth the bottom of the groove with a chisel.

Cutting a stopped dado or groove

Mark a line on the top edge of the stock indicating the end of the recess, and a corresponding line on the rip fence to show the location of the front of the dado head. Turn on the saw and feed the stock through until the line on the stock is aligned with the line on the fence. Holding the stock still, turn off the saw. Once the blade stops, remove the piece and square up the end of the recess with a chisel; if necessary, also chisel the bottom smooth.

Using a radial-arm saw

TOOLKIT
- Dado head
- Clamp (to cut several pieces)
- Chisel
- Handscrew or C-clamp for stopped cut

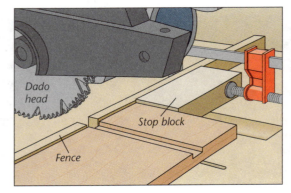

Dado head

Stop block

Fence

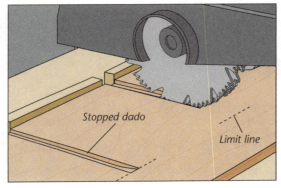

Stopped dado

Limit line

Cutting a dado or groove

Install a dado head on the saw's arbor. Adjust the saw for the depth of the cut; test on scrap. If necessary, correct the depth or adjust the width of the dado head (*page 80*). To cut a dado, place the stock against the fence, aligning the dado lines with the dado head. To cut several pieces, clamp a wood block to the fence (*above*). Pull the saw over the stock; hold the stock against the fence. To cut a groove, rotate the saw's motor 90° to the in- or out-rip position; then with the stock against the fence, line up the dado head with the groove lines. Feed the stock into the blades, going against their rotation. Chisel the recess smooth.

Making a stopped cut

This cut is easy with a radial-arm saw; mark the desired end of the cut and set up a stop. For a stopped dado, clamp a handscrew to the saw's arm at the appropriate place to halt the yoke's travel when the blade reaches the limit line. Cut until the clamp stops the yoke, then return the saw's motor behind the fence.

For a stopped groove, line up the end mark with the rear of the blade, and clamp a stop block to the outfeed side of the fence against the board's end. Make the cut, and when the board hits the stop block, turn off the saw (wait for the head to stop spinning before removing the board). Square up the end of the cut with a chisel.

Using a standard blade to cut a recess

Although a dado head makes a clean cut in one pass, you can use a standard blade to cut a dado or groove. Make a cut on each side of the recess, then make additional cuts between the first two until the waste material is nearly gone. Chisel out the remaining waste (*page 78*).

LAP JOINTS

Half-lap joints (halved joints) are woodworking's most common lap joints. You'll find them holding together frame-and-panel doors, and legs and stretchers. Half-lap joints differ according to where the boards are joined, as shown below.

Following are instructions for cutting half-lap joints with a router, table saw, or radial-arm saw. The setups are similar to those for cutting a standard dado or rabbet, but in this case, the joint is wider—the same width as your stock. If you prefer using hand tools, refer to the instructions for rabbet joints (*pages 75-76*). Full laps are made the same way as half laps, but only one board is rabbet-

ed or dadoed. To cut edge laps use a table saw, as shown on page 84.

Instead of measuring shoulder lines, clamp the boards together at 90° and mark along the edges of each to obtain the cutting lines. If you'll be using a table saw, which cuts on the underside of the stock, mark on the stock's edge; with the radial-arm saw you can see as you cut. In some projects, you may need to reinforce end and T half-lap joints; use dowels or mechanical fasteners (*page 29*). Cross half laps usually don't need reinforcing, as the extra shoulder helps lock the pieces together.

A LAP JOINT FOR EVERY SITUATION

End half-lap joint
Formed with two rabbets; joins two boards at their ends.

Full-lap joint
Used when one board is thicker than other; dado or rabbet cut in thicker board to house thinner one, which is not cut.

Edge half-lap joint
Variation on cross lap; dadoes notched into edges instead of faces of two boards. Used to build "egg-crate" structures.

T half-lap joint
Also called mid half lap. Formed with dado and rabbet; joins end of one board to point anywhere along length of other board.

Cross half-lap joint
Formed with two dadoes; joins faces of two boards along their lengths.

Cutting laps with a router

TOOLKIT
• Clamps
• Straight bit
• Straightedge guides
• Chisel or block plane

Routing a wide rabbet
Begin by clamping the stock to your workbench. If you're cutting two rabbets for an end half-lap joint, make the cuts in both pieces at the same time, as shown. Clamp a piece of scrap of the same thickness on each side of the stock for the router to ride on; all ends and shoulder lines must be aligned. Install the widest straight bit you have in the router, adjusting the bit depth to exactly half the thickness of the stock. Carefully measure the distance from the cutting edge of the bit to the edge of the router's base plate. Then mark off this distance from the shoulder line on the stock. Clamp the edge of the straightedge on this line, perpendicular to the boards' edges.

Remove most of the waste by moving in from the ends toward the straightedge, always cutting against the direction of rotation of the bit. Then make a final pass, using the straightedge as a guide (*right*). Smooth the rabbets with a chisel or block plane.

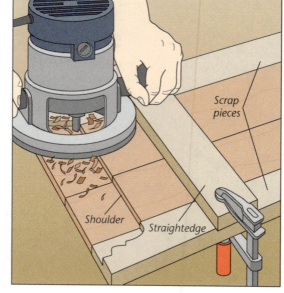

Scrap pieces

Shoulder   *Straightedge*

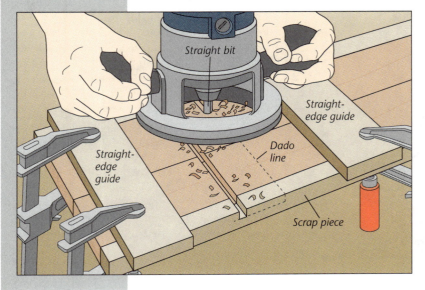

Straight bit

Straight-
edge guide

Straight-
edge
guide

Dado
line

Scrap piece

Routing a wide dado

Use a jig *(page 79)*, or two straightedge guides. Clamp stock to the workbench, adding a scrap piece along each edge to prevent tearout. For a cross-lap joint, cut both pieces at once; align the dado lines. Insert a bit in the router and adjust the depth of cut to exactly half the stock's thickness. Carefully measure the distance from the edge of the bit to the edge of the router's base plate. Mark this distance on both sides of the dado lines, and clamp straightedges to these lines, perpendicular to the boards' edges. Make two cuts to define the outline of the dado, keeping the router's base plate against the guides *(left)*; the cuts should be just to the waste side of the dado lines. Remove the remaining waste with passes down the middle; the guides will keep the router within the dado's outlines. Smooth with a chisel.

Using a table saw to make lap joints

TOOLKIT
- Dado head
- Clamp
- Miter gauge
- Chisel or sanding block

OR (for wide rabbet only)
- Standard blade
- Miter gauge
- Tenoning jig

Cutting a wide rabbet

Install a dado head, using as many chippers as possible; set the depth of cut for half the stock's thickness, and test it on a scrap piece. Clamp a wood block to the rip fence, placing it several inches in front of the cutting edge, as shown. Align the waste side of the shoulder with the outside face of the dado head; butt the wood block against the end of the stock and lock the rip fence in position. With the edge of a scrap piece against the miter gauge (set to 90° and with an extension if necessary) and the end against the wood block, make a test cut, then make any necessary adjustments.

For the actual workpiece, make the initial cut along the waste side of the shoulder line. Make successive cuts, moving the work away from the rip fence for each pass *(right)*, until all the waste is removed. Smooth with a chisel or sanding block.

You can also cut a wide rabbet with a standard blade, as long as the width of the rabbet is less than your blade's maximum depth. Guide the shoulder cut with the miter gauge and use a tenoning jig to make the cheek cut *(page 91)*.

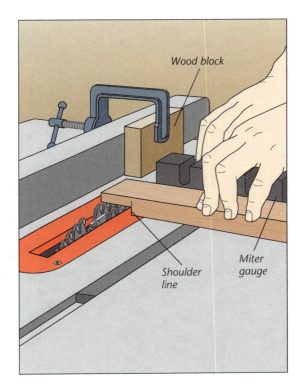

Wood block

Shoulder
line

Miter
gauge

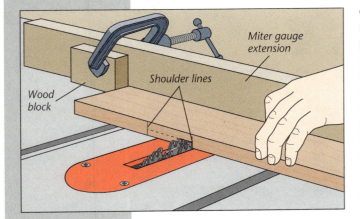

Miter gauge
extension

Shoulder lines

Wood
block

Cutting a wide dado

Install the dado head on the saw, using as many chippers as possible; adjust the depth to cut exactly half the stock's thickness. Move the rip fence out of the way and screw a straight board to the miter gauge as an extension; this added surface makes it easier to guide the stock while cutting. Align the waste side of one shoulder line with the outside face of the dado head, and clamp a stop block to the extension at the end of the stock. Cut one shoulder of the dado *(left)*, then repeat this for any other pieces. Change the setup to cut the other shoulder, then make successive passes, moving the stock before each one, until all the waste between the outside cuts is removed. Smooth the bottom with a chisel or sanding block as required.

Miter gauge extension

Cutting an edge half-lap joint

Install a dado head, setting its width to that of the dado. For an edge dado wider than the dado head, follow the stop-block setup and procedure for cutting a wide dado *(page 83)*. Adjust the dado head to the correct depth. Screw an extension board onto the miter gauge. The board should be at least 1" wider than the depth of the dado and long enough to project beyond the dado head. Holding the stock tight against the miter gauge extension, make the cut. You can cut both dadoes for the joint at once *(left)*; cut the boards separately if you don't want the cuts at the same spot on the stock. For extra stability, clamp the stock to the extension fence. If necessary, use a chisel to smooth the cuts.

Using a radial-arm saw to make lap joints

TOOLKIT
- Dado head
- Carpenter's square
- Chisel

Setting up for the cuts

You'll need a dado head, and if you're cutting dadoes, you'll also need a wood block and a clamp. To cut either a wide rabbet or dado, mount the dado head on the saw's arbor; use a square to check that the dado head is at an exact 90° angle to the fence. Adjust the depth of cut to go halfway through the thickness of the stock. Make test cuts on a piece of scrap before you cut the stock. For either an end half-lap or a cross half-lap joint, you can make the cuts in both pieces together, resting both against a stop block. To make it easier to position the stock when making identical cuts in similar pieces, clamp a wood stop block to the fence at the end of the stock to line up one shoulder. Butt subsequent pieces against this block.

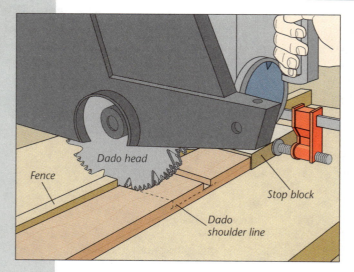

Fence

Dado head

Stop block

Dado shoulder line

Cutting a wide dado

Line up the dado head on the waste side of one shoulder line. If you will be making the same cut on more pieces, butt a stop block against the end of the stock and clamp it onto the fence to quickly locate the shoulder line. Make the cut, repeat for any other identical pieces, then line up the other face of the dado head with the other shoulder line, reposition the stop block, and cut *(left)*. Check that the outlines of the dado match the width of the connecting stock. Then, on each piece, make successive cuts, moving the stock before each cut until all the waste is removed. Smooth the bottom of the dado as required using a chisel.

Cutting a wide rabbet

Cut rabbets for an end half-lap joint together. Position the stock with its edge against the fence; align the outside face of the dado head with the waste side of the shoulder line. Then turn on the saw and make the cut, as you would for a regular crosscut. Make successive cuts, moving the stock along the fence before each pass, until all the waste is removed. This is just like cutting a dado *(above)*, except there is only one shoulder line, and the cut goes right to the end of the board. Smooth the cheek of the rabbet with a chisel.

MORTISE-AND-TENON JOINTS

From the times of the Egyptian pharaohs, woodworkers around the world have used mortise-and-tenon joints to connect two pieces of wood at right angles. Today, mortise-and-tenons—which are among the strongest joints known—are used in everything from doors and furniture to timberframe buildings and wooden ships. The three most common types of mortise-and-tenon joints are blind, through, and open (shown below). They differ primarily in the style of mortises; the tenons vary only in length and whether they have two or four shoulders. Another joint, the slot mortise-and-tenon, is a varia-tion on the blind type, and has rounded edges on both the mortise and the tenon. Commercial router jigs are available to make this type of joint quickly and easily.

It's not surprising that beginners are intimidated by mortise-and-tenon joints, because accomplishing these with hand tools, the method favored by many purists, requires experience, precision, and patience. Yet the inexperienced woodworker, using power tools, can make perfectly acceptable mortise-and-tenons. The secrets to success are careful design, accurate layout, sharp tools and lots of practice.

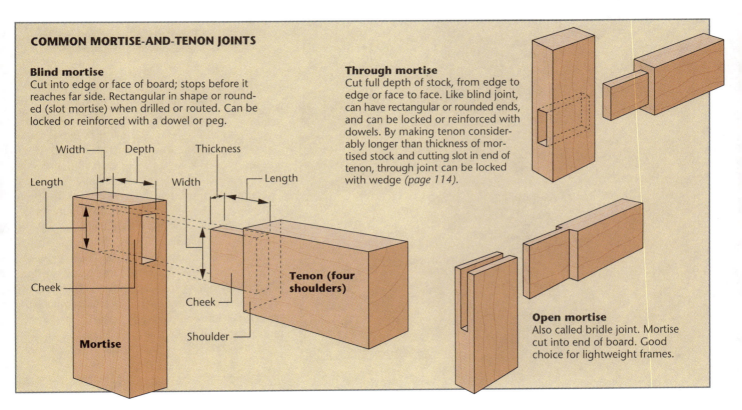

COMMON MORTISE-AND-TENON JOINTS

Blind mortise
Cut into edge or face of board; stops before it reaches far side. Rectangular in shape or round-ed (slot mortise) when drilled or routed. Can be locked or reinforced with a dowel or peg.

Through mortise
Cut full depth of stock, from edge to edge or face to face. Like blind joint, can have rectangular or rounded ends, and can be locked or reinforced with dowels. By making tenon consider-ably longer than thickness of mor-tised stock and cutting slot in end of tenon, through joint can be locked with wedge *(page 114)*.

Width Depth Thickness
Length Width Length
Cheek
Mortise
Cheek
Shoulder
Tenon (four shoulders)

Open mortise
Also called bridle joint. Mortise cut into end of board. Good choice for lightweight frames.

MARKING OUT THE JOINT

For maximum strength, cut a mortise or tenon so that its length goes with the grain, not across it. The thickness of the tenon, and thus the width of the mortise, is deter-mined by the size of the tenon stock; typically, the thick-ness of the tenon—and each of the mortise cheeks—is one-third the thickness of the stock. Cut the mortise at least 1/2 inch away from the end of the stock so that the wood doesn't split out when the tenon is inserted.

In order to hide the joint line between the tenon and mortise, most tenons (except those for open mortises) are cut away on the narrow edges as well as the faces, resulting in a four-shouldered tenon, as shown above.

However, these edge cuts don't have to be as wide; even 1/8 inch will do if the top of the tenon piece will not be flush with the end of the mortise piece. An example of this would be the tenons on the bed rails going into the posts *(page 114)*. Otherwise cut the tenon so as to leave a flush joint with the top of the mortise workpiece.

Lay the pieces out and mark the best face of each—the one that will show the most in the finished project. Then place the pieces in their relative assembly posi-tions and mark matching sides of each joint with a let-ter or number. This will help you to assemble the cut pieces in their correct positions later.

Marking cutting lines

TOOLKIT
- Combination or try square
- Mortise marking gauge

1 ▶ Marking the mortise length

Woodworkers often debate which should be cut first, the mortise or the tenon. Here, the mortise is marked and cut before the tenon. If something goes awry, it's much easier to cut a tenon to fit a mortise than the other way around. An alternate method is to cut one test mortise in scrap wood, then a tenon, and use that tenon to mark the actual mortises. In either case, start by marking the mortise's end lines with a square *(right)*.

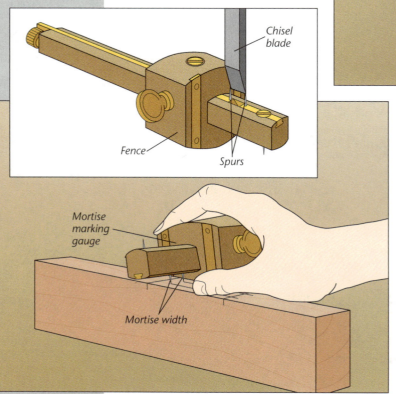

Chisel blade

Fence

Spurs

Mortise marking gauge

Mortise width

Length mark

Stock

2 ▶ Marking the mortise cheeks

Though you can use a try or combination square, it's easier and quicker to use a mortise marking gauge, similar to the marking gauge, but with two spurs, or pins. Adjust these spurs to the mortise width, using the chisel, drill bit, or router bit you'll be cutting the mortise with *(inset)*. Adjust the fence so the lines will be centered on the edge of the stock. Place the fence against the best face of the stock and scribe the cheek lines into the wood *(left)*. For a through mortise, mark the opposite edge of the stock, too; for an open mortise, mark both edges and the end. Note: Always locate the fence against the same face so any error due to the fence adjustment will be the same for all pieces. Before you go on to mark the tenon, cut the mortise.

3 ▶ Marking the tenon

If your tenon stock is the same thickness as your mortise stock, double-check the gauge setting against the mortise, then reuse it on the tenon. If the thicknesses differ, reset the gauge to mark the tenon. Most tenon pieces have a tenon at each end. Though the length of each tenon matches its mortise (it will be about 1/8" shorter in a blind joint, to leave space for the glue), the distance between the tenon shoulders is the actual length of the tenon piece. Measure and mark the shoulder lines on all four sides of one end of the tenon stock. With the gauge's adjustable fence against the best face of the stock, scribe the cheek lines for the tenon on the end and edges of the stock *(right)*. After you've cut the tenon, repeat the marking and cutting at the other end.

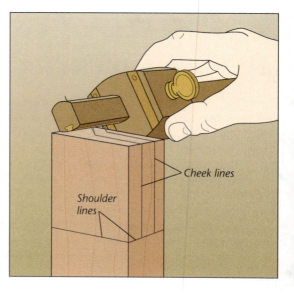

Cheek lines

Shoulder lines

CUTTING A MORTISE

You can use hand tools, power tools, or a combination of the two to cut a mortise. For example, a mortise chisel, an electric drill and bench chisel, or a router will all cut blind and through mortises.

The traditional way, with a mortise chisel, is easier than it appears. The thick blade of the chisel resists twisting, and the parallel sides guide the chisel once it's started correctly. A through mortise is cut in the same way as a blind mortise, but it goes the full depth of the stock. For greater accuracy, and to make a deep through cut, mark cutting lines on both sides of the stock, so you can go from both sides toward the center. An open mortise could be cut using the same basic methods. However, you'll find the going easier if you treat the open mortise as a simple slot, using the hand or power tool techniques shown on page 89.

Cutting a blind mortise with a chisel

TOOLKIT
- Marking knife
- Mortise chisel
- Mallet

1 ▶ Cutting and levering out the waste
First, clamp the stock securely to the bench. Make sure to cut the cheeks of the mortise parallel to the face of the stock. You can wrap a piece of masking tape around the chisel to indicate the depth of the mortise.

To make the cuts, first score the mortise guidelines with a knife to help you position the chisel. Starting with the chisel blade 1/8" from one end of the mortise outline—with the bevel toward the mortise—and centered between the cheek lines, strike the chisel sharply with a mallet, driving the blade about 1/4" into the wood. Then move the chisel about 1/8" toward the other end, keeping the beveled side toward the mortise and repeat *(right, above)*. Continue until you're about 1/8" from the other end, levering out the waste as you go *(right, below)*. Repeat the process in the other direction. Continue until the mortise is at the right depth and the bottom is flat.

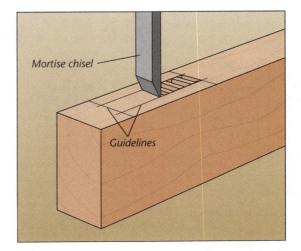

Mortise chisel

Guidelines

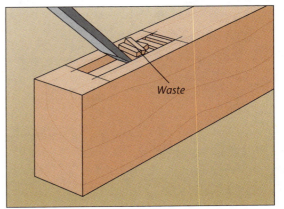

Waste

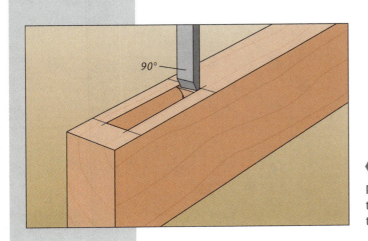

90°

◀ 2 Finishing the ends
Remove the 1/8" of waste left at the ends of the mortise. Place the chisel blade in the score mark at one end, bevel toward the mortise. Strike the chisel sharply, being careful not to undercut the end; keep the chisel vertical. Repeat at the other end *(left)*.

Chiseling a through mortise

Using a chisel
Make sure that the mortise guidelines are marked on both sides of the stock. Cut the mortise halfway through the stock following the instructions above for cutting a blind mortise with a chisel. Then turn the stock over and proceed to cut the mortise through from the other side. Finally, square up both the cheeks and ends of the mortise.

Cutting a blind mortise with a drill and chisel

TOOLKIT
- Drill press, electric drill, or hand brace
- Brad-point or Forstner bit (or auger bit for hand brace); bit must be same size as—or slightly smaller than—mortise width
- Stop collar (optional)
- Bench chisel
- Mortise chisel

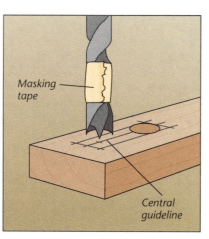

Masking tape

Central guideline

1 ▶ Drilling

With this method, you drill a series of overlapping holes, then pare away the remaining wood with a chisel. Control the depth of the mortise with a stop collar or a piece of tape wrapped around the bit. The holes must be drilled exactly between the cheek lines; an extra guideline in the middle of the mortise will help you center the bit. The holes also must be perpendicular; the stationary drill press is ideal for this. A doweling jig, drill stand, or portable drill press attachment for your electric drill also will help you keep the drill bit upright. Drill a hole at each end *(left)*, then continue with a series of slightly overlapping holes.

2 ▶ Chiseling

Remove the excess stock by paring the cheeks with a bench chisel *(right)*. Then, unless you want a slot mortise, square up the ends with a bench chisel slightly narrower than the width of the mortise or with a mortise chisel the same width as the mortise. Hold the chisel perpendicular to the stock, as shown on page 87 *(step 2)*.

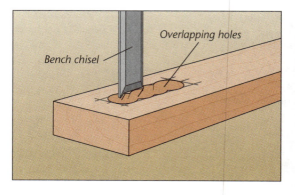

Bench chisel

Overlapping holes

Cutting a through mortise with a drill and chisel

Boring holes and paring out the waste

Drill a series of perpendicular overlapping holes partway through the stock, following the technique for cutting a blind mortise described above. Then turn the stock over and drill the holes from the other side. Remove the waste material by paring the cheeks with a wide bench chisel, working from both sides, as shown in step 2 *(above)*. Square up the ends of the mortise with a bench chisel slightly narrower than the width of the mortise, or with a mortise chisel the same width.

Cutting a blind mortise with a router

TOOLKIT
- Straight bit the same diameter as the width of the mortise
- Edge guide
- Screwdriver
- Chisel to square ends (unless cutting a slot mortise)

Setting up a routing platform

This is a fast way to cut mortises, limited only by the maximum depth of the bit. Clamp stock between 2x4s in a vise with tops of all three pieces flush to form a platform. Screw a stop block across them beyond each end of the mortise at a distance equal to that between the edge of the base plate and the edge of the bit. Adjust the edge guide so the bit is centered between the mortise's cheek lines. Set the bit's depth to 1/4". With the guide tight against a 2x4 and part of the router's base plate resting on the platform, make a plunge cut by pivoting the bit into the work *(right)*; cut from block to block (a plunge router is ideal for this). Lower the bit 1/4" and repeat until the mortise is the right depth. You can chisel ends square.

Edge guide

2x4 platform

Stop block

Vise

Cutting a through mortise with a router

TOOLKIT
• Same as for a blind mortise (facing page)

Cutting an open mortise

TOOLKIT
• Drill and bit the same diameter as the mortise's width
• Backsaw and bench chisel

OR

• Radial-arm saw, and dado

OR

• Table saw, dado head, square, and tenoning jig

Flipping the stock over

If you want to cut a through mortise with a router, the depth of the mortise cannot exceed twice the maximum cutting depth of the router bit. Set up and rout the mortise partway through the stock as you would for a blind mortise (facing page). Then turn the stock over and re-insert it in the 2x4 platform, positioning the end marks of the mortise the correct distance away from the stop blocks. This distance should be equal to the measurement between the edge of the router's base plate and the edge of the bit. Turn the router so that the edge guide is pressing against the same side of the platform as for the first pass. (This ensures that both halves of the mortise will be lined up.) Turn on the router and cut the rest of the mortise. Square up both rounded ends of the mortise with a chisel, unless you want a slot mortise.

Using a drill and backsaw

Drill a hole at the bottom of the slot from one edge to the other, making sure that the hole is exactly parallel to the end and faces of the stock. Unless you have a stationary drill press, you'll find it much simpler to drill in from both edges toward the center. A doweling jig, drill stand, or portable drill press will make the job easier with an electric drill.

Turn the stock on end and clamp it in a vise. With a backsaw, cut straight down on the waste side of the cheek lines to the hole (right). Square up the corners with a bench chisel, unless you're cutting a slot mortise.

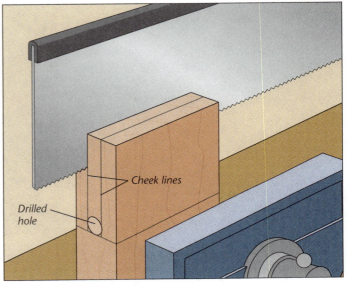

Cheek lines

Drilled hole

Using a radial-arm saw

Mount a dado head on the saw's arbor, using enough chippers to cut the desired width of slot. Adjust the saw's yoke so the blade is horizontal, or parallel to the table. Adjust the height of the dado head to align it with the marked lines for the slot. If you can't lower the dado head enough, use a piece of wood as an auxiliary table, as shown, to raise the stock. Install a fence in the table that is higher than the stock; cut a notch in the top edge of the fence to allow clearance for the arbor and blade guard.

Position the stock against the fence so the dado head will cut to the bottom of the mortise. Holding the stock against the fence with one hand well beyond the blade, turn on the saw and pull the the dado head through the fence and stock. Because of the unusual position of the blade, be extremely cautious.

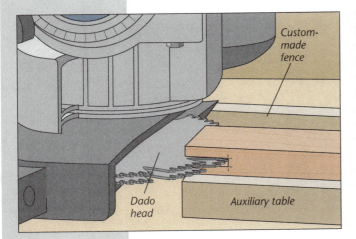

Custom-made fence

Dado head

Auxiliary table

Using a table saw

In addition to a dado head, you'll need a tenoning jig, which you can buy or make yourself (page 91). Install the dado head on the saw's arbor, using enough chippers for the correct width of the slot. Raise the dado head to its full height and make sure that it's at a 90° angle to the table. Set the blade's height to cut the depth of the slot. Clamp the stock on the end of the jig, making sure the stock is perpendicular to the table. Adjust the rip fence so the dado head is aligned with the lines marking the slot. Turn on the saw and run the stock through.

CUTTING A TENON

Tenons, whether for a blind, through, or open mortise-and-tenon joint, vary only in their length and in the number of shoulders (they can have shoulders on two sides or on all four).

You can cut a tenon with a backsaw, router, table saw, or radial-arm saw. Once a tenon is cut, test its fit by inserting it in the mortise. It must fit snugly in the mortise, but you should be able to push it in with light pressure, using a few mallet taps at most. Make any adjustments with a block plane or chisel. If you're cutting a tenon for a slot mortise, round off the ends with a rasp to match the mortise.

Cutting a tenon with a backsaw

TOOLKIT
- Backsaw
- Miter box
- Clamp (optional)

1 ▶ Cutting to the shoulder line

Clamp the stock at a 45° angle and, holding the saw level, cut to the waste side of cheek lines until you reach the shoulder line *(near right)*. Turn the stock around, keeping it at a 45° angle, and saw the other side of the tenon to the shoulder line. Clamp the stock upright and finish both cuts to the shoulder line *(far right)*. If making a four-shouldered tenon, cut extra shoulders on the narrow sides of the tenon.

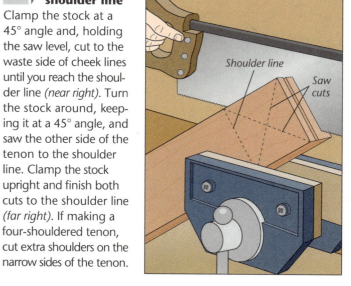

Shoulder line
Saw cuts

Waste

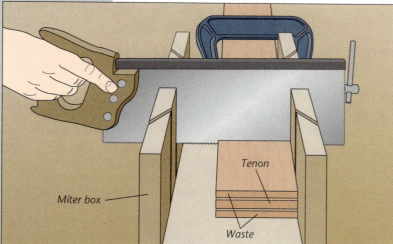

Miter box

Tenon

Waste

◀ 2 Removing the waste

Lay the stock flat in a miter box, aligning the waste side of the shoulder line with the 90° cut in the box. Clamp the stock in place, or hold it firmly, and saw off the waste at the shoulder line. Flip the piece over to cut off the waste on the other side. For a four-shouldered tenon, turn the piece up on edge to remove the waste; repeat on the other edge.

Cutting a tenon with a router

Using a straightedge
Cutting a tenon with a router requires a straight bit and a straightedge to guide the router's base plate. Set up scrap wood the same thickness as the stock on each side to support the router's base plate. The routing technique is the same as that for cutting a wide rabbet for a lap joint *(page 82)*, except that you set the bit depth to cut one-third of the stock's thickness, and once you have cut one face, you turn the stock over and repeat the cut on the other side.

Using a tenoning jig

Build a jig using ³/₄" plywood. Install auxiliary fences tightly around the rip fence, then cut 6"x10" side pieces, and screw a cleat to support the stock onto one, near the end and parallel to it. With the side pieces straddling the auxiliary fences, cut pieces to join them so they can slide along the fence without any play. Mount a standard blade on the saw's arbor. Adjust the blade height so it corresponds to the length of the tenon. Clamp the stock upright on the jig, against the cleat, using a protective wood pad. Then adjust the rip fence so the blade is aligned with the waste side of a cheek line. Turn on the saw and run the stock through. Reposition the rip fence and jig to cut the other side *(below)*. Remove the stock from the jig and place it flat on the table to make the shoulder cuts as you would normal crosscuts, using a stop block clamped to a miter gauge extension as for a wide dado *(page 83)*.

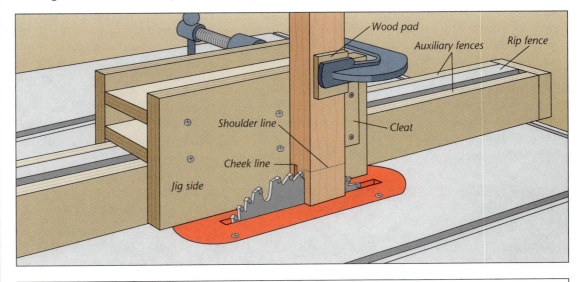

Wood pad
Auxiliary fences
Rip fence
Shoulder line
Cleat
Cheek line
Jig side

Using a dado head

Set the dado head's height so the top tooth lines up with a cheek line when the stock is flat on the table. To make the cuts, follow the instructions on page 83 to cut wide rabbets for lap joints.

Turn the stock over and repeat on the other face. For a four-shouldered tenon, turn the stock on edge, readjusting the cutting height if necessary. Repeat the cuts on both edges.

Using a dado head

Mount the dado head, adjusted to its maximum width, on the saw. With the yoke in the crosscut position, check that the blade is at a 90° angle to the table. Lower the blade until the bottom tooth lines up with the top cheek line on the end of the stock. Then position the stock against the fence, and align the waste side of the shoulder line with the outside face of the dado head; the rest of the blade should be on the waste side of the line.

Make the cut as you would for a regular crosscut *(right)*, then repeat, moving the stock along the fence before each pass, until all the waste is removed. Turn the stock over and make the same cuts on the other side. For a four-shouldered tenon on a narrow workpiece (less than 2"), turn the stock on edge, readjust the cutting height to the waste side of the shoulder line and repeat the cuts on both edges. For wider workpieces, use a backsaw to make the extra shoulders *(page 90)*.

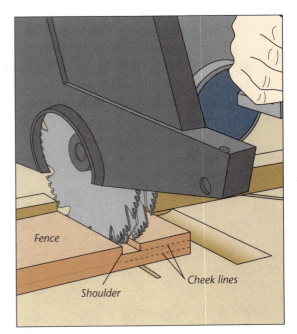

Fence
Cheek lines
Shoulder

DOVETAIL JOINTS

The hallmark of fine woodworking, dovetail joints are both attractive and strong. For many centuries, the pins and sockets of dovetails were cut with a handsaw and a chisel and mallet; these hand-tool procedures are described on the following pages.

Today's woodworkers also have the option of using a router and a dovetail jig to create uniform, tight-fitting joints. The fixture holds the two pieces of stock in the correct alignment and the router, with a dovetail bit, cuts the pins in one piece and the sockets in the other at the same time. Jigs are available in a wide range of prices, but unless you want features such as variable spacing, one of the less-expensive models should meet your needs. To use the jig, follow the manufacturer's instructions for your model. Make several test joints in order to adjust the router and fixture for the cuts you

want; use a piece of scrap wood the same width and thickness as your stock.

Finely made dovetails, whether hand-cut or machine-made, have traditionally had a half-pin at the top and bottom of the joint. Size the piece to allow for these half-pins, which can be wider than half the actual pin size. Before you begin cutting the dovetails, mark a big X on the best face; this will be the outside of your piece. If you are cutting dovetails at all four corners of an assembly, set up the pieces for the best appearance and label the inside face of each piece with its name (back, front, left, and right) to make sure that you cut the pins and tails on the appropriate pieces.

When you assemble a dovetail, the pins should enter the sockets with a couple of light mallet taps, and the joint should be flush.

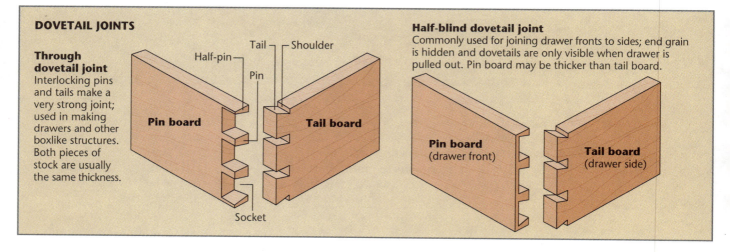

DOVETAIL JOINTS

Through dovetail joint
Interlocking pins and tails make a very strong joint; used in making drawers and other boxlike structures. Both pieces of stock are usually the same thickness.

Half-pin — Tail — Shoulder

Pin

Pin board

Tail board

Socket

Half-blind dovetail joint
Commonly used for joining drawer fronts to sides; end grain is hidden and dovetails are only visible when drawer is pulled out. Pin board may be thicker than tail board.

Pin board
(drawer front)

Tail board
(drawer side)

Cutting a through dovetail

TOOLKIT
- Marking gauge
- Dovetail template (shop-made or store-bought)
- Try or combination square
- Dovetail saw
- Coping saw
- Bench chisel no wider than the narrowest part of the waste
- Mallet

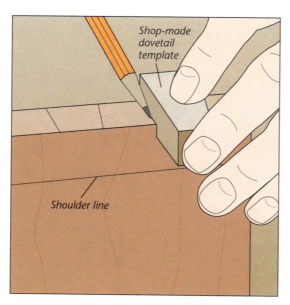

Shop-made dovetail template

Shoulder line

1 Laying out the pins
Set a marking gauge to the thickness of the stock, and mark the shoulder line on all four sides of the pin board. The angle of the pins should be approximately 80° for softwoods (a 1-in-6 slope) or 83° for hardwoods (a 1-in-8 slope). Use a commercial dovetail template, or make your own with rabbeted stock cut to the correct angle, as shown. Determine the size of the pins—you can make them equal to the stock's thickness—and the spacing between them. Always start with a half-pin at each edge, then space the pins equally (or not, for more of a hand-crafted look) within the remaining space. Experiment on paper first, then clamp the pin board in a vise and mark the pins on the end of the board (left). With a square, continue these lines down to the shoulder line. Indicate the waste by marking an X in all the spaces between the pins.

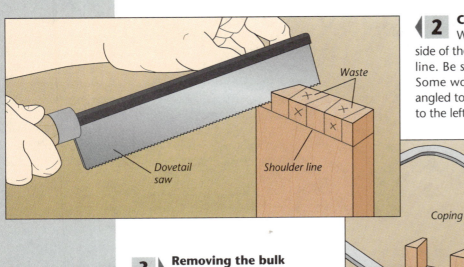

Dovetail saw

Waste

Shoulder line

2 ▸ Cutting the pins

With a dovetail saw, cut just to the waste side of the pin lines *(left)*, stopping at the shoulder line. Be sure to keep the saw perfectly vertical. Some woodworkers prefer to make all the cuts angled to the right first, then to do all those angled to the left.

Coping saw

Waste

3 ▸ Removing the bulk of the waste

Use a coping saw to remove most of the waste from between the pins *(right)*. Don't go too close to the pins' cutting lines or the shoulder line; it's best to use a chisel to remove the remaining wood down to the marked lines.

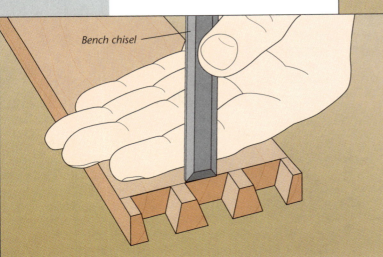

Bench chisel

4 ▸ Paring to the line

Clamp the pin board facedown and use a chisel to remove the rest of the waste between the pins. Choose a bench chisel that is as wide as the narrowest part of the waste area. Follow the instructions for chiseling techniques *(page 58)*, starting with a mallet. Go partway through the board, then flip it over and continue from the other side. When you are very close to the cutting lines, finish paring by hand. Make sure that all the cut surfaces are perfectly flat, and that the corners are well-defined.

5 ▸ Laying out the tails

Use the pin board you have just cut as a pattern to mark the tail board. With the marking gauge set to the thickness of the stock, mark shoulder lines on all four sides of the tail board. With the board lying flat, outside-face down, place the pin board on top, outside-face out (the thinnest end of the pins toward the outside). Line up the pin board with the shoulder line on the tail board; its outside face should be flush with the end of the tail board. Without moving the pin board, mark the outline of the pins on the tail board *(right)*. Now remove the pin board and use a square to continue the lines on the end of the tail board. Mark Xs in all the waste areas.

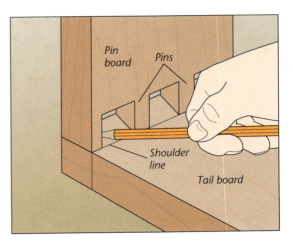

Pin board

Pins

Shoulder line

Tail board

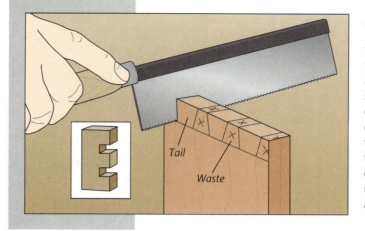

6 Cutting the tails and removing the waste

Clamp the tail board end-up in a vise. Then, with a dove-tail saw, cut down to the shoulder line, just to the waste side of the tail lines *(left)*. Some woodworkers find it easier to stay on the angled line by angling the stock in the vise instead and cutting straight down. Adjust the board so the cutting lines angled to one side are vertical, make these cuts, then angle the board the other way and make the cuts on the other side of the tails. Remove the waste and chisel to the line as you did for the pins. Assemble the joint, using a wooden or rubber mallet to tap the pieces together. If the joint is too tight, pare away wood as necessary. To glue up the joint, make special clamping blocks *(inset)* with notches cut away so as to press only on tails, and not on pins.

Cutting a half-blind dovetail

TOOLKIT
- Marking gauge
- Dovetail template (shop-made or store-bought)
- Try or combination square
- Dovetail saw
- Bench chisel no wider than the narrowest part of the waste
- Mallet

1 Marking and cutting the pins

Start with the pin board, which, on a drawer, would be the front; clamp it upright in a vise. Set a marking gauge to the thickness of the tail board (the drawer side), and mark a shoulder line on the inside face of the pin board. Readjust the gauge to about two-thirds the pin board's thickness and mark a lim-it line along the end grain with the gauge's fence on the inside of the board. Use a dovetail template to mark the pins on the end as you would for a through dovetail *(page 92)*, and continue these lines to the shoulder line with a square. Waste areas should be identified with Xs. Cut to the waste side of the pin lines with a dovetail saw held on an angle *(right)*, being careful not to cross the shoulder line on the face or the limit line on the end.

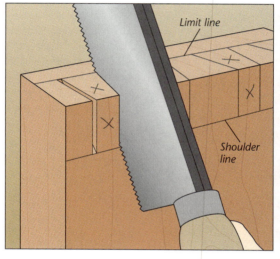

2 Removing the waste

Clamp the pin board to your workbench inside-face up. Hold the chisel on the shoulder line with its bevel toward the waste, keeping it perfectly vertical as you hit it with a mallet to define the shoulder line. (You can clamp a straightedge along the shoulder line as a guide.) Repeat for the other pins; then, with the chisel horizontal and about 1/8" below the surface, remove the chip. Continue chiseling vertically and horizontally in this way *(left)* until you are near the limit line. (See page 58 for basic chiseling instructions.) Finish off paring by hand for precise cuts; the inside corners must be well defined.

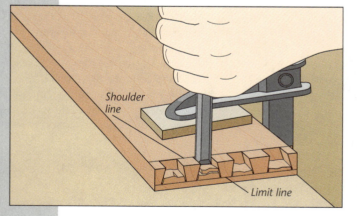

3 Marking and cutting the tails

First make a shoulder line on all four sides of the tail board with the marking gauge set to two-thirds the pin board's thickness. To mark the tails, use the same basic technique as for a through dovetail *(step 5, page 93)*. Place the tail board flat, outside-face down and position the pin board you just cut upright on the tail board, with its inside face on the tail board's shoulder line. Keeping both boards in place, carefully mark the pins' outline on the tail board, then use a square to continue the lines onto the end of the tail board. Mark Xs in all the waste areas, and cut the tails exactly as described for a through dovetail *(step 6, above)*.

BASICS OF FURNITURE MAKING

Designing and building fine furniture is the zenith of the woodworker's art. The following pages will introduce you to traditional furniture making, covering the elements basic to most simple types of furniture: building a carcase, a drawer, a door, and legs, rails, and stretchers. We then take you through the design and assembly steps for some generic types of furniture—a rudimentary bookcase, table, and bed.

One of the keys to good furniture design is to combine all these elements in a single statement, customizing the piece you're building to your own needs. You can add components to a basic structure; doors turn a tall carcase into a wardrobe, for instance.

As you work, you'll want to turn back frequently to the previous chapters for information on tools and materials, and for detailed how-to instructions on cutting, joinery, and assembly techniques. Keep in mind the importance of accurate measuring and marking *(page 32)*, and always have a sharp pencil and a tape measure within reach. Do not be concerned if some aspects of the design and construction seem to be over your head. Simply choose the technique best suited to your ability level. The information on components, proportions, and assembly can easily be applied to simpler projects. Then, as you become more proficient, you can advance to more complicated designs and joinery. Take time to look at the furniture pieces around you. Analyze the design, measure the dimensions, and examine the joinery. You'll learn a lot—and it's good preparation for tackling your own project. Once you have completed your furniture piece, turn to the next chapter for finishing information.

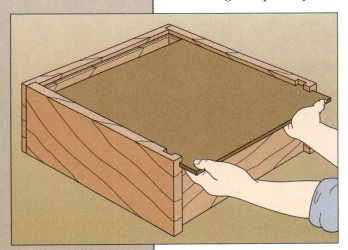

There's a great sense of satisfaction in sliding a drawer bottom home into a perfectly square drawer carcase. Drawer making is among the many techniques explained in this chapter.

BASIC CARCASE CONSTRUCTION

In this book, we limit ourselves to the two simplest types of furniture structure: frame and carcase construction. Frame, or leg-and-rail, construction, entails connecting four vertical members (legs or posts) to four horizontal pieces (rails), thus forming the frame. This simple frame is used for a bed; but change the dimensions of the frame, add height to the legs, secure a top to the rails, and you have a table; fit the table with drawers and you have a desk. Information on how to build a frame is shown in the sections on tables *(page 110)* and beds *(page 113)*.

Building a carcase, shown below, is really just putting together a box; add shelves and you have a bookcase; add doors for a wardrobe; add a lid for a chest; or add drawers—smaller carcase structures—for a chest of drawers. Of course, these boxes can be joined in a variety of ways, from simple reinforced butt joints to beautiful, albeit more complicated, dovetails.

Making a carcase

TOOLKIT
- Appropriate tools for type of joinery
- Saw
- Sander
- Clamps
- Square
- Straightedge
- Screwdriver
- Drill and bits for counterbore, body, and pilot holes
- Mallet
- Flush-cutting saw or chisel
- Router and rabbeting bit
- Hammer

1 **Preparing and joining the stock**

You may choose to make your wide carcase components from plywood, which is stronger, more stable, and less expensive than a series of edge-joined solid boards. If so, choose a type of joinery appropriate for this type of sheet material—rabbets or plate joints are good choices. Otherwise, select your stock and if you need pieces wider than the available stock, make panels by edge-joining, as shown on page 72.

Determine which type of joinery you will use to attach the four pieces of the carcase. In the following act, rabbets are used, an easy and fairly common way to put together a carcase. Cut the rabbets in the side panels, to hide the end grain in the top and bottom panels. Look through the chapter on joinery *(page 70)* for how-to instructions about this or any other joint that connects two pieces at a 90° angle. Keep in mind that you must keep the wood grain on all four pieces run-

ning in the same direction when they are joined, to allow for wood movement; start with a side panel, whose grain should run vertically.

Cut the panels to length and width, and consider whether you need to make any cuts on the panels—such as dadoes in the side pieces for shelves—before they are joined. Do this now, and then make any cuts necessary for the joints. Remember to sand any areas now that will be difficult to reach once the carcase is glued up.

Finally, dry-fit the carcase pieces together to check that all the joints fit properly. If you want, you could cut the rabbets for the back *(step 5)* at this point; this will help you in step 3, as the back will help hold the carcase square. However, you may find it easier to rout the rabbet if the carcase is already glued up. In either case, make any necessary adjustments to the fit of the joints, then disassemble the carcase.

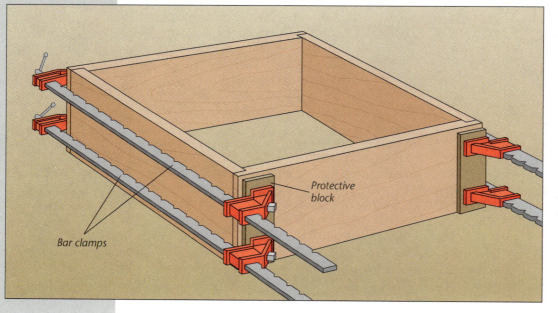

Protective block

Bar clamps

2 **Gluing up the carcase**

Apply glue to one side of each joint, spreading it evenly along the edge. Assemble all four sides and put on clamps, centering the clamp jaws over the joint; insert wood pads or blocks between the jaws and carcase to protect the wood. Don't tighten the clamps all the way yet.

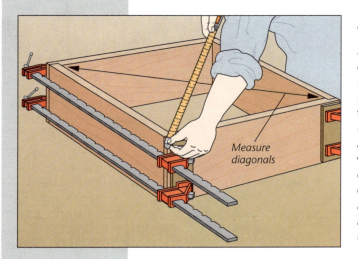

Measure diagonals

3 ▶ Checking for square

Before tightening the clamps all the way, check the assembly's alignment carefully. Measure the corner-to-corner diagonals of square or rectangular carcases: The measurements must be identical. Check 45° and 90° intersections with a combination or carpenter's square, and use a long straightedge to verify whether or not parts are in the same plane. If anything is off, now is the time to make adjustments. Loosen the clamps slightly and realign the offending parts by pulling the carcase into line with bar or pipe clamps, or shift it by pushing firmly on the long diagonal (you can use a bar or pipe clamp for this). Then retighten the clamps and check again. When everything is perfectly aligned, tighten the clamps until they're snug, but not too tight; a thin bead of glue should be squeezed out of the joint. (Don't remove the excess glue until it is dry.)

4 ▶ Reinforcing the rabbet joints

Use screws to strengthen the rabbet joints. Install a screw approximately every 4 inches, first drilling counterbore, body, and pilot holes (page 65). Conceal the screw head with a wood plug: Put a drop of glue in the hole, then fit the plug in, lining up its grain pattern with that of the stock, and knock it home with light taps of a mallet. Once the glue is dry, cut off the protrusion with a flush-cutting saw (right) or a chisel, and chisel off any excess glue.

Flush-cutting saw

Wood plug

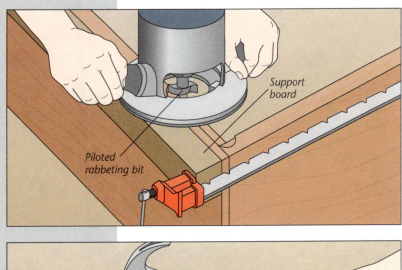

Piloted rabbeting bit

Support board

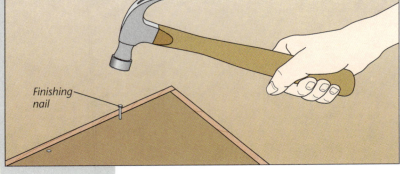

Finishing nail

5 ▶ Installing a back panel

To provide an adequate base for the router, clamp a support board flush with the edge, as shown. Install a piloted rabbeting bit in your router; the bit should make a rabbet about one-third to half as wide as the thickess of the panel, often 3/8". Set the depth slightly deeper than the thickness of the back panel (often made from 1/4" plywood).

With the bit's pilot running along the inside of the carcase, and the router's base plate flat on the carcase edge and support board, rout a rabbet along the edge (left, above). Repeat on the three other carcase sides, installing the support board on each side first. Then, use a chisel to make the corners square. Measure and cut a piece of 1/4" plywood to fit inside the rabbeted carcase. Spread a thin, even layer of glue on the rabbets and install the back panel. Every 4" to 6", drive in a small finishing nail to hold the panel securely (left).

MAKING DRAWERS

For first-rate drawer making, you must size, cut, and join five or six pieces of wood and fit the drawer precisely into a furniture opening. Drawers come in the three basic styles shown below: flush, lipped, or overlay. The type of stock and joinery for all three types can be varied to suit your budget, skill level, and ambition. Cut the pieces and assemble them as shown on the following pages; several installation options are illustrated on page 100. The final touch would be to add the drawer pull.

Designing a drawer: Choose your materials and joinery, and calculate the sizes exactly. For drawer fronts red and white oak, birch, pecan, and vertical-grain fir look good for a natural or stain finish. If you opt for plywood, choose $3/4$-inch lumber-core panels. The material and style for the fronts should match that for any adjacent doors *(see page 103)*. If the door style is frame-and-panel, drawer fronts are typically solid lumber of the same species as the door's frame. Baltic birch plywood, $1/2$ inch thick, is excellent for sides and backs; solid stock is also widely used. Drawer bottoms are typically plywood or hardboard; hardwood plywood adds a touch of class.

Joinery options: Rabbet, through dovetail, and half-blind dovetail joints are all good choices for joining a drawer front to the sides. A drawer back is commonly dadoed into the drawer sides, and the drawer bottom slides into grooves in the sides and front. It's easier to build flush and overlay drawers with a false front, since you can construct the basic box, hang it, then align the false front exactly with the opening in the piece.

Dimensions: Unless you're using bottom runners to hang it, make the height of the drawer the same as the opening in the piece of furniture minus $1/4$ inch. Drawer width is also nominally the opening minus $1/8$ inch, but you'll have to subtract extra for side guides—most require $1/2$-inch clearance on each side. As a general rule, make the drawer length $1/4$ inch less than the depth of the recess, unless your guides require additional space in back.

Take your front style into consideration: Measure flush drawers from the back of the cabinet's front, add the thickness of the overhang for lipped drawers, and measure from the cabinet's front for overlay drawers. Make the height and width of a lipped front at least $1/2$ inch more than your opening. Make a flush false front's dimensions the exact size of the opening—you'll plane it later. Overlay false fronts will overhang the faceframe at least $1/4$ inch on all four sides.

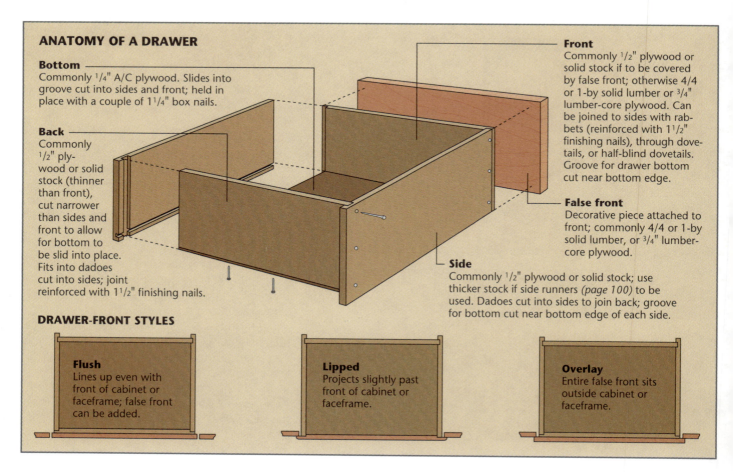

ANATOMY OF A DRAWER

Bottom
Commonly $1/4$" A/C plywood. Slides into groove cut into sides and front; held in place with a couple of $1^1/4$" box nails.

Back
Commonly $1/2$" plywood or solid stock (thinner than front), cut narrower than sides and front to allow for bottom to be slid into place. Fits into dadoes cut into sides; joint reinforced with $1^1/2$" finishing nails.

Front
Commonly $1/2$" plywood or solid stock if to be covered by false front; otherwise 4/4 or 1-by solid lumber or $3/4$" lumber-core plywood. Can be joined to sides with rabbets (reinforced with $1^1/2$" finishing nails), through dovetails, or half-blind dovetails. Groove for drawer bottom cut near bottom edge.

False front
Decorative piece attached to front; commonly 4/4 or 1-by solid lumber, or $3/4$" lumber-core plywood.

Side
Commonly $1/2$" plywood or solid stock; use thicker stock if side runners *(page 100)* to be used. Dadoes cut into sides to join back; groove for bottom cut near bottom edge of each side.

DRAWER-FRONT STYLES

Flush
Lines up even with front of cabinet or faceframe; false front can be added.

Lipped
Projects slightly past front of cabinet or faceframe.

Overlay
Entire false front sits outside cabinet or faceframe.

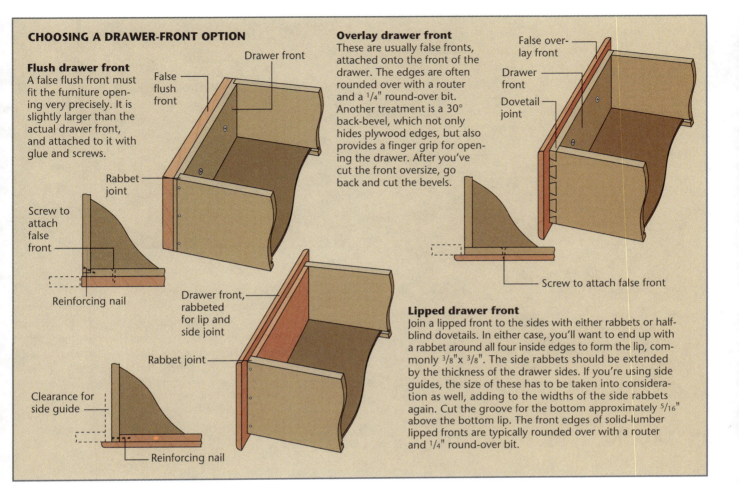

CHOOSING A DRAWER-FRONT OPTION

Flush drawer front
A false flush front must fit the furniture opening very precisely. It is slightly larger than the actual drawer front, and attached to it with glue and screws.

Drawer front

False flush front

Rabbet joint

Screw to attach false front

Reinforcing nail

Drawer front, rabbeted for lip and side joint

Rabbet joint

Clearance for side guide

Reinforcing nail

Overlay drawer front
These are usually false fronts, attached onto the front of the drawer. The edges are often rounded over with a router and a $1/4$" round-over bit. Another treatment is a 30° back-bevel, which not only hides plywood edges, but also provides a finger grip for opening the drawer. After you've cut the front oversize, go back and cut the bevels.

False overlay front

Drawer front

Dovetail joint

Screw to attach false front

Lipped drawer front
Join a lipped front to the sides with either rabbets or half-blind dovetails. In either case, you'll want to end up with a rabbet around all four inside edges to form the lip, commonly $3/8$"x $3/8$". The side rabbets should be extended by the thickness of the drawer sides. If you're using side guides, the size of these has to be taken into consideration as well, adding to the widths of the side rabbets again. Cut the groove for the bottom approximately $5/16$" above the bottom lip. The front edges of solid-lumber lipped fronts are typically rounded over with a router and $1/4$" round-over bit.

Cutting drawer stock

TOOLKIT
• Saw
• Appropriate tools for type of joinery

Making dimension and joinery cuts

Make sure all the pieces are flat and square. Rip the stock for the sides, back, and front to width. (The back won't be as wide as the other pieces, to allow space for the drawer bottom to slide in underneath; once the grooves for the bottom have been cut in the sides and front, you'll rip the back to final width.) If you're adding a false front, cut it now. Next, crosscut the parts to length, making sure to add or subtract any extra for the type of joinery to be used. Choose a front style *(see above)*; flush and overlay drawers are simplest to build, since either can have a sepa-

rate false front. Lay out and cut the desired front-to-side joinery, and then cut $1/2$" wide, $1/4$" deep dadoes in each side piece (set in approximately $1/2$" from the end) to join the back. Cut $1/4$" wide and deep grooves about $5/16$" from the bottom edge of the sides and front for the installation of the bottom. Cut the drawer bottom, making it $1/16$" shorter than the distance to the bottom of the grooves on each side and on the front; this will allow the piece to expand and contract. Once all the stock is cut to size, cut the front-to-side joints, and shape the edges.

Assembling a drawer

TOOLKIT
• Hammer
• Clamps
▼

1 Joining the back to the sides

Before you actually glue up the drawer, take the time to dry-fit the drawer components carefully and check for square *(page 97)*. Begin assembling the drawer with the back-to-side joints (if you're dovetailing, start with the front-

to-side joints). Spread the glue inside the dadoes and along the end grain of the back. Push the ends into their dadoes. Drive three $1 1/2$" finishing nails through each of the sides into the back to lock it in place.

- Glue and applicator
- 1½" finishing nails

2 ▶ **Installing the drawer front**
Next, add the front (but not the false front yet). Again, use glue and finishing nails *(right)* to reinforce the joints; you can nail at an angle if necessary. However, if you're joining dovetails, glue alone is sufficient. Clamp up the drawer assembly.

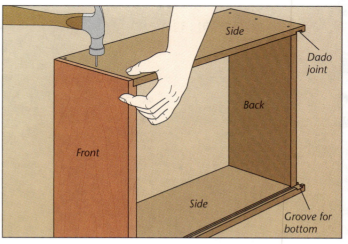

◀ **3** **Installing the drawer bottom**
Flip the drawer upside down and slide in the bottom until it's flush with the back. Check for square with a try or combination square and by measuring corner-to-corner diagonals *(page 97)*. Make any necessary adjustments, then nail the bottom to the back with a couple of 1¼" box nails. Once the basic box is together, ease the sharp edges with a folded piece of sandpaper.

INSTALLING A DRAWER

The simplest way to support a drawer of moderate size and load is on wooden runners; a coat of wax cuts friction. Plastic guides or rollers help, but the best choice is prefabricated metal, ball-bearing guide sets attached to the bottom or sides. Side guides handle more weight and operate more smoothly than bottom ones, which typically require ³⁄₁₆-inch clearance top and bottom and ⅛ inch on the sides. For side guides, ½ inch on both sides is standard. If you're using side guides, use filler strips to bring the mounting surface flush with the edge of the faceframe, as shown. The carcase must be plumb, level, and untwisted. Mark the centers of the elongated screw holes on the guides; install only these screws. Test the drawer; for fine adjustments, loosen the screws slightly and reposition the guide. Once everything is aligned, remove the drawer and drive in the remaining screws. If you're using a false front, align it carefully and fasten to the drawer from inside with screws and glue.

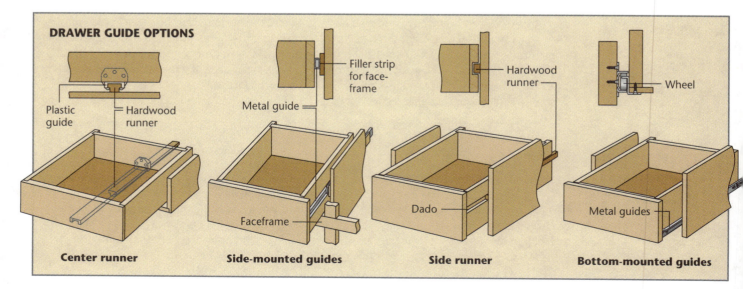

DRAWER GUIDE OPTIONS

Center runner — Plastic guide, Hardwood runner

Side-mounted guides — Filler strip for faceframe, Metal guide, Faceframe

Side runner — Hardwood runner, Dado

Bottom-mounted guides — Wheel, Metal guides

BUILDING DOORS

Study any furniture door and you'll most likely find it's made either from plywood (called a flat door) or from a panel surrounded by a frame (frame-and-panel construction); both of these are shown at right. You'll also notice that there are several ways to mount a door with respect to the cabinet face—flush, lipped, or overlay. To design a door, first decide on the type of door and its mounting style. Finally, you'll need to determine its dimensions and the type of stock to use.

The size of any door—flush, lipped, or overlay—depends on the exact size of the opening and, in some cases, on the mounting hardware you choose (*page 105*). To determine the size, first accurately measure the height and width of the opening, then follow the specifics for the different mounting styles (*below*).

Instructions for making flat plywood doors begin on page 102; the frame-and-panel type starts on page 103. Frame-and-panel designs break down into three basic panel types: flat, raised-bevel, and square-shoulder. You can secure a panel to the frame either in grooves or in rabbets. Solid-wood panels must be hidden in grooves so their seasonal movement doesn't create gaps on the inside of the door frame; plywood panels can go into either rabbeted or grooved frames.

Once you have built your door, the final step is to hang it onto the piece of furniture (*page 105*).

BASIC DOOR TYPES

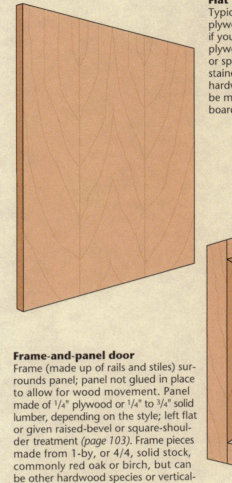

Flat plywood door
Typically made of ³/₄" lumber-core plywood; A/B fir plywood is sufficient if you plan to paint, but hardwood plywood, such as birch—either shop or special paint-grade—is better. For stained or natural finish, lumber-core hardwood plywood is ideal. Can also be made by edge-gluing solid boards together.

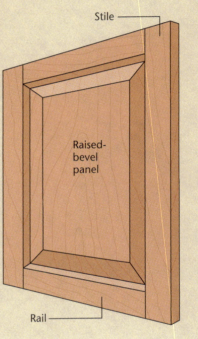

Stile

Raised-bevel panel

Rail

Frame-and-panel door
Frame (made up of rails and stiles) surrounds panel; panel not glued in place to allow for wood movement. Panel made of ¹/₄" plywood or ¹/₄" to ³/₄" solid lumber, depending on the style; left flat or given raised-bevel or square-shoulder treatment (*page 103*). Frame pieces made from 1-by, or 4/4, solid stock, commonly red oak or birch, but can be other hardwood species or vertical-grain fir.

DOOR-MOUNTING STYLES

Flush door
Mounted inside opening; face flush with front of cabinet or faceframe. Make door exact size of opening; plane or sand it to fit later.

Lipped door
Rabbet cut around inside edges of door so half its thickness projects beyond cabinet front or faceframe; should overlap at least ¹/₄" all around, so add at least ¹/₂" total to each dimension. (Exception: Double doors aren't rabbeted where they meet; don't add for rabbets along these edges.)

Overlay door
Overlaps edges of opening; mounted with inside face against cabinet front or faceframe. Can overlap opening as much as you like, but must not interfere with other doors or drawer fronts; ¹/₄" overlap is sufficient. Add extra if edges are to be back-beveled or undercut in some other way.

FLAT PLYWOOD DOORS

A flat plywood door is the simplest type to make, be it flush, lipped, or overlay. Plywood is highly resistant to warping, and, unlike solid lumber doors, you don't have to cut and fit several pieces of wood together.

Lay out the plywood for the fronts of the doors and drawers *(page 98)* at the same time, then cut them from the same panel, as shown on page 103. The grain typically runs vertically. Make the cross-grain cuts first; that way, if the ends tear out slightly, you can clean them up when you rip with the grain.

Cutting procedures and edge treatments for plywood doors vary, depending on whether they're flush, lipped, or overlay, and whether you plan a natural, stain, or opaque (painted) finish. This type of door can be livened up with some sort of edge treatment, as shown below; some do double duty by hiding the plywood's veneers.

Making plywood doors

TOOLKIT
• Saw
For flush doors:
• Iron (optional)
For lipped doors:
• Router
• Round-over or chamfering bit
• Sander
For overlay doors:
• Block plane

Flush plywood doors
A flush door may be cut to the exact size of the opening, with a slight back-bevel on the latch side. If you opt for veneer banding to cover plywood edges, be sure to cut your doors a bit shorter in height and width to allow for the banding's thickness. Glue the strips to the edges and "clamp" them with masking tape *(inset)*, or apply heat-set veneer tape with an iron.

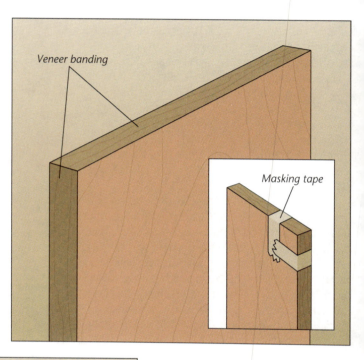

Veneer banding

Masking tape

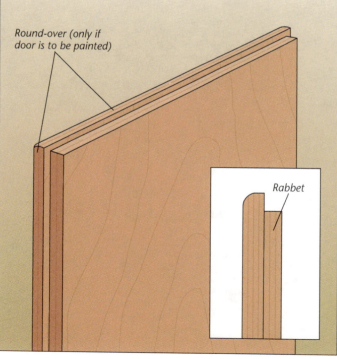

Round-over (only if door is to be painted)

Rabbet

Lipped plywood doors
A lipped door must be rabbeted on the back. Cut 3/8" x 3/8" rabbets on all edges, unless you're making double doors. In this case, cut both doors as one panel, rabbet the edges, then rip the door down the center to divide it into two pieces. If the door is intended for a natural or stained finish, it is not usually shaped on the front edges because the plywood veneers show up. However if you're planning to paint, you can round-over the edges with a router and 1/4" round-over bit, as shown, or a chamfering bit. Fill any veneer voids carefully, then sand.

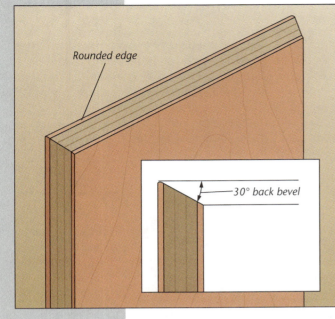

Rounded edge

30° back bevel

Overlay doors

These doors can either be cut to size with squared edges, or cut oversize and then back-beveled about 30°; the back-bevel allows you to hide the veneers more effectively and serves as a finger pull. For best results, cut the bevels on a table or radial-arm saw, then round off any sharp edges with medium-grit sandpaper or a sharp block plane.

FRAME-AND-PANEL DOOR CONSTRUCTION

FRAME-AND-PANEL DOORS: SOME OPTIONS

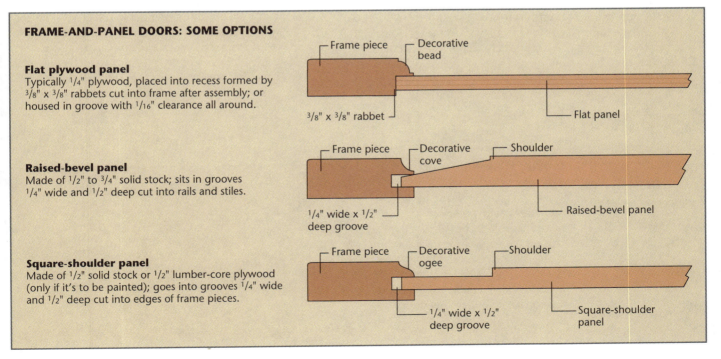

Flat plywood panel
Typically 1/4" plywood, placed into recess formed by 3/8" x 3/8" rabbets cut into frame after assembly; or housed in groove with 1/16" clearance all around.

Frame piece · Decorative bead
3/8" x 3/8" rabbet · Flat panel

Raised-bevel panel
Made of 1/2" to 3/4" solid stock; sits in grooves 1/4" wide and 1/2" deep cut into rails and stiles.

Frame piece · Decorative cove · Shoulder
1/4" wide x 1/2" deep groove · Raised-bevel panel

Square-shoulder panel
Made of 1/2" solid stock or 1/2" lumber-core plywood (only if it's to be painted); goes into grooves 1/4" wide and 1/2" deep cut into edges of frame pieces.

Frame piece · Decorative ogee · Shoulder
1/4" wide x 1/2" deep groove · Square-shoulder panel

Making the frame

TOOLKIT
- Saw
- Router
- Clamps

Choosing the type of joinery

You have a wide choice of joints to connect the stiles and rails that form the frame: doweled butt joints, half-laps, open mortise-and-tenons, and blind mortise-and-tenons. Cut the frame members to size; make all the joinery cuts. If joining the panel to a grooved frame, cut the grooves at the same time with a router, table saw, or radial-arm saw, stopping them short of the areas to be joined. If you plan to use rabbets to affix the panel, assemble and glue up the frame, but wait until it's dry to cut the rabbets. For either style, now is the time to shape the inside edges of the frame: Dry-clamp the frame and use a router with the desired decorative bit.

Cutting the panel

TOOLKIT
For flat panel:
- Saw
For raised-bevel panel:
- Clamps
- Table saw, radial-arm saw, or router table with panel-raising bit
For square-shouldered panel:
- Table saw

Making a flat panel

This type of panel is easy to make from $^1/4$" plywood; there won't be any problem with wood movement. Cut the panel to fit the space, adding on the width of the rabbets or grooves that it will fit into. If it will be placed into a rabbeted frame, make it the exact size; if it will be let into grooves, add $^1/16$" clearance all around for ease of assembly.

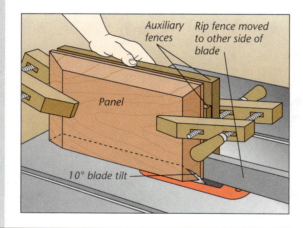

Auxiliary fences

Rip fence moved to other side of blade

Panel

10° blade tilt

Making a raised-bevel panel

This type of panel is made from $^1/2$" to $^3/4$" solid stock (plywood doesn't bevel well). Make panels less than 6" wide from a single piece of wood; for wider panels, select and edge-glue narrower pieces *(page 72)*. Before you cut the panel, with the frame dry-assembled, measure the bottom-to-bottom distance between the grooves. Cut the panel $^3/16$" to $^1/4$" short on each side to allow the panel to "float" in case of wood movement.

The table saw is the tool of choice to cut raised bevels (although you can use a radial-arm saw or router). Tilt the blade approximately 10° away from the rip fence (you may have to move your rip fence to the other side of the blade, as shown), and make test cuts until the cut piece fits into the groove the correct distance. Make the bevel cuts on all four panel faces, clamping the stock to auxiliary fences as shown for support *(left)*. Test the panel for fit; if necessary, adjust the blade and repeat the cuts.

Making a square-shouldered panel

Proceed the same way as for a rabbet cut on the table saw with a standard blade *(page 77)*. Make the cuts on the face first, then make the edge cuts with the panel held vertically the same way as for a raised-bevel panel *(above)*, with the shouldered side of the panel facing out to prevent the waste from binding between the blade and the rip fence.

Assembling a rabbeted frame-and-panel door

TOOLKIT
- Router and rabbeting bit
- Clamps (optional)

Cutting the rabbet and installing the panel

To attach a flat plywood panel to rabbets, once the glue on the frame pieces has dried, cut $^3/8$" by $^3/8$" rabbets on the back of the frame with a router and rabbeting bit. Apply glue sparingly, and evenly, to the rabbets, press the panel in place, and secure it with clamps or hammer in brads.

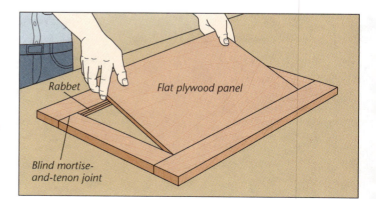

Rabbet

Flat plywood panel

Blind mortise-and-tenon joint

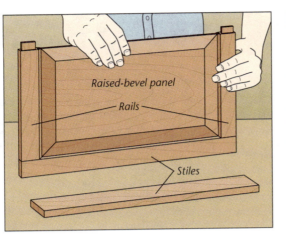

Raised-bevel panel

Rails

Stiles

Joining the rails, stiles, and panel
To assemble your door, you'll need two bar or pipe clamps—one centered under each rail. Be sure the clamps lie on a flat surface; if they're not flat in relation to each other, the door will wind up twisted. First, apply glue and join one stile and one rail, using dowels or other reinforcement if the joint calls for it; the blind mortise-and-tenon shown doesn't. Slide the panel into the grooves of these two pieces; don't apply any glue to the panel. (Note: To avoid gluing the corners of the panel to the frame, you can round them off slightly and coat the edges with paste wax before inserting it.) Attach the other rail *(left)*, and finally, the second stile, then clamp the assembly securely.

HANGING A DOOR

Door hinges are available in a wide variety of styles, sizes, and finishes to fit flush, lipped, and overlay doors; representative hinge styles are illustrated below. When possible, opt for self-closing hinges; the standard types require a separate door catch to keep them closed.

The European hinge is gaining popularity. It's easy to install, and can be adjusted with the turn of a screw to bring a door into line. It's usually mounted directly to the carcase side, and is hidden when the door is closed; because it's spring-loaded it requires no catch.

Before hanging a door, be sure the carcase is upright, plumb, and level. If you're installing flush doors, plane them to match the opening. Your hinge setup will require careful positioning and cutting of any mortises or other recesses. To hang the door, follow the sequence of steps listed at right; drill body and pilot holes for the screw first *(page 65)*. There are a few tricks: When hanging a lipped door, set the side to be hinged on two pieces of folded sandpaper—one at each end. This will raise the door enough to prevent binding. If hanging overlay doors, construct a simple jig to hold them at the correct height while you install them.

DOOR-HANGING SEQUENCE

To hang a door on a piece of furniture, proceed as follows:
1. Fasten the hinges on the door;
2. Line up the door and mark the upper screw holes on the carcase or faceframe;
3. Install the top screws;
4. If the swing and alignment check out, install the bottom screws.

European hinge

Recess fits in hole bored in door

Mounting plate screwed to carcase

Arm attached to mounting plate

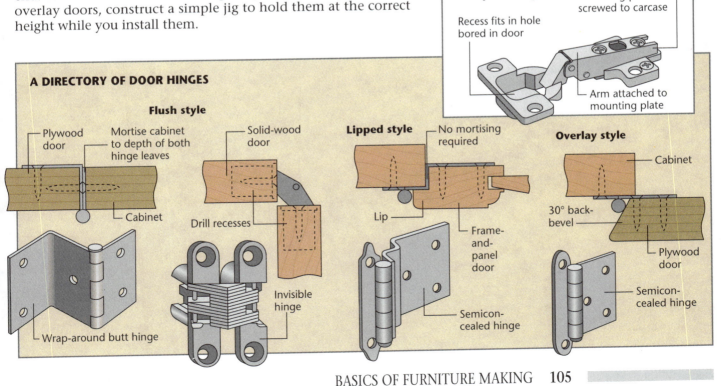

A DIRECTORY OF DOOR HINGES

Flush style

Plywood door

Mortise cabinet to depth of both hinge leaves

Cabinet

Wrap-around butt hinge

Solid-wood door

Drill recesses

Invisible hinge

Lipped style

No mortising required

Lip

Frame-and-panel door

Semiconcealed hinge

Overlay style

Cabinet

30° back-bevel

Plywood door

Semiconcealed hinge

MAKING LEGS, RAILS, AND STRETCHERS

Leg-and-rail (frame) construction, as its name suggests, comprises legs connected to one another by horizontal rails. Furniture pieces such as tables, desks, and beds are built in this way—with other elements added for distinctive form. Stretchers are installed on some desks and tables as a sort of lower rail, although you will mostly see them between chair legs.

Legs: More than any other single component, legs express furniture style. As shown below, legs come in a wide variety of shapes—tapered, round, oval, square, curved, or with a combination of these characteristics.

Contemporary furniture tends toward undecorated straight or tapered legs. The more ornate, usually curved, legs of period furniture often feature fluting (long narrow channels), reeding (ridges), carving, and turning. The most widely used traditional style is the cabriole leg, which forms a double curve, like an elongated "S".

You can easily cut square and rectangular legs with a table saw. Many curved legs, including the cabriole, can be shaped with a band saw, but round legs must be turned on a lathe. In general, you should cut straight and slightly curved legs with the grain running the length of the leg. Take special care when you're laying out legs with large-radius curves, taking the grain into account at each of its weakest points. (Try moving a template around on the stock.) Heavily curved or bent legs may be bent-laminat-ed for greater width and strength. You may find it's more practical to buy ready-made turned and highly decorative legs unless you own a lathe or enjoy carving. Though most manufactured legs come only shaped and sanded, some are fitted with hardware that will fit most rails, and they may include glides (metal or nylon tips on the feet). Mail-order woodworking outlets are your best sources of supply for these items.

Rails: These components provide support for tabletops and desktops and help discourage these slabs from cupping and warping. Often called aprons, rails also visually define the outlines of a piece of furniture. For this reason, you'll have to consider proportion as well as strength when you choose the width of the rail stock for a particular design. Remember also to account for any top overhang that will obscure the top of the rail.

Rails are typically made from 4/4 or 5/4 stock and are seldom narrower than 2 inches or wider than 5 inches.

Stretchers: These horizontal members hold legs or posts rigidly apart, also keeping them from splaying more than intended and reducing the stress on the leg-to-rail connections. Stretchers may be the same size as the rails, or much narrower. Their shape ranges from round or oval to square or rectangular. Use them singly (as in a trestle table) or in combination, such as the H-shaped assembly installed under a harvest table.

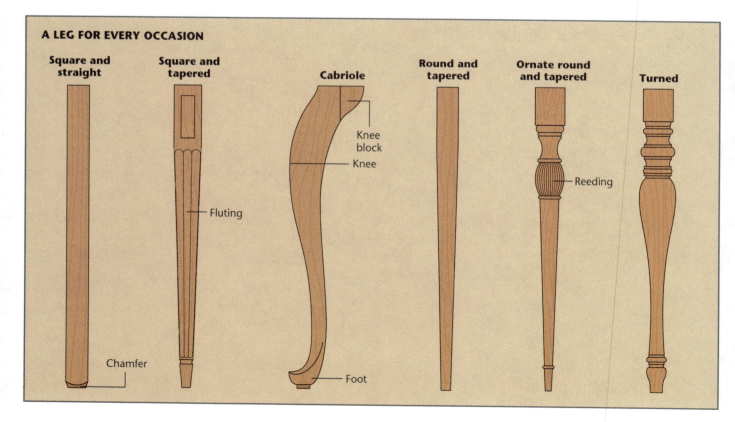

A LEG FOR EVERY OCCASION

Square and straight

Square and tapered

— Fluting

Chamfer

Cabriole

Knee block

Knee

Foot

Round and tapered

Ornate round and tapered

— Reeding

Turned

BUILDING A BOOKCASE

There are few homes that couldn't use more shelves for storage. On the following pages, we'll show you how to design and build a basic bookcase—a set of shelves with a frame and back. This bookcase is geared toward portability and can be made with inexpensive softwood. If you're after something special—a room divider or a built-in, for example—combine the guidelines that follow with information from earlier chapters, then create a bookcase to suit your needs exactly.

To design a bookcase, keep in mind that it's essentially a box: The top, sides, and bottom shelf define the space, and the back (like the bottom of a box) holds the other components rigid and square. When planning your bookcase, balance your storage requirements against strength, economy, and aesthetics. Though the basic components don't vary, you do have many choices in size, materials, shelving design, and joinery.

On the bookcase illustrated below, the top and sides are connected with rabbet joints (other options shown on page 108). Fixed shelves are dadoed to the sides; the bottom shelf is raised off the floor, resulting in a kickspace. To recess the back, rabbet the inside edges of the top and sides (below, left), and cut the back smaller than the overall dimensions of the bookcase. Some design guidelines follow.

Dimensions: The size of your bookcase depends largely on your storage needs and available space. The only design restriction is shelf span: Bookshelves longer than 24 inches have a tendency to sag if they're made from $3/4$-inch particleboard. Better grades of fir and pine will span about 32 inches; $3/4$-inch plywood and most hardwoods will stay relatively straight at 36 to 40 inches in length. Support longer shelves along the back with cleats, or use partitions, as shown below (right).

Materials: Most large storage units are made from plywood for ease of construction, economy, and strength, but solid lumber is also good; No. 1 and 2 Common pine is an economical choice. If you prefer to use hardwood, go with 1-by stock. For a small case, you can make the back from $1/8$-inch tempered hardboard; use $1/4$-inch hardboard or plywood for a larger case.

Shelves: Your bookcase can have fixed or adjustable shelves, or as is frequently done, a combination of both. Some options are shown on the next page. Fixed shelves —dadoed into the sides—will make the case stronger. Generally, the bottom and top shelves are both fixed; if the case is over four feet tall, fasten at least one middle shelf as well. On a backless case, the majority of the shelves should be solidly attached. Joined shelves,

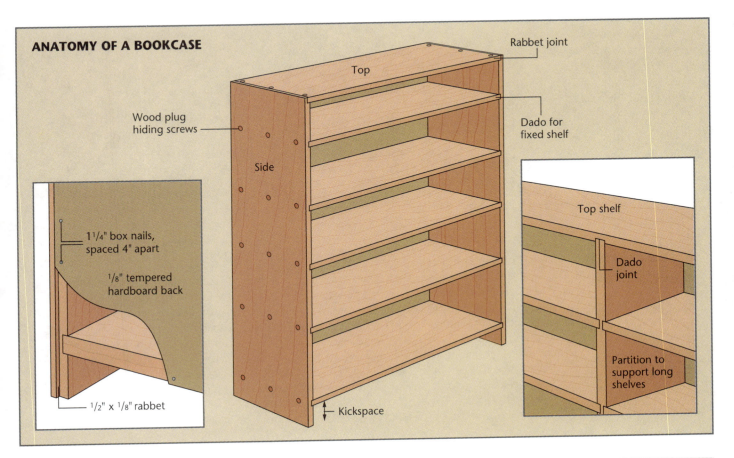

ANATOMY OF A BOOKCASE

Rabbet joint

Top

Wood plug hiding screws

Dado for fixed shelf

Side

Top shelf

1 1/4" box nails, spaced 4" apart

Dado joint

1/8" tempered hardboard back

Partition to support long shelves

1/2" x 1/8" rabbet

Kickspace

though rigid and good-looking, require major surgery if you want to make changes later.

Adjustable shelves offer a lot more flexibility; they can be supported with slotted metal tracks and clips, or with pegs. The tracks can be surface mounted or, for a neater look, recessed into grooves. With pegs, you can choose between short lengths of 1/4-inch-diameter hardwood dowel and a variety of manufactured styles. Whichever type of peg you decide on, you'll need two rows of 1/4-inch holes in each side piece or partition.

Cutting and assembly: It's vital to cut and join pieces carefully. To attach a fixed shelf to the sides of the case, use a dado joint *(pages 78-81)*; for a more finished effect, stop the dado an inch from the front edge. To join the top to the sides, choose from the options shown below. These varieties of rabbets are strong and relatively simple to cut *(see page 75)*. If you don't want fasteners to be visible on the outside of your case, try butt joints, reinforced by biscuits *(page 73)*; no plugs or putty will mar the surface.

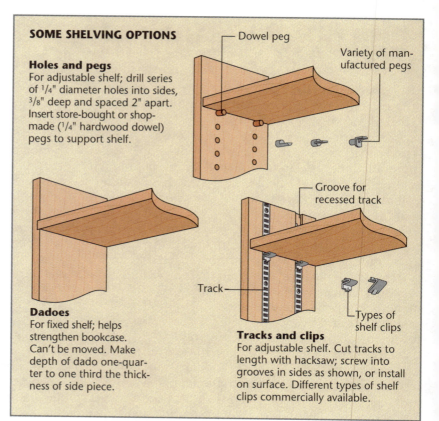

SOME SHELVING OPTIONS

Holes and pegs
For adjustable shelf; drill series of 1/4" diameter holes into sides, 3/8" deep and spaced 2" apart. Insert store-bought or shop-made (1/4" hardwood dowel) pegs to support shelf.

Dowel peg

Variety of manufactured pegs

Groove for recessed track

Track

Types of shelf clips

Dadoes
For fixed shelf; helps strengthen bookcase. Can't be moved. Make depth of dado one-quarter to one third the thickness of side piece.

Tracks and clips
For adjustable shelf. Cut tracks to length with hacksaw; screw into grooves in sides as shown, or install on surface. Different types of shelf clips commercially available.

TOP-TO-SIDE JOINTS

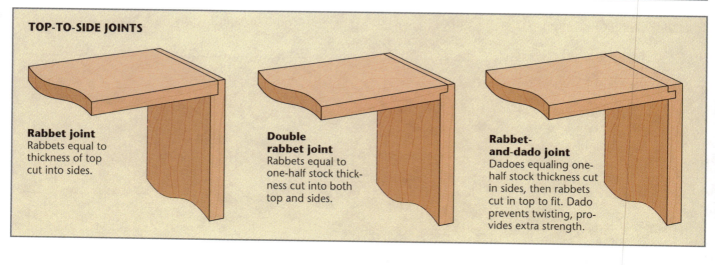

Rabbet joint
Rabbets equal to thickness of top cut into sides.

Double rabbet joint
Rabbets equal to one-half stock thickness cut into both top and sides.

Rabbet-and-dado joint
Dadoes equaling one-half stock thickness cut in sides, then rabbets cut in top to fit. Dado prevents twisting, provides extra strength.

Assembling a bookcase

TOOLKIT
- Square
- Saw
- Sander
- Appropriate tools for type of joinery
- Clamps
- Router, rabbeting bit

▼

1 Cutting the stock
Make sure all the stock is flat and square. When ripping boards to width, use the same fence setting (for a stationary or portable circular saw) or marking gauge setting for each. Because you're recessing the back in a rabbet, the shelves and any interior partitions must be narrower than the top and sides. When you crosscut the shelves and top to length, add for the joinery, and check the shelf ends for square. The back must also be square or the finished bookcase will list to one side; measure both diagonals, and if the measurements match up, the back is square.

After cutting the basic components to size, rough-sand any flaws, lumber stamps, or pencil marks. Cut the corner joints, then dry-assemble the case (minus the shelves) and rout the rabbets for the back. Disassemble to drill or cut recesses for shelf hardware, or cut shelf dadoes. (Cut the dadoes on scrap first and test their width with your shelf stock. The fit should be snug but not tight.)

- Drill and bit for peg-type shelf supports
- Screwdriver or hammer (optional)
- Hammer or mallet

2 ▶ Gluing up the assembly

Dry-fit all the pieces first; make any adjustments. For the shelf dadoes and rabbet-type joints, use fasteners and glue. Screws (counterbored and plugged, or countersunk) pull joints together and keep them that way. Nails (set and filled) don't offer much strength, but hold the joint while the glue dries; if necessary, use clamps to hold everything in alignment while nailing. For glue only, use two clamps for the top and for each fixed shelf.

To glue up the assembly, lay one side piece facedown on a flat surface. Spread glue evenly in all dadoes and rabbets; coat the end grain of the matching pieces. Put bottom shelf into its dado and tap it home with a beating block and hammer. Once all the fixed shelves are upright in their dadoes, quickly add the other side piece before the glue dries. If you have a few shelves, put them in using only hand pressure, then tap them further in with a beating block and hammer *(right)*. Attach the top to the sides.

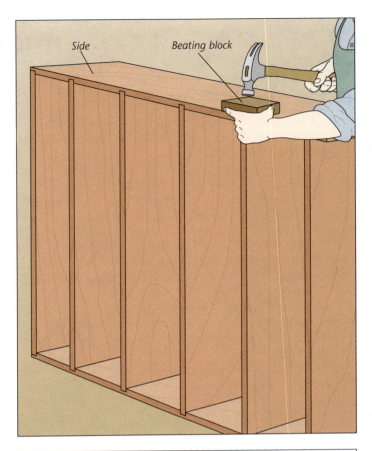

Side

Beating block

3 Fastening and clamping

To tighten up the shelves in the dadoes, use pipe or bar clamps—unless you're fastening them with screws. Rotate the assembled case to the upright position. Starting with the bottom shelf, place one clamp across the front of the case and another across the back, aligning them over the dadoes. (Positioning the clamp—and adding wood scraps to protect the sides—can be maddening; get a helper.) Slowly tighten the clamps, alternating between them. Stop when you feel the shelf bottom out in the dado, or when you see glue squeeze out. If you're using nails, drive one in the center of each side between the two clamps. Then remove one of the clamps and, on each side, drive a nail in its place. Repeat for the other clamp. If you're relying on glue alone, clamp the front and back of each shelf, square the case, and leave the clamps overnight.

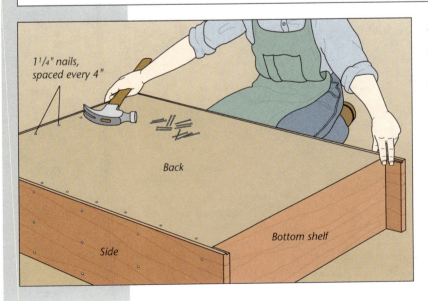

1¼" nails, spaced every 4"

Back

Side

Bottom shelf

4 Squaring the case

After drawing all the joints tight—and before the glue dries—you must square the case. The textbook method, as described on page 97, is to measure the diagonals, position a pipe clamp diagonally across the longer dimension, and tighten slowly. Once the case is square, let the glue dry, then attach the back with a small amount of glue and 1¼" box nails spaced every 4". A quicker method to square a bookcase with screw-reinforced joints is to use the back as a guide. If your joints are snug and the back is absolutely square, nail one side of the back flush, then rack the case to fit the back, nailing as you go to keep it square *(left)*.

Now you're ready to finish the bookcase: Plug or fill any holes, sand, and finish *(page 115)*. Install any hardware and add any nonfixed shelves.

CONSTRUCTING A TABLE OR DESK

A table, like a desk, is nothing more than a stable horizontal surface—a top—held up off the floor at a convenient height by legs. The length and width of your table or desk depend mainly on your space and needs; the height is more critical. Suggestions for designing and building tables and desks—desks being combinations of tables and carcases (page 96), with drawers—follow.

Dimensions: When you're planning a table or desk, two elements are crucial: the height of the top and the placement of the legs and stretchers. Correct height depends on the ultimate purpose of the piece. Where you place the legs and any stretchers will affect the comfort of the people using the furniture; ensure that the stretchers won't interfere with seating.

Standard heights for tables and desks, as well as comfortable minimums for dining tables are shown on page 111; take these as a starting point and adapt them for your situation.

Tops: Tops for tables and desks, as illustrated on page 111, are built from either edge-joined hardwood lumber or hardwood plywood. The edge-joined type are typically 4/4 or 5/4 stock that's at least 3/4 inch thick when planed and sanded or scraped. Face-laminating—gluing the faces of boards together—produces an informal look known as butcher block.

Because of its size and dimensional stability, hardwood plywood is often used for a large, high-quality top. The specialty furniture grades of plywood, featuring carefully matched veneers, make beautiful surfaces. Plywood edges are typically covered, or banded, with solid stock. Less expensive plywood can be used as an underlay for tile, plastic laminate, or veneer.

Joinery options: It's essential that your table or desk be rock steady; the joinery between legs, rails, stretchers, and top will ensure this rigidity. There is a variety of joints that you can use for the legs to rails, and then for the leg-and-rail assembly to the top, as shown for assembling a table or desk (page 112).

TWO TABLES YOU CAN BUILD

Occasional table

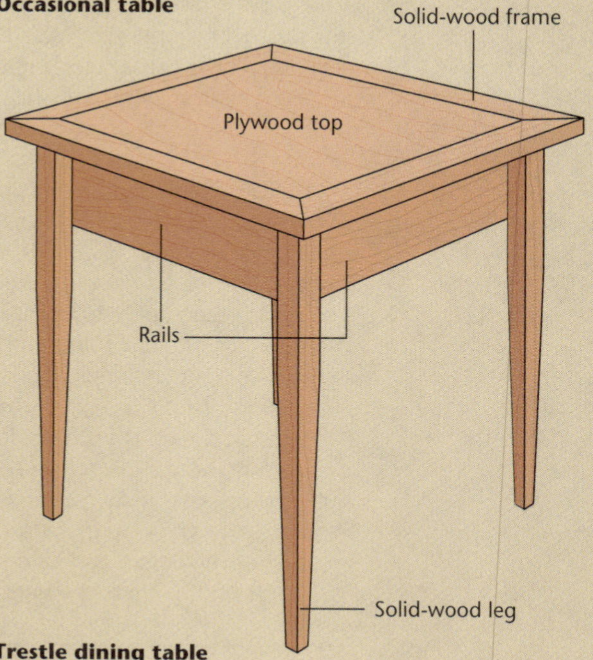

Solid-wood frame

Plywood top

Rails

Solid-wood leg

Trestle dining table

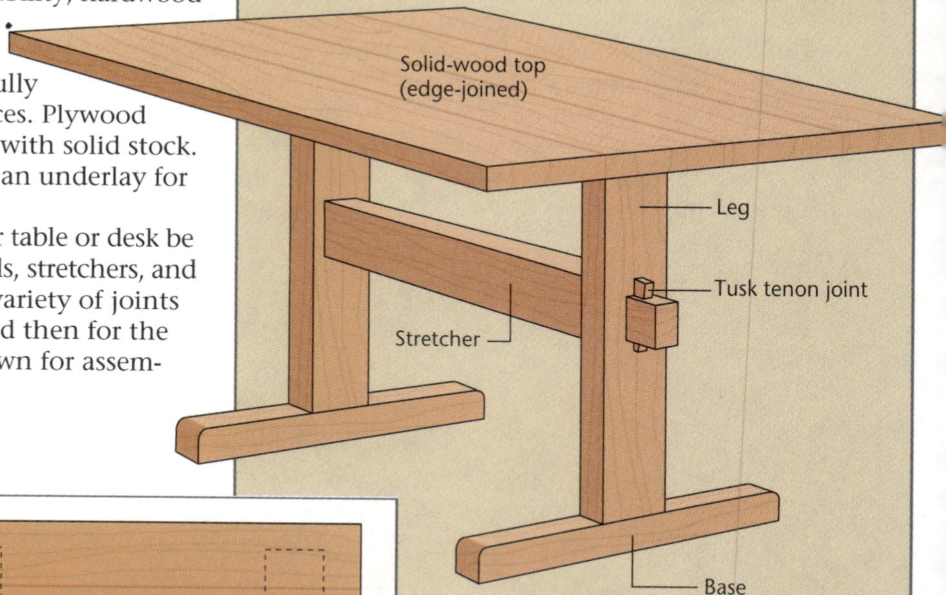

Solid-wood top (edge-joined)

Leg

Tusk tenon joint

Stretcher

Base

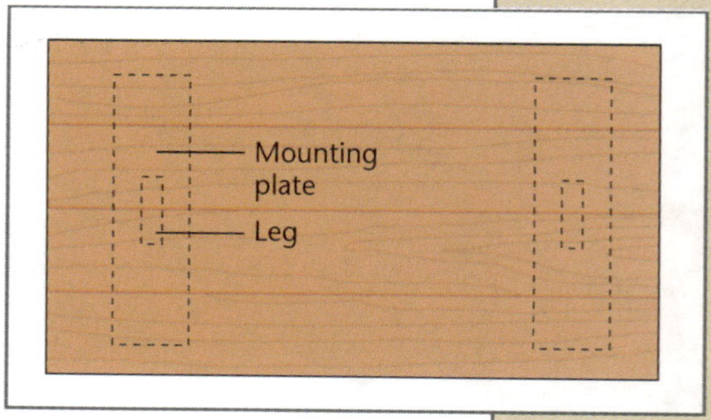

Mounting plate

Leg

This top view of a trestle table shows the position of the mounting plates that join the legs to the top.

A TRIO OF TABLETOPS

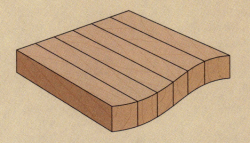

Solid-wood top
Narrow pieces edge-joined together *(page 72)*; typically ³/₄" thick. After glue-up, router used to shape decorative edge.

Butcher-block top
Made of solid stock 1¹/₄" to 2¹/₂" thick, glued face-to-face *(page 72)*. Planed to thickness, then decorative edge may be routed, if desired.

Plywood top
Made of ³/₄" hardwood plywood. Edges concealed by solid-wood molding, as shown, with plywood rabbeted and glued into groove in molding. V-grooved, tongue-and-grooved, or splined connection can be used instead, or top can rest in a frame.

SIZING YOUR TABLE OR DESK

The height of a table varies depending upon its purpose; for instance, an occasional table may be sized according to the sofa it will be placed next to. Some standards for desks and different types of tables are shown at right. Both tables and desks vary enormously in their horizontal dimensions. When determining the length of a dining table, measure out 24 inches (along the edge) for each diner. Widthwise, plan on a minimum of 12 inches from the table's edge toward the center for a place setting, then add 4 to 6 inches for serving dishes.

A 32-inch square table, as shown, can accommodate four diners, but a 40-inch size is more practical. The minimum diameter for a round table is about the same, but if you have the space, a 48-inch table will seat four people more comfortably—and six in a pinch. Round tables rarely exceed 66 inches in diameter. Keep in mind that you can fit more diners around a rectangular table than a square table of the same square footage, and of all the shapes, oval tables are the most space-efficient. No matter what shape you choose, plan the position of the legs carefully so as not to limit seating; leave a minimum of 20 inches between the legs for each chair and occupant.

Desks can range anywhere from 20 to 36 inches deep; 30 inches is a good average. The length will depend on the planned use of the desk and the available space.

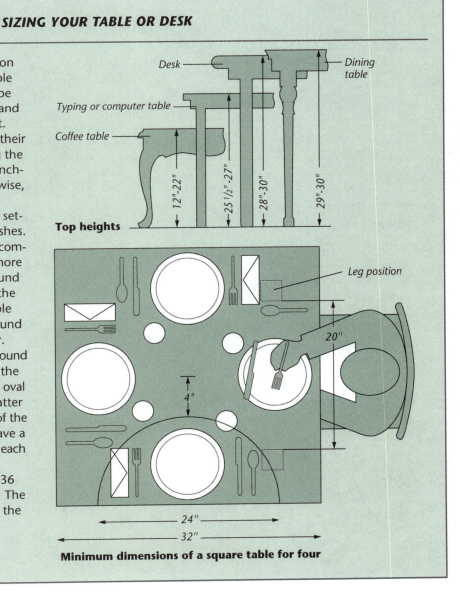

Desk
Dining table
Typing or computer table
Coffee table
12"-22"
25¹/₂"-27"
28"-30"
29"-30"
Top heights

Leg position
20"
4"
24"
32"

Minimum dimensions of a square table for four

Assembling a table or desk

TOOLKIT
- Saw
- Appropriate tools for type of joinery
- Clamps or appropriate tools for knock-down fittings
- Sander

1 ▶ Joining legs and rails
Cut the legs and rails to size, leaving any extra for the joinery method to be used. Decide how you will join the top to the leg-and-rail assembly *(step 2)* and make any necessary cuts in the rails now, such as pocket holes, mortises for desktop clips, or grooves for wood buttons or tabletop fasteners.

Next, choose a type of joint to attach the legs and rails *(right)*, and glue up the assembly—or fasten it together, if you are using knock-down fittings. Also attach any stretchers at this time; a mortise-and-tenon joint is commonly used for this. Leg-and-rail construction traditionally has used various types of mortise-and-tenon joints, but a faster solution is a butt joint reinforced with blind dowels. If the top overhangs the legs and rails, you can use a dovetail dado or, for light-duty tables, a stub (short) tenon in an open mortise. Legs and rails of any table can also be joined with knock-down fittings, such as metal corner blocks or bolts and cross-dowels.

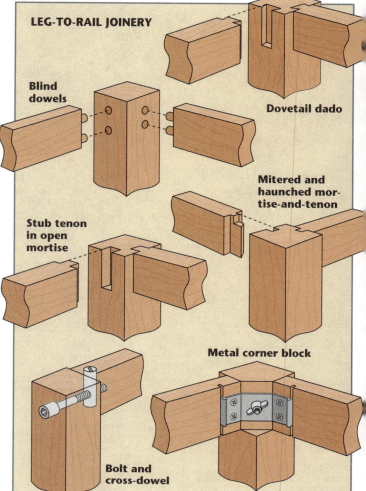

LEG-TO-RAIL JOINERY

Blind dowels

Dovetail dado

Mitered and haunched mortise-and-tenon

Stub tenon in open mortise

Metal corner block

Bolt and cross-dowel

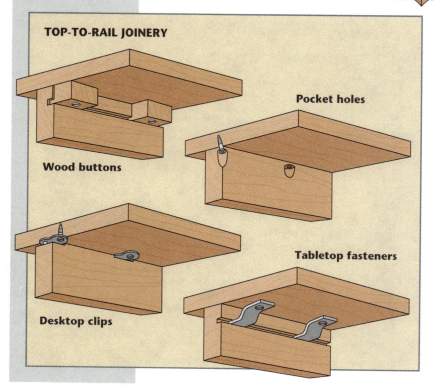

TOP-TO-RAIL JOINERY

Wood buttons

Pocket holes

Desktop clips

Tabletop fasteners

2 ◀ Making and installing the top
Top-to-rail connections require careful joinery to avoid the seasonal wood movement problems common with solid-wood tops; choose from the methods shown at left. The principle here is that the top cannot be tightly fastened to the rails; it must be able to move if the wood swells or shrinks. Traditional solutions are wood buttons or pocket holes (drilled up through the rail or angled in from the inside face of the rail to accommodate an undersized screw and a washer). An easier alternative is metal slotted angles *(page 31)*, tabletop fasteners, or desktop clips.

A trestle table is made with rail-less construction: Use lag screws to fasten a piece of wood almost as long as the table's width to the top of each leg as a mounting plate. Then, make elongated screw holes in this piece and screw it into the underside of the tabletop. Use lag screws or bolts and cross-dowels to attach the base to the legs.

To complete a table, do a final sanding and apply a moisture-resistant finish to all surfaces, including the underside of the top.

PUTTING TOGETHER A BED

The headboard, footboard, and side rails of a bed not only define its perimeter, but also give the bed its distinctive style. The four end posts may extend well above the rails to further emphasize the space. Many beds have more than one rail at both the head and the foot, creating the headboard and footboard; these rails can be connected with vertical spindles or slats, or the uppermost rail can be widened for a solid look. Either way, the bottom end rails are typically the same width as the side rails, and all of them are placed at the same height on the corner posts. The top of the headboard should be at least a foot above the top of the mattress; the footboard is often lower than the headboard. Most headboards, footboards, and side rails are made from 4/4 or 5/4 solid stock.

Though posts are typically made from thicker stock—such as 8/4 or 12/4—sized to support the joinery for the side rails, they also have to be in proportion with the rest of the bed. Posts can be turned, tapered, rectangular, or square.

Mattress supports—either 3/4-inch plywood or 1x3 solid-wood slats laid close together—should rest on cleats that are either housed in grooves cut into the side rails, or glued and screwed to the rails.

Dimensions: If you plan to use a commercial mattress, you'll have to build the inside dimensions of the bed to the nominal mattress sizes listed in the chart at right. Measure your mattress for exact dimensions and add at least 1/4 inch on all sides for clearance.

If you prefer, you can make a bed to your own specifications and use a high-density foam mattress cut to size with an electric carving knife. In this case, keep in mind that, though the width of a bed is mostly a matter of preference, its length is critical. For maximum comfort, add eight inches to the height of the person using the bed. If you're planning a child's bed, be sure to take the child's growth into account.

Though most people aren't particular about how far off the floor they're sleeping, other considerations do count. If the bed will also be used for sitting, the best height is a mattress 18 inches off the floor. But beds need to be changed too, and for that, 24 inches is ideal. Most beds fall between these two heights.

Joinery options: Beds are cumbersome to move or store unless they're made, at least in part, with knockdown joinery. Typically, end rails are permanently fixed to the posts with mortise-and-tenon joints. Side rails disengage; you can connect them with knock-down hardware or bolt them to the inside of an extra-wide post, using threaded inserts.

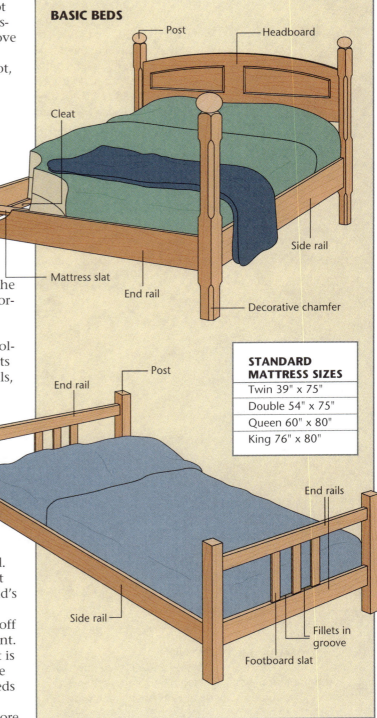

BASIC BEDS

Post — Headboard

Cleat

Mattress slat

End rail

Side rail

Decorative chamfer

End rail — Post

Side rail

End rails

Fillets in groove

Footboard slat

STANDARD MATTRESS SIZES	
Twin	39" x 75"
Double	54" x 75"
Queen	60" x 80"
King	76" x 80"

Constructing a bed that's through-bolted, as described on page 114, requires a variety of demanding joints. If you decide to choose one of the other joinery options shown, you can follow the same basic construction sequence as for through bolts to build the bed.

Building a bed using through bolts

TOOLKIT
- Saw
- Tools to cut mortises or grooves, and for type of joinery
- Router and decorative bit
- Sander
- Clamps
- Drill and bit larger than through bolts, adjustable drill stand, and doweling jig
- Chisel
- Screwdriver

1 Cutting the stock
Do all the cutting at once, rather than joint by joint; this way you can use the same saw setting to achieve the required uniformity. The posts must be square, straight, and identical in size. Square-cut the bottom of each post, but don't cut them to length yet. Rip the rails to width; don't trim them to their exact length until you've double-checked that there's enough extra stock for the tenons. If the end rails form open headboards or footboards that will receive slats or spindles, make the cuts now: Mortise or drill the edges of the rails, or groove them and insert fillets (small wood strips) to fill the voids between the slats. Also cut any grooves on the inside face of the side rails to receive the mattress-support cleats.

2 Joining the posts and end rails
Lay out and cut the mortise-and-tenons to join the posts and end rails. For a solid head or footboard, don't make one big tenon, make two small ones instead. Just attach the top few inches of a large headboard or footboard to reduce problems with wood movement later on. Make the mortise for the bottom tenon longer than the tenon's width so that the tenon can expand or contract. Cut the tops of the posts to length and then do any shaping required, such as chamfering the edges of the posts or rounding-over the headboard and footboard. Also do the finish-sanding at this time. Next, glue up the end rails and posts, leaving them clamped until the glue has completely cured.

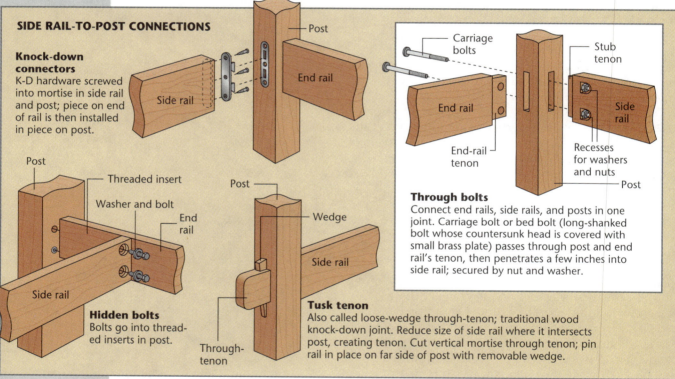

SIDE RAIL-TO-POST CONNECTIONS

Knock-down connectors
K-D hardware screwed into mortise in side rail and post; piece on end of rail is then installed in piece on post.

Post — End rail — Side rail

Carriage bolts — Stub tenon — End rail — Side rail — End-rail tenon — Recesses for washers and nuts — Post

Through bolts
Connect end rails, side rails, and posts in one joint. Carriage bolt or bed bolt (long-shanked bolt whose countersunk head is covered with small brass plate) passes through post and end rail's tenon, then penetrates a few inches into side rail; secured by nut and washer.

Post — Threaded insert — Washer and bolt — End rail — Side rail

Hidden bolts
Bolts go into threaded inserts in post.

Post — Wedge — Side rail — Through-tenon

Tusk tenon
Also called loose-wedge through-tenon; traditional wood knock-down joint. Reduce size of side rail where it intersects post, creating tenon. Cut vertical mortise through tenon; pin rail in place on far side of post with removable wedge.

3 Attaching the side rails
To join the side rails to the end-rail assembly, use through bolts, or you can choose from some other options (above). For through bolts, cut stub (short) tenons on the ends of the side rails and corresponding mortises in the posts. Clamp side rails to end-rail assemblies. Drill two holes for the bolts through each post into each side rail, passing through the end-rail tenon. Use an adjustable drill stand to keep the drill on target (page 64). Unclamp the side rails and use a drill and a doweling jig to extend the bolt holes 2" or 3". Drill out recesses for the nuts and washers on the inside face of the side rails; leave at least 1/2" of material at the end of the rail. Then use a chisel to square off the hole so the washer will rest against a flat surface. Sand all the pieces and attach the cleats to support the mattress slats to the rails, then assemble the bed with carriage or bed bolts. Finish as desired and add the mattress slats, which can be screwed in place.

FINISHING YOUR PROJECT

A fine finish not only protects wood from dirt, abrasion, moisture, heat, and chemicals, but also can greatly enhance the "feel" of the surface. You can choose from two types of finishes—those that penetrate wood pores and those that are built up in layers on top of the surface. The chart on page 120 will help you size up your basic choices. Keep in mind, though, that the use of synthetic resins is blurring the distinctions between some traditional finishes, as well as creating new ones. If you're confused, ask an experienced paint or hardware dealer for help. In any case, it's best to test the finish on a piece of scrap wood left over from your project to make sure you'll be getting the result you want.

Though choosing a finish is the first step, before you can apply any finish you'll have to do the preparatory steps—repair all surface flaws, finish-sand, and then fill, seal, and stain as required. At last, you're on to the top coat, the actual "finish"—oil, shellac, lacquer, varnish, or enamel. In this chapter, you'll find information about the pluses and minuses of each type, and descriptions of application techniques. Finally, if you want to rub down or wax your finished project to a custom sheen, we explain how that's done on page 126.

If you've used plywood or other sheet material for your project and want to cover up the unattractive edges, use either solid wood edge-banding or the veneer type—available with an adhesive backing and applied quickly and easily with a hot iron.

Whether you want to brush, wipe, or spray on a finish, in the pages that follow you'll find the information you need to make your project look beautiful.

PREPARING THE SURFACE

Proper surface preparation is one of the secrets to any successful finish. Admittedly, it's probably the least enjoyable step; just when you're ready to celebrate putting together the last successful joint by brushing on a fine finish, you have to focus on the minute details involved in making the outer layer of wood virtually flawless.

Though the biggest part of surface preparation is repairing the wood and finish-sanding, prepping also means filling open-grain woods, sealing wood pores, and staining. Whether or not you do this work—and the order in which you do it—depends on your wood, your finish, and the look you want to achieve. All these procedures are explained on the following pages.

Making wood repairs: Before you sand, study the surface of your project in a low-angle light and identify any imperfections. Some, like shallow scratches, can be sanded out; if any millmarks are left, planing or heavy-duty sanding is the prescription now. Other surface imperfections—deep scratches, checks *(page 24)*, chips, gouges, nail holes, open joints, and grain tear-out—will also have to be filled with a type of patching material.

Using patching materials to make surface repairs can be a problem if you're planning to apply a clear finish. These materials have a different rate of absorption than the surrounding wood, and patched areas tend to look lighter or darker than the rest of the piece once stain or a clear finish is applied. The solution, though you may find it time-consuming, is to first do a test with your patching material, stain, and top coat on a piece of scrap wood left over from your project. You can then adjust the color of your patching material. You'll find information on the various patching materials—and how to apply them—opposite.

Finish-sanding and grain-raising: To sand wood effectively, you must use progressively finer grits of sandpaper each time you sand, as described on pages 68-69. Now's the time to finish up the job with the finest grits.

Finally, you may want to raise the grain, particularly if you are planning to use a water-base finish. When wood is exposed to moisture, the surface fibers begin to swell, making the wood look and feel fuzzy; by wetting down the wood now and removing the raised fibers with steel wool or sandpaper, you will avoid this problem later. Instructions on finish-sanding and raising the grain are shown opposite.

Filling and sealing: Open-grain woods such as oak, mahogany, ash, and rosewood have large pores that are exposed when the wood is cut. If you're finishing with shellac, lacquer, or enamel and you want a glass-smooth surface, you'll have to fill up these pores first with a filler.

The term sealer refers to any product capable of sealing wood surfaces. Typically used just before applying the top coat, a sealer can also be useful before you stain. Both of these procedures are explained on page 118.

ASK A PRO

WHAT DO I HAVE TO CONSIDER WHEN I CHOOSE PRODUCTS TO PREP THE SURFACE?
Any filler, sealer, or stain you use must be compatible with the finish you've chosen, or the finish layers won't bond properly. You'll know that two products are compatible if they can be dissolved in a common thinner.

Repairing a dent in wood

TOOLKIT
• Iron

Steaming out a dent
Most dents can be steamed out; simply cover the crushed wood fibers with a damp towel and hold a hot iron on the towel until it begins to dry out *(right)*. Remoisten the towel and repeat the procedure several times. Be patient, and you'll find that this usually works.

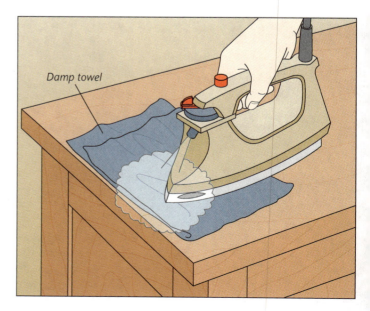

Damp towel

Filling surface imperfections

TOOLKIT
- Putty knife
- Sander (for large holes)

OR

- Soldering gun or other smokeless heat source

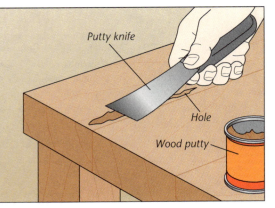

Putty knife

Hole

Wood putty

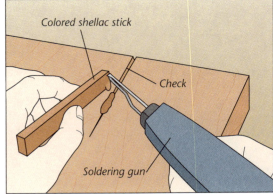

Colored shellac stick

Check

Soldering gun

Using wood patching compound

Wood dough comes in many shades and soaks up a lot of stain. Wood putty, whitish-gray in color, comes premixed or in powder form. Some putties accept stain, but they're typically used under opaque finishes. Plastic wood (in many tones) absorbs very little stain. Apply any of these by flexing a putty knife blade to drive in the patching compound *(above)*. On large voids, use a few thin applications; leave the last layer higher than the surface and sand later.

Using a shellac stick

Shellac sticks (also called burn-in sticks), used often for furniture repairs, also work well for a range of surface imperfections on new wood, including small checks, dings, joint lines, and scratches. The sticks are available clear or in a range of wood tones; choose the color closest to your finish, since shellac absorbs little stain. Press the tip of a soldering gun on the shellac stick to heat it, melting the shellac directly into the flaw *(above)*.

Finish-sanding

TOOLKIT
- Sander
- Vacuum cleaner (optional unless a water-base finish will be used)

Sanding with fine-grit paper

To spot-sand patching materials, small gouges, or scratches, return briefly to a coarser grit and sand them out. Remember to sand only with the grain, and sand end grain in one direction only. Use a hand scraper, an emery board, or the crisp, folded edge of a new sheet of sandpaper to reach into corners and crevices. As you progress with finer grits of paper, check your work again with a low-angle light. When all the scratches made by the previous grit have been removed, you're ready for the finest grit. Finish by vacuuming the entire piece to pick up fine dust particles, or, for any finish other than water-based ones, you can wipe the surface with a tack cloth *(see below)*.

  ASK A PRO

CAN I MAKE A TACK CLOTH?

Tack cloths are best used on nonporous woods; never use one on wood that will receive a water-base finish. To make one, wet a piece of cheesecloth with mineral spirits and wring out any excess. Add a few drops of varnish and work it in until the cloth feels tacky. When it begins to lose its stickiness, add more varnish. Store it in a clearly labeled plastic bag or airtight coffee can.

Raising the grain

Swelling and smoothing the wood fibers

If you'll be using a water-base stain or finish, you should raise the wood's grain and remove the raised fibers; with other types of finishes, you won't need to do this unless the wood has a naturally fuzzy surface. To raise the grain, swell the wood fibers by wiping the surface with a damp sponge *(right)*; let the wood dry. Then use medium-grade steel wool to cut off the fibers, or sand them down with a fine-grit sandpaper. Repeat the process once or twice.

Damp sponge

Swollen wood fibers

Filling the grain

TOOLKIT
• Sander

Applying wood filler

Paste fillers are the most common; silicate formulas such as silex do the best job. They are neutral-colored and typically have the consistency of peanut butter. Thin filler according to the label instructions and color it with stain pigments. Or buy premixed filler, available in a number of shades. If you'll be using light-colored stain, apply the filler first. For darker stains, make your filler at least one shade darker than the stain and apply it after staining. Apply the filler with burlap or a soft cloth, using a circular motion to work it into the pores. Do a final light wipe with the grain, then allow the filler to dry for 24 hours. For sanding, follow the label instructions for the product you're using.

Sealing wood

TOOLKIT
For a wash coat:
• Same application tool as for actual coat
For commercially available sealer:
• Application tool recommended by manufacturer

Applying a sealer

A sealer, sanded after it dries, forms a solid bond between wood and the top coat, sealing off the stain and filler so the finish won't get cloudy. Often, the best sealer is a wash coat, a thinned-down coat of your final finish—compatibility won't be an issue. If you'll be finishing with shellac or lacquer, try a 1-pound cut of shellac *(page 122)* as a sealer after filler and stain coats. There are also quick-drying sealers and sanding sealers on the market; follow the manufacturer's application and sanding instructions. Don't use these under any top coat but lacquer unless the sealer's label states otherwise.

Sealers can also be used at earlier stages. On softwoods, a coat under the stain gives more even penetration, eliminating the mottled look of stained pine or the high-contrast stripes of darkly stained fir plywood. Seal end grain before applying stain, since these areas tend to drink up stain at a faster rate. Because sealers absorb stains differently, always try out your stain and sealer on a test patch. Remove all sanding residue.

STAINING

Stain is probably the most misunderstood and misused product in wood finishing. Many woods—cherry, walnut, and mahogany, for example—have beautiful natural color that requires no stain at all. But on light-colored, non-descript wood, stain gives the wood some color and a bit of character; it can also highlight the grain figure.

Wood stains fall into two general categories: pigments and dyes. Pigmented stains are composed of finely ground particles of color held in suspension in oil, resins, or solvent. Essentially a thin, opaque paint, this type of stain coats the wood fibers and tends to conceal the grain. Most wood dyes are aniline (a coal tar derivative) dyes, which are dissolved in a number of mediums. These dyes are actually absorbed by the wood fibers, allowing the grain to show through.

The basic stain categories are discussed below. The tendency toward "one-step" products has led to stain/filler combinations, pigmented sealers, and all-in-one stain finishes. Many of these products work well, although you have less control over each step.

Applying pigmented oil stains

TOOLKIT
• Natural-bristle paintbrush (optional)

Natural-bristle brush

1 Brushing on the stain

These popular, ready-mixed stains, sold as oil stain, wood stain, and pigmented wiping stain, are nonfading, nonbleeding, and easy to apply. However, they aren't compatible with shellac or lacquer and should not be used on unfilled open-grain woods such as oak, because their heavy pigments fill up surface pores and cloud the finish. Keep in mind, too, that cracks, dents, or scratches in the wood will catch more than their share of the pigments and will stand out when the finish is applied. Stir these stains well before and during use. Brush the stain into the wood *(left)*, or wipe it on with a lint-free cloth using small, circular motions.

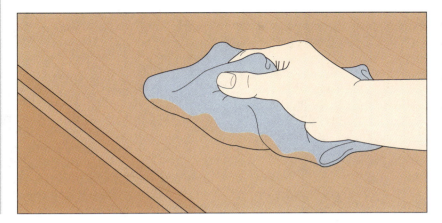

2 **Removing the excess**
Wipe off the excess stain immediately with a clean cloth *(left)*. Wait 12 to 24 hours before sealing the wood.

Applying penetrating oil stains

Wiping on the stain

Though often confused with pigmented stains, these are actually dyes carried by an oil/resin medium. Commonly known as colored Danish oil, or colored penetrating oil, these stains are popular because they provide color and finish in the same coat, while allowing the wood grain to show through. Apply penetrating oil stains with a clean, lint-free cloth, then use the same cloth to remove any excess oil and to equalize the surface color as much as possible. Wipe the stain while it's still wet, making the last strokes parallel to the grain.

Applying water-base aniline dyes

TOOLKIT
• Synthetic-bristle paintbrush or spray gun

Brushing or spraying on the dye

Generally sold in powdered form and mixed with hot water, these stains are clear, permanent, and brilliant in color. They contain no flammable solvents, have no odor, and clean up easily. However, water stains swell the wood fibers, so you'll have to raise the grain first *(page 117)* or sand after staining. These stains also take at least 24 hours to dry. Water-base stains are effective on woods such as oak, cherry, and walnut that require only a slight boost in color. Remember, though, that the stain will appear slightly darker in solution than when dry. Applying water-base aniline dye is as simple as brushing or spraying *(page 124)* it on. Don't flood the surface of the work or you may loosen glue joints and extend the drying time.

Applying alcohol-base aniline dyes

Spraying on the dye

A spray gun *(page 124)* is the best way to apply alcohol-base aniline dyes (sometimes called spirit soluble stains); use the type of sprayer powered by an air compressor. These dyes don't raise the grain, but on the other hand, they aren't very light-fast. Aniline dyes are very quick-drying, and this is why they should be sprayed on—otherwise, lap marks will be visible.

Applying non-grain-raising stains

Brushing or spraying on the stain

A favorite of the furniture and cabinet making industries, non-grain-raising (NGR) stains are available premixed. Combining the best qualities of water and alcohol-base stains with none of their disadvantages, these stains are light-fast and—as their name promises—won't raise the grain. They're also quick drying and can be used under nearly any finish. However, NGR stains are not recommended for softwoods because of uneven penetration. It's best to spray these stains on, though you can add a retarder to make them brushable.

FINISHING THE SURFACE

Today's finishes are different from those of the past; both clear and opaque finishes have gone through a chemical revolution. Though finishing products are vastly improved over their predecessors, it can be confusing to choose one. The chart below sets out the basics, and divides finishes into those that penetrate right into the wood—primarily natural oils and oils fortified with synthetic resins—and finishes that sit on the surface of the wood, such as shellac, lacquer, varnish, and enamel. This is not to say that a thinned-down varnish won't penetrate the wood's pores when used as a sealer, or that polymerized tung oil won't build up on the surface. But for a "bare wood" look, you'll generally want to turn to penetrating finishes; for more complete protection and a glassier appearance, use a surface finish.

Because many finishes are not easily categorized, it's important to read the label on the can very carefully. Examining the list of solids—primarily resins and oils—will help you determine what type of finish it is. You'll also be able to compare brands by looking at the percentages of solids in each one—better finishes will have a higher percentage of the resin or oil that gives the product its name. If you're still in doubt, ask your paint dealer for help. Comparing notes with other woodworkers is also an excellent way of finding a reliable finish.

Instructions on applying the various finishes are covered on the following pages: oil finishes (page 121), shellac (page 122), lacquer (page 123), varnish (page 124), and enamels (page 125). If you want to finish your finish, giving it even more sheen, turn to page 126 for information on rubbing and waxing.

Before you begin to work with any finishing product, read pages 41-42 for some safety tips, and also look for safety information on the product label. Make sure you wear a respirator when necessary, and provide adequate ventilation when you're using a flammable product.

TYPE OF FINISHES

Penetrating finishes	Characteristics
Boiled linseed oil	Lends warm, slightly dull patina to wood. Dries very slowly; requires many coats. Moderate resistance to heat, water, and chemicals. Easily renewable.
Mineral oil	Clear, viscous, nontoxic oil good for cutting boards and serving and eating utensils. Leaves soft sheen; easily renewed. For better penetration, heat in double-boiler before applying.
Tung oil	Natural oil finish; hard and highly resistant to abrasion, moisture, heat, acid, and mildew. Requires several thin, hand-rubbed applications (heavy coats wrinkle badly). Pure tung oil has low sheen; best with polymer resins added. Polymerized tung oil also builds a surface finish.
Penetrating resin (Danish oil, antique oil)	Use on hard, open-grain woods. Leaves wood looking and feeling "natural." Easy to apply and retouch; doesn't protect against heat or abrasion. May darken some woods.
Rub-on varnish	Penetrating resin and varnish combination; builds up sheen as coats are applied; dries fairly quickly. Moderately resistant to water and alcohol; darkens wood.
Surface finishes	**Characteristics**
Shellac	Lends warm luster to wood. Easy to apply, retouch, and remove. Excellent sealer. Lays down in thin, quick-drying coats; can be rubbed to a very high sheen. Little resistance to heat, alcohol, and moisture.
Lacquer	Strong, clear, quick-drying finish in both spraying and brushing form; very durable, but vulnerable to moisture. Requires 3 or more coats; can be polished to a high gloss. Available in less-flammable water-base form, similar to standard type, but slower drying time; non-yellowing.
Alkyd varnish	Widely compatible oil-base interior varnish; produces a thick coating with good overall resistance. Dries slowly and darkens with time. Brush marks and dust can be a problem.
Phenolic-resin varnish (spar varnish)	Tough, exterior varnish with excellent weathering resistance; flexes with wood's seasonal changes. To avoid yellowing, product should contain ultraviolet absorbers.
Polyurethane varnish	Thick, plastic, irreversible coating; nearly impervious to water, heat, and alcohol. Dries overnight. Incompatible with some stains and sealers. Follow label instructions to ensure good bonding between coats. Water-base type less resistant than solvent type.
Water-base varnish	Water base makes for easy cleanup but raises wood grain. Not as heat- or water-resistant as alkyd varnish, nor as chemical-resistant as polyurethane.
Enamel	Available in flat, semigloss, and gloss finishes in wide range of colors. May have lacquer or varnish (alkyd, polyurethane, or acrylic) base; each shares qualities as same type of clear finish.
Wax	Occasionally used as a finish, but more often applied over harder top coats. Increases luster of wood. Not very durable, but offers some protection against liquids when renewed frequently.

OIL FINISHES

Probably the original wood finish, oil is still very popular. Today there are a number of products that are oils by name but that contain polymers, resins, and driers, giving them some of the superior properties of varnish and other harder, more durable finishes. The application techniques for the most popular choices—traditional or modern—follow.

Penetrating resins: These products are simple to apply, and thus very popular. Commonly sold as Danish oil, teak oil, antique oil, or penetrating oil sealer, they preserve the wood's feel and produce a relatively durable finish that can easily be patched or renewed. They are best for hard, open-grain woods such as oak or teak, producing mixed results on softwoods and closed-grain hardwoods, and darkening the surface of some woods objectionably. Test the product on scrap first.

Mineral oil: This clear, viscous, nontoxic oil is a good choice for wooden bowls, eating utensils, and cutting boards. But don't expect much more than a warm glow and a slight renewing of the surface.

Tung oil: This natural oil, built up in thin coats, produces a relatively hard finish that resists abrasion, water, heat, and acid. Its sheen increases with each coat, but it will never develop a high gloss. A true tung oil finish should be either 100 percent tung oil or polymerized tung oil. The latter has polymer resins and driers added for a faster-drying hard finish with a higher sheen.

Boiled linseed oil: Old-timers may swear by this finish, but the hours or even days it takes each coat to dry, and the number of coats required, make it impractical for most projects. In addition, it's a rather soft finish that doesn't take kindly to water, heat, or chemicals.

Applying penetrating resin

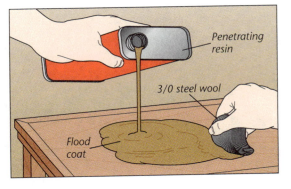

Penetrating resin

3/0 steel wool

Flood coat

1 ▸ Applying the flood coat
You can either stain the wood first (use a water-base aniline dye or a lightly pigmented stain to keep the pores from filling up), or use a tinted penetrating resin. Don't use a filler or sealer. Be generous with your first application, called a flood coat: Pour on the resin directly from the can and spread it around the surface with 3/0 steel wool *(left)*.

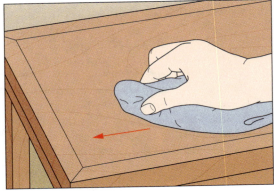

2 ▸ Wiping the surface dry
Allow the flood coat to sit for 15 to 30 minutes, then wipe it off with a soft cloth, following the direction of the wood grain. You can apply a second or even a third coat if you want to build up the finish. Consult the manufacturer's directions for drying time.

4/0 steel wool

3 ▸ Increasing the sheen
If you want greater luster, once the surface is completely dry, rub briskly in the direction of the grain with 4/0 steel wool and a little resin. Wipe the surface clean, let it dry overnight, and follow up by applying two or more coats of paste wax, as described on page 126.

Applying mineral oil

Dipping the object or rubbing on the oil
Buy mineral oil at any pharmacy; it will penetrate better if you heat it—the safest way is in a double-boiler. Submerge small objects briefly in the warm oil; rub oil on larger pieces with a soft cloth. Apply the oil sparingly or you'll end up with a sticky film. You'll need to renew this finish often.

<table>
<tr><td>

Applying tung oil

</td><td>

Rubbing in the oil

You'll need a soft, lint-free cloth and a lamb's wool buffer. Thin 100% tung oil with mineral spirits—thick coats may wrinkle, hiding the wood below.

</td><td>

Rub the oil into the wood with the cloth. Apply at least two coats, letting each dry as long as the product label recommends, then buff the surface.

</td></tr>
</table>

<table>
<tr><td>

Applying boiled lin-seed oil

</td><td>

Brushing or wiping on the oil

If you opt for this finish despite its disadvantages, dilute it with an equal amount of turpentine or mineral spirits and apply it sparingly with a nat-

</td><td>

ural-bristle paintbrush or lint-free cloth. When the wood pores have absorbed all the oil they can hold, wipe the surface briskly with a clean, dry cloth.

</td></tr>
</table>

SHELLAC

Warm and subtle, shellac has been associated with fine furniture for hundreds of years. Made from the secretions of the Asian lac bug, shellac can be purchased in dry or liquid form, and it is available in orange and white types. The orange type is the standard; white shellac has been bleached so it won't impart an amber tone to the wood, but it's significantly less moisture-resistant and has a much shorter shelf life than the orange type.

Because it's thinned with alcohol, shellac is a pleasure to work with. It's quick-drying and layers are built up easily because the alcohol in each new coat softens the previous coat, bonding the two. French polish—the prized piano finish so popular with 17th- and 18th-century furnituremakers—owes its glasslike depth to this characteristic.

On the other hand, shellac is vulnerable to a spilled cocktail, strong soaps and detergents, and even hard water. Also, if exposed to much heat or moisture, it turns cloudy.

You must build up the surface with several coats before the finish takes on luster. But because it dries dust-free in 15 to 30 minutes and can be reapplied in an hour or so, the finish can take just a day to complete.

BUYING AND MIXING SHELLAC

Shellac deteriorates with age. Always buy it in small quantities from a dealer with enough turnover to ensure a fresh stock. When in doubt as to the shellac's age, test it on scrap. If it takes a long time to dry or remains tacky it should not be used.

Flake (dry) shellac is sold by the pound. The amount you add to a gallon of alcohol determines the strength of the solution, measured in "cuts." A 1-pound cut is made by dissolving 1 pound of flakes in 1 gallon of denatured alcohol; a 2-pound cut requires 2 pounds of flakes to a gallon, and so on. If you've never worked with shellac before, begin with a 1-pound cut. Once you have some experience, move to a 2- or 3-pound cut.

Liquid (dissolved) shellac is typically sold in 3- or 4-pound cuts. To make a 1-pound cut from a 4-pound one, add 3 parts alcohol to 1 part dissolved shellac.

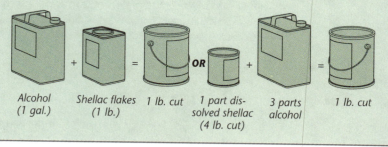

Alcohol (1 gal.)   Shellac flakes (1 lb.)   1 lb. cut   1 part dissolved shellac (4 lb. cut)   3 parts alcohol   1 lb. cut

<table>
<tr><td>

Applying shellac

TOOLKIT
• Natural-bristle paintbrush
• Sander (optional)

</td><td>

1 ▶ Brushing on shellac
Begin by brushing on a full coat of shellac, using a slow, smooth motion. Take special care to overlap all adjoining brush strokes *(right)* and to maintain a clean, smooth surface. This will help keep ridges and streaks to a minimum.

</td><td>

Natural-bristle brush

Overlapping stroke

</td></tr>
</table>

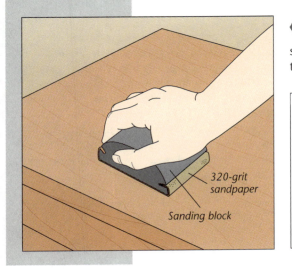

2 Sanding the surface
After about an hour, sand or rub off ridges and brush strokes with 320-grit sandpaper or 4/0 steel wool (in line with wood grain). The shellac should sand to a powder; if it clogs the paper, wait a few more minutes before continuing.

320-grit sandpaper

Sanding block

3 Building up the finish
Apply a second coat the same way as the first, then sand or rub it down after 1 hour of drying. The third coat should be smooth enough for final rubbing; if not, sand one last time and apply more shellac. Continue until you build up the finish you desire. Then use 4/0 steel wool and lubricating oil *(page 126)* to even up the surface gloss. For a classic high-gloss look, allow at least 3 days for the finish to harden, then polish with pumice, rottenstone, or 600-grit wet-or-dry sandpaper. Follow with wax.

LACQUER

Clear lacquer that's sprayed on dries within seconds, eliminating any dust problems. This also lets you lay down many coats in the time it takes one coat of other finishes to dry. Though not as moistureproof as varnish, a lacquer finish is very durable and can be rubbed to a high gloss. Lacquer is more heat- and chemical-resistant than shellac, but shares the quality of invisible layering where each additional coat softens and bonds to the previous one. Lacquer won't fill pores in open-grain wood; use a filler and follow with a sealer.

The lacquer available today is basically nitrocellulose modified with oils and resins, then dissolved in solvents. Spraying and brushing lacquer are basically the same, and will produce essentially the same finish, but brushing lacquer evaporates more slowly, giving brush marks time to level out. Both types are available in flat, semigloss, and gloss finishes. Never apply spraying lacquer with a brush, or vice versa. For best results, thin lacquer according to the label instructions. Never work with lacquer that won't flow easily. If you've used pigmented oil stain, use a wash coat of shellac or sanding sealer for extra protection.

Brushing lacquer: This produces a first-rate finish, but you may need to sand between coats. Use gloss lacquer, which is stronger, to build up the surface, then the final coat can be semigloss or flat, or you can add a flattening agent. Create a matte finish by scrubbing gloss lacquer down with fine steel wool.

Spraying lacquer: Buy lacquer in a spray can for small projects, but for best results use the equipment shown on page 126 (you can rent it). Never use an electric spray system with lacquer, since this could cause an explosion. Follow directions or consult a paint dealer.

Brushing on lacquer

TOOLKIT
• Wide natural-bristle paintbrush
• Sander

Natural-bristle brush

1 Applying the first coat
Begin by brushing the lacquer onto the wood in a smooth coat. Working rapidly with a wider than normal brush to speed things along, spread the lacquer with long strokes without too much back-and-forth brushing, and with little overlap between adjacent strokes *(left)*. Keep your working area small and finish one area at a time.

2 Applying additional coats
Even though your surface will dry dust-free in minutes, wait at least 1 hour before sanding or applying a second coat. Then carefully level any high spots or defects with 400-grit sandpaper. Apply additional coats until you build up the desired finish; two coats over a sealer is a bare minimum. If you want an even higher gloss, after the final coat has dried overnight, rub the surface with rottenstone, pumice, or 600-grit wet-or-dry sandpaper *(page 126)*.

Spraying on lacquer

TOOLKIT
• Air compressor
  and spray gun
OR
• Lacquer in
  aerosol can

Using a spray gun

If possible, set your project up in a spray booth to prevent overspray from spreading beyond a limited area and to keep dust off your work. Always wear a respirator, and avoid any possibility of open flame or sparks in the area. Follow the manufacturer's instructions to set up the spray gun, and thin the lacquer according to the label directions. Holding the spray gun 8" to 10" away from the work surface, spray from side to side, making overlapping passes (below, left). Let it dry, then continue applying coats of lacquer (with each coat sprayed in a pattern perpendicular to the previous one) until you have built up the finish to your satisfaction. If you choose to use lacquer in an aerosol spray can as shown below (below, right), hold the can 10" to 12" from the work while you're spraying. This method produces good results for small surfaces, but requires many coats, since the lacquer is thinned greatly to force it through the can's spray nozzle.

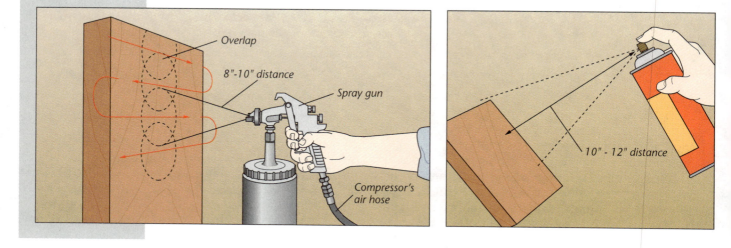

VARNISH

For durability and moisture-and heat-resistance, you can't beat varnish. Available in gloss and semigloss sheens (sometimes called matte or satin), varnishes vary widely in their characteristics. A description of the major types follows; the brushing technique for all types of varnish is shown on page 125.

Polyurethane varnish: The ultimate in resistance to abrasion, moisture, heat, and chemicals, polyurethane is a "miracle finish" for tabletops, floors, and other high-use areas. Though it's somewhat brittle, it's widely used because of its toughness. One further consideration: Once this finish has cured, it's permanent—no solvent will remove it, and new coats won't bond to it chemically. The only way it can be completely stripped off the wood is by sanding.

Never use polyurethane as a sealer for anything but a polyurethane top coat, and don't put it over shellac, lacquer, or most enamels. If you want to apply an additional coat, make sure the first coat isn't completely cured, or the next coat won't bond.

Alkyd varnish: Often referred to as oil-base varnish, this is the traditional interior type. Though not as hard as polyurethane, it's more flexible, so you can recoat without worrying about bonding. A tung-oil base makes it particularly moisture-resistant. Because alkyd varnish is thinned with mineral spirits, it's compatible with most stains, fillers, and sealers. Like most varnishes, it's susceptible to darkening with time, but can be removed with paint stripper.

Phenolic-resin varnish: This exterior varnish, often called spar varnish, is harder and more moisture-resistant than alkyd varnish. Unlike polyurethane, it's flexible enough to withstand wood's seasonal changes without splitting or cracking. Phenolic-resin varnishes tend to yellow; to avoid this problem, choose one that contains ultraviolet absorbers.

Water-base varnishes: Nontoxic and easy to clean up, these "latex" acrylic varnishes perform reasonably well, but lack the chemical resistance of polyurethane and the heat and moisture resistance of other varnishes.

Because water-base varnishes are about 70 percent water, it takes several coats to achieve the same build up as one coat of alkyd varnish. The water content will also raise the grain, which you can either sand off after the first coat has dried or raise intentionally beforehand (page 117).

Rub-on varnish: This penetrating resin and varnish mixture is rubbed in like a penetrating resin finish (page 121), but because of its higher solids content, it builds up in layers on the surface. Each application increases the sheen. However, rub-on varnish trades durability for ease of application. Like other penetrating finishes, it darkens wood; also, it's irreversible on open-grain woods.

Applying varnish

1 Preparing the workpiece

Fillers are seldom used with varnishes, but a sealer is always a good idea. Use a thinned-down solution of the varnish as a sealer. Since varnish remains tacky for 2 to 6 hours, dust is its main enemy. Pick a clean workspace and vacuum all surfaces a few hours before setting up. Make sure the room is warm enough—this can make a big difference in drying time.

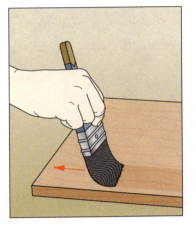
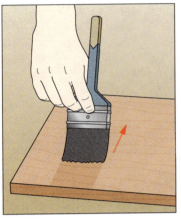
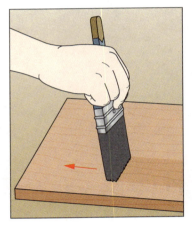

2 Brushing on varnish

Avoid runs and drips by not loading up your brush and by keeping the work horizontal when possible. It's particularly important to be spare when applying varnish to minimize the "plastic" look. Do a test first; if you find that air bubbles remain in the finish after it's cured, use about 15% mineral spirits to thin the varnish. Apply the varnish evenly with long, smooth, continuous strokes parallel to the grain (above, left). Then quickly brush this same area across the grain (above, center). Complete the process by "tipping off" along the grain, stroking lightly using only the very tips of the bristles (above, right). Use the least number of brush strokes you can, and work in only one small section at a time. This will allow you to finish the entire piece section-by-section without creating disfiguring lap marks. Side-lighting the work will help you avoid leaving dry spots.

3 Applying additional coats

Follow the manufacturer's recommendation for drying time, then use 400-grit stearated (self-lubricating) sandpaper to remove the gloss and provide better adhesion for the next coat. Build up the surface with gloss varnish, then switch to the sheen of your choice for the final coat. Once the final coat is completely dry, you can rub the surface lightly with 4/0 steel wool for a satin finish, or with pumice, rottenstone, or 600-grit wet or dry paper for a high gloss (page 126).

ENAMELS

Enamels are the best choice if you want bright color, or if you wish to mask lower grades of wood. They are available in flat, semigloss, and gloss finishes, and in a wide range of colors. Enamels are essentially clear finishes (lacquers or varnishes) with pigments added. The four basic types are described below; application tips are found on page 126.

Colored lacquers: To identify these enamels, check the product label for nitrocellulose content. Colored, or pigmented, lacquers provide a durable and beautiful finish. Like clear lacquers, they are available in spray or in brush-on form; to spray, follow the instructions on page 124.

Alkyd-base enamels: These oil-base paints use paint thinner as a solvent; their characteristics are similar to alkyd varnishes. The resulting finish is durable and flexible.

Polyurethane enamels: Like polyurethane varnish, these enamels are highly abrasion-resistant, but are somewhat brittle. They can be used for both interior and exterior projects. Clean them up with paint thinner.

Acrylic (water-base) enamels: Also called latex or vinyl enamels, colored acrylic varnishes are odorless, nonflammable, and easy to apply, resulting in a glossy and durable finish. Their big advantage is that they can be cleaned up with water.

Applying enamel

TOOLKIT
- Paintbrush (natural-bristle for oil-base enamels; synthetic for water-base), 3" paint roller, or pad applicator.
- Sander

1 Preparing the surface
Always begin your paint job with an undercoat, or primer. Not only does the undercoat seal the wood, but it also shows any remaining surface flaws, which can then be patched and sanded. After priming, smooth the surface with 220-grit sandpaper.

2 Brushing on enamel
Brush enamel generously onto the wood, then feather it out with lighter strokes in the direction of the grain. Another technique—useful for large areas—is to lay on the paint with a small paint roller, then smooth it out with light brush strokes. Pad applicators also work very well on large areas.

3 Applying additional coats
Let the first finish coat dry for at least 24 hours, then if you're planning to apply another coat, sand the surface first with 320- or 400-grit sandpaper. For a finish with remarkable depth and clarity make the last coat clear varnish (or apply two coats of water-white clear lacquer over the colored lacquer).

RUBBING OR WAXING THE FINISH

Rubbing, and/or waxing, lends elegance to any finish. Done with one of several fine abrasives, rubbing removes lint, dust, and brush marks from the finish so that it reflects light uniformly, increasing its sheen. Waxing adds depth and luster, and protects the finish.

Rubbing: You'll need both an abrasive and a lubricant for rubbing. The traditional lubricant is paraffin oil, but almost any kind of oil, or even water, will do. You can also rub with mineral spirits and wet-or-dry sandpaper (400, 500, then 600 grits wrapped around a felt- or rubberlined sanding block). This matte finish can be improved by buffing with a lamb's wool pad; for extra gloss, try commercial products for power buffers.

Waxing: Wax is inexpensive, easy to apply and to renew. Make your own by dissolving pure beeswax in turpentine until a soft paste forms. Commercial floor or furniture paste waxes, which contain carnauba wax, are more durable and may be tinted for dark-stained wood.

Rubbing a finish

TOOLKIT
- Cork sanding pad or blackboard eraser

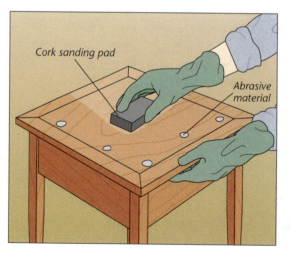

Cork sanding pad

Abrasive material

Applying the abrasive and rubbing
Spread lubricant (paraffin oil, mineral oil, or water) in a thin film over the surface of the wood. Then, for a matte finish, rub with FFF-grade ground pumice. Shake it on sparingly—an old saltshaker works well. If you prefer a glossier finish, choose rottenstone. Commercial rubbing compound can be used instead. Rub the abrasives across the lubricated surface, using a cork sanding pad (*left*) or a blackboard eraser. Keep your strokes long and even, and rub in the direction of the grain. Once you've rubbed the entire surface, wipe off the slurry that's formed, and check the surface for any spots that still gleam. Keep rubbing until they're gone. Complete the job by wiping off all the oil with a soft cloth.

Waxing a finish

TOOLKIT
- Power buffer (optional)

Applying wax
Spoon the wax onto a moist cloth (old socks are useful), then fold the cloth around the wax to make an "applicator." Rub the wax into the finish, using large, circular motions. Apply just enough to create a thin film; excess wax will dull the surface and make it gummy. Let the wax dry for a few minutes (or for the time indicated on the label), then buff the surface with a soft cloth or with a power buffer fitted with a pad made of felt or lamb's wool.

WOODWORKING GLOSSARY

Banding
A decorative edge or trim applied to a surface to hide end grain or the edges of sheet materials, such as plywood layers.

Bent-lamination
The joining of thin pieces of stock which have been bent to shape and are held together with glue.

Bevel
An incline between two faces or edges, on a piece of wood. Also used to describe the incline on a tool blade from face to edge. Includes any angle other than 90°.

Blind cut
A cut that is not visible on the outside of a joint or workpiece.

Brad
A small, almost headless nail that resembles a miniature finishing nail; useful for joining thin pieces and nailing into delicate ends or edges.

Carbide
A super-hard alloy used on the cutting edge of blades and bits; stays sharp longer than steel. Carbide-tipped cutters require less maintenance and have a longer life than regular steel or high-speed steel cutters, but are more expensive.

Carcase
The outer framework of a piece of furniture; boxlike construction.

Casework
Furniture construction based on the joining of panels to each other.

Chamfer
A decorative incline between two surfaces that are perpendicular to each other.

Counterbore
Drilling a hole in advance of setting in a screw at a depth that leaves the head of the screw below the surface of the stock. Allows for the hole to be plugged, concealing screw head.

Countersink
Beveling the opening of a hole for a flathead screw to allow the head to sit flush with the surface.

Crosscut
A cut running perpendicular to the direction of the wood grain.

Cut, interior; cutout
The removal of stock from within the surface of a workpiece, leaving all the outside edges intact.

Dado
A channel cut across the grain of a workpiece with square sides and bottom.

Dress
The act of finishing a cut edge to a precise line with a hand tool such as a plane or chisel when the rough cut done with a saw or power tool is not precise enough.

Ease
To remove a sharp corner with sandpaper or a plane.

Edge (of a board)
The narrow side that runs parallel to the grain direction, as compared to the end.

End (of a board)
The part that reveals the cross-cut end grain, as compared to the edge.

Extension
A shop-made addition to a guiding accessory on a machine table that facilitates the movement of stock through the cutter.

Face (of a board)
The wider surface; the good face, which will show on the finished project, is chosen for its attractive appearance.

Faceframe
The structure composed of horizontal and vertical members that makes the opening for drawers and doors on a cabinet.

Featherboard
An antikickback device designed to hold and guide a workpiece while it is being worked on a stationary power tool.

Fence
Device attached to a stationary power tool surface to guide stock; known as auxiliary fence. Also, the part of a tool that guides it along the edge of the stock.

Figure
The wood grain on the face of a board.

Frame-and-panel
A type of structure in which a floating (nonattached) panel is supported by a grooved frame made up of rails and stiles.

Fret saw
A type of coping saw with the same thin, fine toothed blade but a frame with a much deeper throat.

Grain
The direction and arrangement of the wood fibers.

Groove
A channel cut in the edge or face of a workpiece, going with the grain.

High-speed steel (HSS)
Steel that is tempered to withstand the friction and heat created at higher speeds of revolution.

Hole, pilot
A hole drilled into a piece of stock for a screw or nail to follow. It is slightly smaller than the shaft of the nail or the threads of the screw. It guides the fastener and prevents splitting. Also, a clearance hole in a board to start interior cuts.

Infeed
The end on a machine table from which a workpiece proceeds into the cutter.

Jig
Any device designed to aid the guiding of a tool or stock in motion; shop-built or commercially available.

Joint
To make the edge or face of stock straight and even, as with a plane or jointer.

Kerf
The area of a workpiece that is removed by the teeth of a saw blade.

Miter
An angled cut; a joint between two workpieces at any angle other than 90°.

Mortise
A shaped cutout in a workpiece that commonly receives a tenon; also a recess for a hinge.

Outfeed
The end on a machine table to which a workpiece proceeds after having contacted the cutter.

Pilot
The part of a router bit that guides it along the rim of a template or piece of stock.

Plate joiner
A portable power tool that cuts slots into stock with a rotating blade, for plate or biscuit joints.

Plunge cut
A cut made directly into the surface of a workpiece without starting from an open edge.

Push stick (or block)
A tool used to feed wood through the cutting blade or bit of a tool without endangering the operator's hands.

Rail
The horizontal element of a framed structure which joins two stiles.

Resawing
The act of cutting thick stock into two or more thinner boards.

Rip cut
A cut running parallel to the direction of the wood grain.

Sheet material
Any type of manufactured or processed stock that is bought in large panel form, such as plywood or hardboard.

Shooting board
A guide that holds a workpiece at an angle to the blade of a tool.

Square
The achievement of a 90° angle at the point where two workpieces meet.

Stile
The vertical element of a framed structure which joins two rails.

Stock
Woodworking material including solid lumber and sheet products.

Stop block
A clamped-on block of wood that prevents the stock or cutter from passing beyond a certain point.

Stopped cut
An abrupt end to a cut before an edge of the stock is reached.

Stretcher
A horizontal member providing stability between posts in a leg-and-rail (frame) construction.

Surface
To work the face of a board on a jointer or with any other cutting tool to create an even and clean profile.

Template
A device, either shop-made or commercial, that guides a cutting tool along a certain path or in a design.

Tenon
The shaped end of a workpiece that fits into a mortise.

Through cut
A cut that extends from edge to edge on a piece of stock.

True
To achieve a flat surface and squared edge on wood.

Veneer
A thin slice of wood to be glued onto another surface for decorative effect or to hide lower grades of wood.

Warp
The distortion of wood due to uneven shrinkage when drying.

Waste
Excess material to be removed (or already removed) from stock.

INDEX